Farmer-led extension

Concepts and practices

Edited by
VANESSA SCARBOROUGH, SCOTT KILLOUGH,
DEBRA A. JOHNSON and JOHN FARRINGTON

INTERMEDIATE TECHNOLOGY PUBLICATIONS 1997

Intermediate Technology Publications Ltd,
103–105 Southampton Row, London WC1B 4HH, UK

in association with

International Institute of Rural Reconstruction, Silang, Cavite 4118, Philippines
Overseas Development Institute, London, UK
World Neighbors, Oklahoma City, OK, USA

A CIP record for this book is available from the British Libary

ISBN 1 85339 417 3

Technical editing and typesetting by Paul Mundy, Bergisch Gladbach, Germany

Printed in the UK by SRP Exeter

Contents

Acknowledgements

The July 1995 workshop on which this book is based was co-organized by the International Institute for Rural Reconstruction (IIRR), the Overseas Development Institute (ODI), and World Neighbors. The editors are indebted to a large number of staff of these organizations, without whom the workshop could not have taken place. Julian Gonsalvez of IIRR and Larry Fisher, formerly of World Neighbors, generously shared their ideas in initial discussions of the workshop proposals in 1992. The workshop organizing team was composed of Stefan Wodicka and John Jackson of World Neighbors, John Farrington and Vanessa Scarborough of ODI, and Mila Resma, Daniel Selener and Scott Killough of IIRR. Lhai Kasala and Guia Reyes of IIRR provided outstanding administrative and logistical support.

Financial sponsorship for the workshop and preparation of the book was provided by the Ford Foundation's programmes in South and Southeast Asia, by the World Bank Small Grants Programme, by the Southeast Asia office of the International Development Research Centre, and by the Swedish International Development Agency. We are greatly indebted to all of these, especially to Ruth Alsop, Lennart Bondesson, John Graham, Peter Hemsch and Suzanne Siskel, who took continuing interest in the substance of the workshop.

Our keynote speakers, professor George Axinn of Michigan State University and professor Chris Garforth of Reading University, helped very substantially to set the tone of the workshop, without pay and at very short notice. The workshop participants provided the practical experiences chronicled in these chapters and shared their stories so that others might benefit from their knowledge. Special thanks are due to the farmer-extensionists and farmer-promoters who participated in the workshop: Pedro Aspiras, Pedro Baile, Jose Cansancio, Teo Llena, Gabino Lopez, and Simon Mchunu.

Adrienne Watson at ODI compiled with aplomb a complex and fragmented manuscript. Paul Mundy provided invaluable editorial inputs, greatly enhancing the usefulness of the rich experiences presented, and formatted the manuscript for publication.

Finally, the editors alone remain responsible for any errors of interpretation contained in this book.

Abbreviations

AKRSP	Aga Khan Rural Support Programme, India
BAIF	Bharatiya Agro Industries Foundation, India
CALRC	Community Agriculture and Livestock Research Centre, Nepal
CARE	CARE (an international non-government development organization)
CAW	community agricultural worker
CD-ROM	compact disk–read-only memory (computer disk)
CIDSE	Coopération Internationale pour le Développement et la Solidarité
CIP	International Potato Centre, Peru
DAE	Department of Agricultural Extension, Bangladesh
DFID	Department for International Development (formerly the Overseas Development Administration, ODA), UK
EV	extension volunteer
EW	extension worker
FAO	Food and Agriculture Organisation of the United Nations, Italy
FPR	farmer participatory research
GTZ	Gesellschaft für Technische Zusammenarbeit, Germany
IFAD	International Fund for Agricultural Development, Italy
IIRR	International Institute for Rural Reconstruction, Philippines
IPM	integrated pest management
IRRI	International Rice Research Institute, Philippines
ITDG	Intermediate Technology Development Group, UK
KVK	Krishi Vigyan Kendra (rural extension centre), India
MANAGE	National Institute of Agricultural Extension Management, India
MEV	master extension volunteer
NAF	Nepal Agroforestry Foundation
NFEP	Northwest Fisheries Extension Project, Bangladesh
NGO	non-governmental organization
ODI	Overseas Development Institute, UK
PAN	Pesticide Action Network, Indonesia
PC/PS	problem census/problem solving
PCAD	people-centred agricultural development
PRA	participatory rural appraisal
PTD	participatory technology development
RISA	Regional Initiative in Sustainable Agriculture, Thailand
RRA	rapid rural appraisal
SWOT	strengths, weaknesses, opportunities, threats
UNAG	Unión Nacionál de Agricultores y Ganaderos, Nicaragua
UNDP	United Nations Development Programme, USA
USAID	United States Agency for International Development
VAC	garden, fishpond, livestock building (Vietnamese acronym)
VACVINA	National Association of Vietnamese Gardeners
VDC	village development committee
ZOPP	goal-oriented project planning (German acronym)

Tables and figures

Tables

Figures

1 Introduction

John Farrington, Debra A. Johnson, Scott Killough and Vanessa Scarborough

THE MAJORITY OF the poor in developing countries live in rural areas, rely on agriculture for their employment, and spend much of their income on food. Population densities continue to rise and land for agricultural expansion is becoming increasingly scarce. Moreover, labour constraints, particularly in households headed by women, often limit farmers' ability to expand the area they cultivate. Thus, sustainable increases in land and labour productivity in agriculture, through technological and managerial innovation, continue to be crucial ways of reducing poverty and fostering economic growth.

Public-sector agricultural services in developing countries have played a vital role in promoting such innovations. They have contributed to respectable agricultural growth rates in many countries. However, such growth has been largely concentrated in reliably rainfed or irrigated areas, with only minor improvements in living standards in environments which are risk-prone, complex, and diverse in socio-economic and agro-ecological terms. Moreover, changes in the public sector and in the context in which it operates, and the likely nature of future technological innovation, raise questions about whether the institutions that supported the green revolution will be able to meet the challenges of the continued need for increases in agricultural productivity.

It is likely that future gains in agricultural productivity through technological innovation will have to be more incremental, locally specific and directly geared towards specific farmer constraints. Antholt (1994:4) suggests that a repeat of the widespread effects of the green revolution is impossible because of constraints on the role that biotechnology can play in difficult areas, as well as physical limits on the further expansion of land under cultivation and irrigation.

This is particularly true for resource-poor farmers in environments that cannot be made more uniform through irrigation and purchased inputs, that are remote from markets and political centres, and where the natural resource base is fragile. World-wide, about one billion people live in such complex, diverse and risk-prone areas, at or below poverty thresholds. A critical barrier to development in these areas is the failure to find institutionally viable ways to provide appropriate technical support to farm households. It is becoming increasingly accepted that locally specific innovations in technology and management are needed. In turn, this means that agricultural research and extension will have to become more responsive to particular needs and constraints

— i.e., more demand-led. The question, then, is how to achieve this in practice?

Governments and other development agencies (NGOs, donors, etc.) are experimenting with approaches to agricultural extension. For example, some extension services are located alongside research services or in integrated rural development projects. Others are located in a separate government department or in agricultural universities. Some extension services are commodity-specific, others cover the range of farming requirements; some disseminate information through visits to individual contact farmers, others focus on farmer groups.

Public extension networks, however, have limited effectiveness in making available a range of technology options from which farmers can choose. The reasons for this limited impact are widely and often hotly debated. They include the inappropriateness of 'contact farmer' methods, the lack of relevant technological messages, inadequate feedback of farmers' requirements into research agendas, and the increasingly commonplace fact that public sector budgets are too stretched to support a large number of extensionists adequately in the field.

Over the last decade, a growing number of organizations have sought models which might be both more effective in serving farmers' needs and institutionally more sustainable. They have experimented with promoting farmers and other rural people — rather than professional extensionists and researchers — as the principal agents of change. Most of these 'farmer-led extension' projects have been in the voluntary sector; few as yet have been sponsored by government organizations.

This search has been conducted in countries as diverse as Bolivia, Chile, Ecuador, Guatemala, Honduras and Nicaragua in Latin America; Egypt, Kenya and Zimbabwe in Africa, and Bangladesh, India, Indonesia, Nepal and the Philippines in Asia. In other countries, for example China and Vietnam, the transition to a market economy has added impetus to the search for entirely new ways to manage extension services. Moreover, in many countries (Bangladesh, Colombia, Indonesia, Nepal, the Philippines and South Africa) the decentralization of extension services has provided a potentially favourable context for farmer-based approaches. The evidence, as yet fragmentary, suggests that these approaches have achieved considerable success in identifying productivity-enhancing technologies which become widely adopted — and in doing so at relatively low cost.

However, not only are such programmes still rare islands in a sea of conventional approaches, but they also face many problems of their own creation. For example, some continue to face problems in overcoming gender bias and in reaching the poorest. Few rigorous evaluations of farmer-led approaches have been made. Most efforts remain small in scale. With very few exceptions, government extension services have had limited interaction with farmer-led approaches, despite the considerable potential for interaction and the replication of such approaches. Finally, there has been a gap in terms of sharing lessons learned among farmer-led extension experiences, and of comparing the experiences of NGO-supported projects with activities supported by the public sector.

The farmer-led extension workshop

A one-week workshop on farmer-led extension on these issues was organized in July 1995 by the Overseas Development Institute (ODI), the International Institute for Rural Reconstruction (IIRR) and World Neighbors at IIRR's headquarters in the Philippines. The aims of the workshop were to:

o share experiences between those working in farmer-led extension programmes, thus enabling information on innovative approaches to extension to be synthesized and disseminated
o enable leaders of conventional extension services to learn about more responsive approaches, and particularly how public-sector services might incorporate, or better relate to, farmer-led initiatives.

The objectives of the workshop were to:

o draw out guidelines and lessons from farmer-led experiences to date
o examine the constraints and potentials for scaling up farmer-led extension methods
o identify the policy and institutional changes that could facilitate public-sector adoption of such methods to spread them more widely, and analyse other means of doing so
o identify how those already involved in farmer-led extension could help reorientate less farmer-responsive systems
o allow those experienced in farmer-led approaches to assist each other in resolving problems.

The workshop's 70 participants (see Appendix 1) came from a wide range of professional backgrounds. They included farmers and farmer extensionists; community workers and representatives; staff of NGOs supporting farmer-led extension or research; public-sector representatives (some involved in reorienting extension and research to more responsive modes, and others interested to learn about approaches supported by other organizations); donor representatives and academics.

More than 50 papers were submitted to the workshop organizers (see Appendix 2). Together with the workshop discussions, these form the basis of this book.[1] To save time and maintain focus, the papers were not presented individually during the workshop. Rather, the organizers drew together the content of the papers under

---

1. Apart from this book, other outputs from the workshop (some of which were still in production when going to press) include: a book documenting farmer-extensionists' stories about farmer-led extension; 17 case studies published in ODI's Agricultural Research and Extension Network (Scarborough 1996), a video on farmer-led approaches; a practical 'how-to' farmer-led extension kit, based on existing experiences from around the world; a training manual for the establishment and management of farmer-led extension approaches; a broad but rigorous assessment of such approaches; continuing documentation of local experiences in farmer-led extension; and cross visits and training between Latin Americans, Africans and Asians involved or interested in farmer-led extension.

3

five themes, prepared abstracts of all the papers for participants, and provided full copies on request. These materials then served to catalyse discussion in parallel working groups.

The five themes were:

o strategies and methods used in farmer-led extension and research
o roles and responsibilities of different actors
o internal and external factors contributing to success or failure in adoption, implementation and spread of the approaches
o qualitative and quantitative means of assessing the activities
o factors facilitating or inhibiting scaling up.

In response to proposals from participants, two additional sessions were added to the programme:

o a presentation by the seven farmer participants of their experiences as farmer-extensionists
o a discussion of the training and support needs of those engaged in reorienting public-sector, traditional transfer-of-technology extension services.

Finally, in the evenings, individual participants showed slides or videos and expanded informally on their work.

What is farmer-led extension?

At the beginning and at the end of the workshop, participants were requested to define 'farmer-led extension'. This exercise produced a huge variety of definitions — reflecting the diversity of activities on the ground. Whilst all the activities described during the workshop aim to ensure that agricultural extension or research services are responsive to resource-poor farmers' needs and potentials, the particular methods used vary enormously.

A group of participants developed the following definition:

What:	A multi-directional communication process
By whom:	between and among extension staff and farmers,
Doing what:	involving the sharing, sourcing and development of knowledge and skills
Why:	in order to meet farming needs and develop innovative capacity among all actors,
Role of farmers:	in which farmers have a controlling interest; are 'centre stage', are the protagonists and play a key role in technology development and delivery; and involving farmers in training other farmers and trainers, and in sharing, sourcing and transferring knowledge and skills.

As the workshop progressed, a clearer distinction emerged between pure 'farmer-to-farmer' extension, and the wider concept of 'farmer-led' extension. The former, typified by the *campesino-a-campesino* experience in Latin America, is characterized by:

o the emergence of a 'movement' initiated and sustained by farmers
o the generation of most innovations by farmers themselves, with occasional external support, for instance from an NGO
o the provision of training by farmers, to farmers, often through the creation of a structure of farmer-promoters and farmer-trainers.

In other words, farmer-to-farmer extension is largely self-contained and self-reliant. Some see it as a special case within 'farmer-led' extension; others see it as quite distinct. Clearly, 'farmer-led' *can* imply farmers' leadership of their own processes and institutions. However, more generally it implies a relationship with those (usually public-sector) agencies responsible for the design and delivery of extension services in which farmers seek to gain a stronger voice.

We have grouped the diversity of activities presented under the banner of 'farmer-led extension' under five categories. Subsequent chapters in this book deal with each in turn:

o Farmer-to-farmer extension (Chapters 4–7).
o Farmer field schools (Chapter 8)
o Problem census/problem solving approaches (Chapter 9)
o NGO–government collaboration in extension (Chapter 10)
o Other approaches to farmer-led extension (Chapter 11).

Many of the organizations represented at the workshop are engaged in one or more of these strategies. The choice of strategy, or combination of strategies, depends on various factors, including:

o The objectives of the project or programme
o The nature of the farmer organizations, community groups or development institutions involved
o The resources these institutions have available
o The institutional and policy environments, including perceived failures of previous systems.

For example, in the context of war and a total breakdown of public-sector services in Nicaragua, NGOs and people's organizations began to support information exchange already practised by farmers — i.e., farmer-to-farmer extension (Chapter 4). Likewise, in Vietnam, public extension services were available only to large-scale state or co-operative farms. In the absence of such services for family gardens, NGOs began supporting family farming. With very limited resources and few staff, they were forced to rely on farmer-to-farmer extension strategies.

The perceived failures of previous systems of technology generation and diffusion have also led to more farmer-led approaches. For example, in Indonesia and other Southeast Asian countries, the failure to spread integrated pest management technologies, despite the efforts of agencies trying numerous dissemination approaches, led NGOs, government organizations and multilateral agencies to support farmer field schools (Chapter 8) and farmer-to-farmer extension (Chapter 4). In Nepal and Bangladesh, public-sector extension staff realized that the training-and-visit system was not responding to poor farmers' needs and potentials. Accordingly, they adopted ways of giving these farmers a larger say in determining the extension agenda (Chapter 9).

Farmers themselves have probably been the most common generators of farmer-led approaches. For example, in Bangladesh a female farmer approached CARE International with questions about fish growth. This led to a substantial farmer-led research and extension project supported by CARE, the government of Bangladesh and the UK Department for International Development (DFID, formerly the Overseas Development Administration) (Chapter 11).

Whatever their origins and rationale, there are now a large number of activities in the world, using a wide variety of strategies and methods, all aimed at creating more responsive extension and research services. Nevertheless, most remain small in scale and coverage. This book aims to disseminate these experiences more widely, contribute to the debate on why such efforts remain small and rare, and explore what can be done to spread greater responsiveness in the service systems.

Actors in farmer-led extension

As is the case with strategies deployed, a wide range of agencies and combinations of organizations are engaged in farmer-led extension. Government organizations, multilateral and bilateral donors, NGOs, farmer associations and community groups were all represented at the workshop. The papers submitted to the organizers mention the following actors:

o Farmers
o Farmer-extensionists or farmer promoters
o Community or farmer groups or associations (and their leaders)
o Field-level extension agents — government, and international and local NGOs
o Local, state and central government agencies
o National government resource institutions (training, research, etc.)
o Government policy makers (especially at the national level)
o The private sector
o Donors
o Mass media.

These actors undertake numerous activities within farmer-led extension. The lists below are not exhaustive, but reflect some key roles and examples drawn from the case papers.

Farmers
o actively make decisions on technology adaptation
o participate in community-level activities and community organizing, including training, work groups and group meetings
o represent or identify sources of indigenous technologies or knowledge
o participate in on-farm trials and experimentation
o redefine the roles and evaluate the performances of other actors in the process.

Farmer-extensionists or farmer promoters
o organize and conduct farmer learning opportunities, e.g., training, study tours and farmer cross-visits.
o search for, introduce and provide technical information to farmers
o simplify or interpret technical information accessed from other institutions
o lead or conduct farmer experimentation, especially on-farm or adaptive research
o encourage the formation and support of community-level groups, such as farmers' associations or mutual work-sharing groups
o monitor and evaluate progress of farm-level agricultural improvements
o liaise between the community and external agricultural development institutions
o facilitate problem identification
o identify and access resources from outside the community
o support community leadership.

Community or farmer groups or associations (and their leaders)
o serve as a co-ordinating mechanism in the community for sharing information, disseminating technology, planning, monitoring, evaluation, etc.
o facilitate resource access and mobilization.

Field-level extension agents — government and international and local NGOs
o encourage the preparation of farmers to become farmer-extensionists
o organize and conduct farmer learning opportunities, e.g., training, study tours and farmer cross-visits
o facilitate research support (from the national and international research community) for farmers on specific technical areas, e.g., integrated pest management, ecological agriculture
o initiate links between communities or farmers and public- or private-sector institutions
o channel feedback so that farmers can influence the setting of government priorities
o input material, human, technical and financial resources toward the establishment, maintenance and management of farmer-led extension programmes
o help reorientate extension services to be more responsive to farmers' needs
o analyse and prioritize community and agricultural problems with farmers.

Local, state and central government agencies
- o form a tripartite alliance (between farmers and their organizations, NGOs and the public sector) to have farmers' concerns more strongly represented in public-sector agriculture research and extension programmes
- o provide a learning structure or facilitate learning for farmers on specific technical areas, e.g., integrated pest management, improved varieties
- o train farmers to become farmer-extensionists
- o hold bimonthly meetings between NGOs and the public sector to identify and develop collaborative projects which fulfil the information needs of farmers.

National government resource institutions (training, research, etc.)
- o provide technical training to support farmer-extensionists
- o input resources (human, technical and financial) focused on the establishment, maintenance and management of farmer-led extension programmes.

Government policy makers (especially at the national level)
- o form a high-level task force of government organizations, NGOs and private input suppliers to draft a revised policy on extension and co-ordinate the necessary organizational changes within the extension service.

The private sector
- o provides information, materials and equipment (usually through sales) to farmer-extensionists which allow them to carry out their extension function more effectively.

Donors
- o provide critical financial resources and logistical support to experimentation with new farmer-led extension strategies.

Farmer-led extension approaches, especially those supported by NGOs, are often part of broader rural or community development activities. This often means that individual actors may be called on to assume several roles.

Outside organizations, such as an NGO or government extension service, can play a critical role in initiating or facilitating the farmer-led extension process. However, this can be difficult, especially given previous modes of interactions with farmers. It may be necessary to redefine the traditional roles of the various actors. For example, the authority of local government institutions to make decisions must be strengthened if they are to have the flexibility needed to meet farmers' demands. To collaborate and communicate effectively, government, NGOs and farmers' groups each have to incorporate some of each others' skills.

The remainder of the book

Chapters 2 and 3 contain edited versions of keynote papers presented by George Axinn (Michigan State University, USA) and Chris Garforth and Nicola Harford (University of Reading, UK) at the workshop. In Chapter 2, Axinn addresses five key challenges to agriculture in the next century: control and accountability, ecological sustainability, the role of women in farming and extension, participation, and corruption. In Chapter 3, Garforth and Harford identify four trends in the way extension is viewed, discuss the shrinking role of government in extension and the implications for sustainability, and identify seven key issues emerging from the previous 20 years' experience.

Chapters 4–7 focus on the 'pure' form of farmer-to-farmer extension. Chapter 4 describes the origins and evolution of farmer-to-farmer extension networks in Latin America, Indonesia, the Philippines, Vietnam, Nepal and India. Chapter 5 summarizes the principles upon which such networks are based and the field methods they deploy. Chapter 6 outlines the roles of the main actors within them — the farmer extensionists, professional extensionists and support agencies. Chapter 7 examines various reactions to some of the main issues, problems and questions thrown up by farmer-to-farmer extension in practice.

Chapters 8–11 describe various other approaches that might be included under the broader term of farmer-led extension. Chapter 8 discusses farmer field schools, a method increasingly used in Southeast Asia to help farmers to learn and discover for themselves solutions to their problems. The chapter describes field schools implemented by public-sector and NGO integrated pest management programmes in Indonesia and the Philippines, and addresses issues that occur in this approach.

Chapter 9 turns to the problem census/problem solving approach. It describes how projects in Nepal and Bangladesh have tried to use this approach within government extension systems, and highlights some of the problems and possibilities of trying to make the public-sector extension system more responsive to local needs.

Chapter 10 describes a number of efforts aimed at developing collaborative links between farmers, NGOs and public-sector extension systems. The cases present the rationale for collaboration, areas or activities in which the three actors have worked together, and the benefits, problems and lessons of collaboration. The cases present perspectives from both government and non-government agencies, aiming to illuminate both the pros and cons of collaboration.

Chapter 11 provides five further case studies within the broad rubric of farmer-led extension. The first of these describes a project in Bangladesh that supported rural women to do their own research on fish culture using small cages. The second case describes an NGO-supported project in Zimbabwe which helps poor communities prioritize their needs and do research on how to meet these needs. The only inputs provided by the project are staff members; the case shows what can be done merely through facilitation. The third case also demonstrates the enormous potential of facilitation. It describes a project in Egypt which assists farmers to prioritize their agricultural research needs, then arranges for them to visit places (such as research stations) where they can find answers or garner ideas to test on their own farms. The fourth case illustrates how a government institute in India has combined farmer-led approaches in an innovative way with more conventional, institution-based training to promote a sophisticated agricultural technology (hybrid rice production). The final case in the chapter describes an interesting but still relatively rare approach: training farmer-extensionists so they can earn income by providing agricultural services to their neighbours for a fee.

Chapter 12 focuses on assessing the impact of farmer-led extension. This has been a crucial area of weakness: the lack of rigorous evaluations of the approach mean it is impossible to tell how useful and effective the approach is compared to alternatives such as conventional extension or media-based approaches. This chapter describes evaluations that have been made at the farmer-, project- and national levels, and then discusses how to make such assessments and some indicators that are (or might be) used.

Chapter 13 discusses efforts at scaling up farmer-led approaches. This is also a weak area: with a few exceptions (such as the *campesino-a-campesino* movement in Latin America and the farmer field schools in Southeast Asia), most farmer-led extension experiences have been localized and small scale. There have been relatively few attempts to expand the approach to a larger area or to institutionalize it within government extension systems. This chapter describes various approaches to 'scaling up' (increasing the size of a programme) and 'scaling out' (spreading the methodology to other organizations and areas), and lists a range of factors that have been found to promote or inhibit attempts at farmer-led extension.

The final chapter draws together the lessons learned by those involved in the initiation, implementation and management of farmer-led agricultural extension and research services, as well as outlining some priority areas for further action, documentation, research and analysis.

Chapters 4–13 consist largely of selected excerpts from the papers submitted to the workshop organizers, together with editorial comments. For clarity, the excerpts are printed in a smaller typeface from the editorial comments:

Text by the editors is printed in this typeface.

Excerpts from workshop papers are printed in this (smaller) typeface.

Excerpts from other publications are indented into the main text.

Significant passages that have been edited out are marked with '...'. This approach was chosen to preserve as much as possible of the information and flavour of the original papers, but in a structure that draws together common strands from among the papers. A guide at the end of the book shows where readers can find the various parts of papers that appear in several places in the book. Cross-references have been used where necessary to avoid repetition.

Unfortunately in a book of this size it is not possible to include the complete texts of papers, or indeed excerpts from the more than 50 papers submitted to the workshop organizers (listed in the Appendix 2). Chapters 1 and 14, and the editorial comments in the remaining chapters, are based on a careful review of all these papers. Seventeen of the papers are published in full in ODI's *Agricultural Research and Extension Network Paper* 59 (Scarborough 1996), available from ODI. The complete text of the other papers can be obtained from IIRR (see the address at the front of the book).

2 Challenges to agricultural extension in the twenty-first century

George H. Axinn[1]

A world in which 20 per cent of the population enjoys 84 per cent of the annual income, while another 20 per cent struggles for survival on a mere 1.4 per cent of the world's income... can never provide a secure and sustainable way of life for humankind. — *M.S. Swaminathan, 1994*

The changing global scene

IN THE STRUGGLE by agricultural extension toward increased food supplies and rural development, there have been many sustained successes. But many efforts that appeared successful at the time of implementation have proved later to be unsustainable.

This is an era of rapid technical change. Biotechnology in plant and animal breeding, high speed transportation, and global electronic communication networks have already changed the potential for agricultural extension beyond anything expected. Technical change is always accompanied by, and constrained by all types of non-technical phenomena — the cultural, social, economic, political, biological, administrative, and diplomatic dimensions of life are real, and we must take them into account. Global communication has tremendous potential for the exchange of ideas and information, but it has not brought peace and friendship to humankind. Nevertheless, the reality of global e-mail, and the promise of linked computers in every agricultural extension office and every rural NGO office — and potentially on every farm — are some of the reasons why the agricultural information system of the twenty-first century will be very different from what we know today.

The ability of this generation to exploit our ecosystem more rapidly than could our predecessors has given rise to global concern for the environment. Ecologists can identify the problems, but it will take more than ecologists to discover acceptable and implementable solutions.

Thus we see:

o   increasing wealth among smaller numbers in most countries, while ever-larger numbers of people find themselves in poverty
o   a rapidly growing global population putting increasing stress on food production, preservation, and distribution

---

1.   Professor Emeritus, College of Agriculture and Natural Resources, Michigan State University, East Lansing, Michigan, USA.

o a widespread lust for consumption at the expense of the sustainability of the natural resource base

o gender and age roles and statuses collapsing faster than humanity can adjust.

These are times of global political turmoil. The oversimplification of an East, a West, and a Third World, or a North and a South, has faded, and the complexities emerging in its place are enormous. With a global money market, no nation state can control its own currency, much less the multi-national corporations.

All this is happening in a era when new knowledge is being generated and disseminated at a faster rate than ever before. But this knowledge tends to be highly specialized and so fragmented that we have been unable to put it together to solve such serious problems as hunger, natural resource degradation, and the pollution of air, water, soil, and human minds.

The challenge to agriculture

If rural people were allowed by their urban brothers and sisters merely to feed themselves from the lands and waters upon which they toil, rural life would be more pleasant, and the challenges to professional agriculture, forestry, fisheries, and rural development would be much simpler. But that is not the case in today's world. Those who farm must produce enough not only to feed themselves, but to feed increasing numbers of those who live in the urban world. And, realistically, urban people control the political systems, the economic systems, and the military and policy systems.

This trend is not decreasing. As Alex McCalla (1994) put it recently,

> As the world population moves towards 8.5 billion in the year 2025, 83 percent will live in less-developed countries as against 75 percent in 1985. Sub-Saharan Africa will exhibit faster population growth than Asia, and current projections suggest that the number of malnourished people world-wide will rise from 750 million to 1 billion. By 2025 the demand for staple food will be more than double what is currently produced. Based on current trends of production and consumption, the two regions in which some two-thirds of the rural poor live — South Asia and sub-Saharan Africa — will jointly have a food gap of over 460 million tons by 2025, which is more than double the current total for world grain of 200 million tons.

Food security — for rural as well as urban people — is not simply a matter of having a global supply greater than the demand. As Amartya Kumar Sen (1981) demonstrated so effectively with data on several of the world's famines, it is not merely a matter of having hungry mouths to feed, and therefore demand for food. If you don't have what economists call *effective demand*, you don't get the food. Put another way, food security has at least three dimensions: the production of food; the storage, transportation, processing, wholesaling, and retailing of food (marketing); and the entitlement to food. At the close of the twentieth century, we are far from solving the entitlement problem.

14

Agricultural extension must focus on increasing production and productivity of food and fibre in an economically and environmentally sustainable way, and in a way which does not destroy rural livelihoods and communities. In many places in the last few decades increasing the food supply has become the central goal of agricultural extension. A consequence has been the neglect of small mixed-farming systems, usually on less productive lands, where the primary goal is to feed the family. Large government extension systems listened less to farmers, and more to highly specialized agricultural researchers, and tried to deliver appropriate technologies to farmers. Too often, technologies developed for large-scale, specialized operations did not fit the needs and interests of smaller scale, subsistence farmers. Agricultural research emphasized high-input strategies and one commodity at a time. The result, toward the end of the twentieth century, was very large agricultural extension systems which were increasingly useless to people in small, mixed farming systems. And while many international and local NGOs took a much more human, family-welfare approach, most were limited to small areas.

During the last half of the twentieth century, agricultural extension systems have drifted away from the multiple roles which characterize some of their greatest successes, and slipped into excessive emphasis on delivering new technology to farming people. Many of the largest government systems have neglected the opportunity to organize groups, empower their clientele, press for equity, and demand sustainability of fields and streams — all critical aspects of successful long-range rural development. These extension systems are led by government officers, agricultural scientists, and international agencies; they are not farmer-led.

Meanwhile, scholars and practitioners have increasingly observed that everything is connected to everything else. Farming systems research and extension, conducted by a small minority of professionals in Africa, Asia, and Latin America, attempted to comprehend the whole farm as a system. As Richard Bawden (1991:2362) noted:

> Reductionist science with its positivistic philosophical roots and experimental research practices has generally served agriculture well for around 150 years. Technological innovations based on the propositions generated through this paradigm have played a profound role in the extraordinary productivity growth that has occurred in agriculture across the globe. Yet with recognition of its success in this context is the realization of its inadequacies from broader perspectives. There is an increasing sense about degradation of biophysical environments, distortions of socio-economic environments, and dislocations of cultural environments too often associated with agricultural practices. There are calls for a new science and praxis of complexity to deal with these problematic relationships between agriculture and the environment in which it is conducted. Systems thinking and practices are emerging as useful in this regard.

As we move into the twenty-first century, it will be increasingly necessary, and increasingly feasible, to take a whole-systems approach to organized, positive change in rural places. For extension, that means helping farming people toward sustainable increasing productivity — particularly in small-scale mixed-farming systems

15

in rainfed areas, in upland areas, and in other places which have been neglected. It also demands measuring success in terms of the *consumption* of rural people, as well as their *production*. And that, in turn, will require agricultural extension systems which help farm men and women to organize themselves in ways which empower them — to lead extension and to exert enough power and influence over research systems so that they generate useful, practical information which fits the needs and interests of those farming people.

Challenges for extension

I see five major challenges to agricultural extension in the twenty-first century. I believe the most critical global problem and opportunity for extension is that of control and accountability. Next are two overriding concerns: the need to ensure ecosystem sustainability and to serve women farmers. I then turn briefly to two further challenges: participation, and human greed and corruption.

Control and accountability
Extension systems are like other types of human organizations. Whoever owns and operates them, also controls them. Whoever controls an extension system determines its programmes and its staff. Historically, the functions of exploring and testing new techniques in farming (what we now call 'research'), and then sharing information about what works and what doesn't (what we now call 'extension'), have been a part of what farming people do. The early organized efforts at agricultural extension tended to be by groups of farmers, usually as part of organizations they established. From these emerged the early 'master farmer' programmes in Japan, the agricultural societies of Europe, and the Farm Bureaus of the USA (Axinn and Thorat 1972).

These groups made many attempts to serve their own needs and interests: local secret societies, irrigation associations, agricultural fairs and exhibitions, cattle shows, research farms, and general agricultural extension. Later, in an effort to further the interests of rural life, and to help feed growing numbers of people in the cities, governments became sponsors of these extension systems.

It has become increasingly evident, however, that as extension systems have grown in size and complexity, they have ceased to be controlled by farming people. The personnel of such systems feel more accountable to their employers or professions than they do to their farmer clientele. This is reflected in the lack of relevance to local needs and interests in some extension programmes.

Farm families (the circle on the left in Figure 2.1) are usually the client or the 'target system' of both agricultural extension systems and many local NGOs.

The circle labelled 'extension acquisition system' represents organizations of people from farm families who have taken on the function of *acquiring* from the outside world what they believe they want and need. This might be just one individual, an informal grouping which emerges when needed and then disappears, or a rather formal organized group. It is distinguished from circles further to the

16

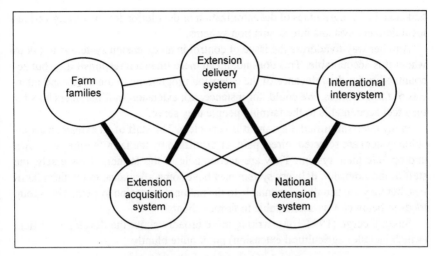

Figure 2.1: Structure and control of agricultural extension
(adapted from Axinn 1978, Ch. 3)

right because it is controlled by the people in the farm families. They own it and operate it.

The function of the 'extension delivery system' in the centre of Figure 2.1 is to *deliver* ideas, information, or sometimes physical inputs to the farm families. Unlike the acquisition system, it is owned, operated and controlled by outsiders (usually by people from cities). Rather than to *acquire* for the village what its residents request, it is designed to *deliver* what these outsiders think the village needs. Examples of such delivery systems are the district extension office or a local NGO office.

The next circle represents a national extension system. This could be the ministry of agriculture or local government, an educational institution, a private firm, or a national NGO, perhaps with a religious base. It may have various links with the farm family: providing goods or services to it, extracting products or information from it, or for other purposes.

Finally, on the far right side of the diagram, are international agencies. These are organizations from outside the country, belonging to another state or to an international organization or NGO.

If a national organization wishes to become more responsive to the needs and interests of farm families — to become more farmer-led — one strategy is to decentralize functions and sometimes decision-making to local delivery systems. Those which are even further decentralized will share functions with acquisition systems. In the middle of the twentieth century, Taiwan demonstrated the effectiveness of farmer's associations as instruments of village development. Malaysia followed by converting some of its delivery systems, particularly in extension, into acquisition systems. By the end of the twentieth century, both the Philippines and Indonesia

17

had launched programmes of decentralization or devolution by converting various local delivery systems into acquisition systems.

Another way to address the issue of control in an extension system is to ask to whom it is accountable. This does not mean mere financial responsibility, but accountability for the relevance of the extension programme to the needs and interests of farm families. We could, for instance, ask extension staff members how far they feel accountable to the farming people they serve.

In my over-simplified diagram, it is very clear. The staff of an extension acquisition system are selected, hired, paid, or dismissed by the farm families who own and operate their system. They are accountable to the farmers. Conversely, the staff of the extension delivery system may have some allegiance to the farm families, but they are usually accountable to the national extension system. This group tends to be much less accountable to farmer clients.

Susan George (1992:168), writing more broadly about the development field (which includes agricultural extension) put it quite bluntly:

> [Some] people working in the field of 'development' are wholly disqualified from claiming 'professional' status. Unlike other, genuine professionals, they are accountable to no one (except in the ordinary hierarchical way). If they make a mess of a development project, they can walk away from their victims, towards the next disaster.

Since extension activities so often involve outsiders, who are invited to participate because of their knowledge or financial inputs, but who have no long-range stake in the consequences of whatever advice they might give, our field is sometimes deserving of such criticism. This lack of accountability to clientele is not unique to extension. It is found in other branches of agriculture, health, forestry, education and other fields. The phenomenon is found throughout the development professions, and is a serious issue.

What are the implications of *control* and *client accountability* for farmer-led approaches to extension? What are the implications of an 'acquisition-system' type of structure and control for farmer-led extension? Whoever controls the personnel and the programme determines relevance to farmers. If there is little accountability to farmers, neither a government extension system nor an NGO is likely to be controlled by farmers.

Sustainability

By the 1970s it had become apparent to many development professionals that things could not get 'bigger and better' forever: there were limits to development and growth (Meadows *et al.* 1972). A major shock of the twentieth century was the awareness that there were no more 'new worlds' left on this planet. Wherever one might venture, others were already there. And the natural resources which fuelled human consumption were not unlimited. In the last twenty years of the century, serious official development efforts began to consider the *sustainability* of what was being planned and implemented.

18

From a global perspective, any change may have negative consequences: some short-term improvements for some people may result in a serious worsening for others, or for those same people in the long term. But the serious issue is the sustainability of this planet for humanity to survive for coming generations.

There are two major types of sustainability problems in agriculture. One arises from over-use of such inputs as fertilizer and irrigation water in large-scale commercial agriculture. The other relates to the marginal lands and fragile ecosystems with small-scale mixed-farming systems and large numbers of poor people trying to survive by producing whatever they can.

What are the implications of the issue of sustainability for agricultural extension? There are technical and economic dimensions — in which extension programmes are already involved. But there are also political, cultural, social and other dimensions, in which agricultural extension has a significant interest. This book explores some of these.

Women farmers and women extensionists

One of the most serious challenges to agricultural extension toward the close of the twentieth century is the very high proportion of farmers who are women — and the even higher proportion of extension staff who are men. Some of my colleagues believe I should not raise this as a separate item, as it is related to all the other issues. But I believe it has been neglected for too long; there are several demonstrations around the world where extension systems have taken women farmers seriously. This is a major opportunity for farmer-led extension.

Contemporary scholarship on sustainable agriculture and rural development places increasing emphasis on gender issues, the necessity of disaggregating data by gender, and designing programmes that take into account the different functions of women and men in rural life.

In Africa, Asia, and Latin America the high proportion of farm work done by women is well documented (Acharya and Bennett 1981, Axinn and Axinn 1969; N.Axinn 1990, Shiva 1988, Cloud 1989). At the same time, the professional personnel who work on agriculture and rural development tend to be mostly men. In some countries, as much as 85 per cent of all farm work is done by women while 99 per cent of the extension personnel are men. Men also dominate the professional staffs of universities, government agencies, and NGOs which deal with farming (Shiva 1991, Sen and Grown 1987, Kardam 1991). While excellent research, teaching, and extension are being done by some men sensitive to the impact of gender on agriculture, there is a global tendency for this problem not to be integrated into mainstream issues. This is a major strategic error.

Janice Jiggins (1994:41) summarized it this way:

> It is a world governed by the public decisions of men who choose to solve problems by force. It is a world in which women and children form the majority of the poor, the displaced, and the hungry. Such a world is not sustainable.

19

Such statements are now accepted by many scholars, but not yet by many practitioners, including high-level policy makers. In fact, *denial* is still the normal response. This situation is changing gradually but slowly.

The gender issue pervades all aspects of extension activity, and is related to the other challenges discussed in this chapter. There are implications for women-farmer-led extension, for the timing, location, and language of many types of extension activities.

Participation

The challenge of participation is not new to those concerned with extension. By the middle of the twentieth century, it was recognized in both extension and community development that a major means of ensuring relevance and therefore success was to design programmes so that those affected by them participated at all stages of their planning, implementation and evaluation. But the idea of participation was not widely accepted, particularly by those in power where top-down authority was the cultural and political norm.

A favourite illustration of mine is the work of a man and a team of oxen in a field. From one perspective, the man and the oxen are all participating in the work. But the oxen do not decide when to work and when to rest. The oxen do not decide when to start, how much work to do, when to drink. The man makes all the decisions, but the oxen share the work. This view of participation is common among the powerful who control social, political and economic systems. But it is not the meaning of participation which is fruitful in extension.

We have plenty of examples of participation in extension. There have been some great successes in this field, as well as many failures. One of the critical differences between the successes and the failures is the extent to which the people who are supposed to benefit from the programme have a voice in deciding the content, the objectives, and the methods used by the system. In other words, *the extent to which the clientele participate in all aspects of planning and implementing the programme is directly related to its success.*

But, in spite of the well-documented evidence, many extension organizations, particularly those controlled by governments, make a different basic assumption. They assume that farmers are really not competent to decide the objectives or content of extension programmes, simply because many farmers have little formal schooling. They take the position that scientists at government research establishments or universities should make those decisions.

This is an example of substituting the knowledge of outside experts for that of the clientele. It results in a 'top-down' delivery approach, in which others decide what farmers need to know, and attempt to deliver it to them. This sometimes works well in specialized situations. But for extension in general, and especially with the small-scale mixed-farming systems in which most rural people live and work, it is almost invariably a failure (Axinn 1988).

Scholars and practitioners observing extension throughout the world have come to a general consensus that 'top-down' approaches tend to be much less effective than participatory, farmer-centred, approaches. The 'top-down' approaches feature technology transfer — such as that of the typical ministry of agriculture delivery system — from central research organizations to extension specialists to field extension personnel to farmers. By contrast, in participatory, farmer-centred approaches, the clientele participate in determining the agenda, the content, the communication channels to be used, and even the personnel to staff the system (Antholt 1991, Arnaiz 1995, Brokensha and Little 1988, Chambers 1983 and 1993, Clark 1991, Esman and Uphoff 1984, Farrington and Martin 1987, Korten 1987, Korten and Klauss 1984, Uphoff 1986 and 1992).

Some of the most effective extension systems have been organized by groups of farmers, such as the farmers' associations of Taiwan in the 1950s and the county Farm Bureaus in the USA early in the twentieth century. The clientele participated in everything, because they *owned and operated* the extension systems. These were extension acquisition systems.

It is easy for outsiders to recommend participation, but it may not be implementable in practice. The nature of participation itself may be different from place to place, from culture to culture. There is not one simple formula which can be implemented everywhere. In some places the assumption is that all people have a right to be treated with equity, and that equity is an essential component of sustainable development. In other places, equity among humans is unknown, and difficult to imagine. From a strategic perspective, it is increasingly clear that change without participation of those people most affected by it is not likely to be viewed as development.

What are the strategies for achieving more participation through farmer-led approaches to extension? I believe there are many. They are significant. And they should guide our future.

Greed and corruption
Human greed and corruption are not concepts which the extension literature typically addresses. But if ignored, they can defeat the best of extension strategies. Self-interest may be viewed as a basic, intrinsic human characteristic. Normal individuals learn that it is actually in their self-interest also to be concerned about the well-being of others. However, the breakdown in 'normal' behaviour patterns, which might be labelled as overt greed, is real; it leads to the corrupt manipulation of extension programmes for individuals' personal benefit.

Increasingly, the literature uses the word 'greed' to account for some of the failure of international development activities. For example, the 1993 UNDP Human Development Report focuses on people's participation. Its section on obstacles states: 'Participation is a plant that does not grow easily in the human environment. Powerful vested interests, driven by personal greed, erect numerous obstacles to block off the roots to people's political and economic power' (UNDP 1993:28). These obstacles include legal systems, bureaucratic constraints, social norms and the mal-distribution of assets. Greed and corruption are an area where

21

well-meaning planners, scholars, experts, and administrators are typically defeated politically by powerful commercial, industrial and agricultural forces.

The evidence of greed by powerful individuals who siphon off large proportions of the funds for development projects is well known. Sometimes referred to as 'leakage', practitioners attempt to keep the proportion of total money used for this purpose to a minimum. Cases have been well documented by Susan George (1988 and 1992) and Graham Hancock (1989).

My personal experience suggests that data on these aspects of extension and other types of development co-operation tend to be deliberately hidden, especially from 'outsiders'. Thus extension professionals may need to acquire greater skills in use of the local language, as well as local social and cultural patterns, in order to understand the situation, and to make appropriate operating decisions. However, serious professionals who are insiders sometimes are able to utilize collaboration with outsiders to strengthen their position in defending themselves from more powerful people within their own countries.

3 Extension experiences in agriculture and natural resource management in the 1980s and 1990s[1]

Chris Garforth and Nicola Harford[2]

Introduction

THIS CHAPTER FALLS into four parts. First it identifies four general trends in the way agricultural extension is thought about and provided. It then reflects on the growing view that the role of the public sector in extension should diminish — a view that in part derives from disappointment with these dominant approaches. The third part explores the implications of the sustainability agenda for how agricultural extension services are organized and managed. The final part identifies seven key issues we must take into account in a more farmer-led approach to extension.

Changing concepts and practice

Among the many changes in the way people view extension over the past two decades, four are particularly relevant to this book: the recognition that extension is not the exclusive preserve of extension agencies; the growing variety of forms of provision; an expansion of the agenda which extension is expected to address; and changes in our understanding of how extension works.

Extension: activity and agency

Most countries have one or more agencies whose primary function is to provide extension support to farmers. But most of the things we usually associate with extension are also done by research agencies, companies, other organizations and individuals for whom extension is a natural part of their main activities (such as selling inputs or buying farm produce), and even more so by farmers who give and seek advice among themselves, share new information and teach one another new skills. The distinction between extension *activity* and extension *agency* is relevant to any discussion of 'farmer-led' approaches to extension: we are not concerned primarily with building farmer-led approaches within extension agencies, but with the broader enterprise of seeing how extension as an activity can become more responsive to, and be led by, the needs and interests of farmers.

1. The research on which this chapter is based was partly funded by the Department for International Development (DFID, formerly the Overseas Development Administration) through research contract R5984.
2. Respectively professor of extension systems, and research fellow, Agricultural Extension and Rural Development Department, University of Reading, UK.

Variety of provision

In the early 1980s, when people spoke about extension agencies, the normal assumption was that these would be public-sector agencies, funded and managed by governments. This is no longer the case, of course, and there is an increasing variety of forms of provision: commercial consultancy firms, government agencies which recover a proportion of their costs in fees from clients, extension organizations run by farmers' associations, and non-profit NGOs. In the public sector, it is still common to have separate research and extension organizations, often under different ministries. With NGOs, research is done more often in partnership with farmers, and the research and extension functions are much more closely integrated. One of the main reasons for NGOs' involvement in extension is that public-sector services have proved not very effective at supporting resource-poor farming households: variety in provision is more likely to meet the needs of a wide range of categories of farmer.

An expanding agenda

Assumptions have also been changing about the proper role of extension in the economic and social development of rural areas. There has always been a debate on the proper balance in the public sector between economic and social goals. This is inevitable given the importance of agriculture, in both developed and developing countries, in the social fabric of rural areas, as well as in producing food for cities and foreign exchange for economic development. Economic goals focus on raising production and productivity. Among extension's social goals are:

○ *equity* — achieving greater equality of access to, and security of, the means of production between communities, households, men and women, and individuals
○ *poverty alleviation* — encouraging labour-intensive technologies to facilitate employment of the landless and near landless, and developing alternative livelihoods for the poor (Jazairy *et al.* 1992)
○ *improved nutrition* — particularly for children.

To this agenda have more recently been added two further suggestions for the role of extension: ensuring food security (at a national level and within rural communities), and conserving the environment. This last demand is made not for the sake of conservation *per se*, but because of the concern that farming should not damage or destroy the resource base on which it depends.

These very different perspectives influence how we view the achievements of extension organizations and the outcome of extension activities. From a social policy perspective, a failure to address the needs of the poorest would be seen as a serious shortcoming; those emphasizing economic goals might argue that using extension to address social goals is inefficient and that other policy tools would be more appropriate.

How does extension work?

Our understanding of how the activity of extension works has also changed. Extension professionals used to speak principally in terms of 'technology transfer': they would pass on new varieties and practices to farmers, who would then incorporate them into their farming systems and thereby improve their productivity or output. This simplistic notion was reflected in the fact that national extension projects were appraised by donors on the basis of predicted levels of uptake of new technology with a known effect on yields. Decision-making processes by which this new technology became integrated into the farming systems were assumed to follow a set sequence (Everett Rogers 1983). It is now, by contrast, more common to hear of helping farmers to identify constraints, problems and opportunities on their farms and then helping them to obtain the information and other support they need to solve the problems and take advantage of opportunities. Alan Rogers (1993) links this trend to developments in models of adult education, from teaching, to interactive and reflexive learning.

This view recognizes the need for greater interaction and dialogue, and acknowledges the farmer's expertise in identifying problems and selecting options for improvement. The frequent call for participatory methods and recognition of farmers' knowledge derives partly from the failures of 'transfer of technology' approaches. But it also comes from better, empirically based, understanding of how farmers compare options, minimize risk, adapt practices, and seek information to assist them in their decisions.

This is not to deny the validity of the notion of transferring technology. Down the centuries and across the globe, technologies have been taken from place to place and have led to radical changes in farming systems and agricultural economies. But with planned technology transfer, it is important to ensure that the technology is appropriate, to recognize that farmers are the only ones who can decide whether the technology is relevant to their farms and resources, to see adaptation rather than straightforward adoption as a valid response to extension, and to ensure that the transfer process itself is based on sound principles of adult learning. The integrated pest management farmer field schools (see Chapter 8) are a good example of a highly interactive and participatory approach to the transfer of a set of technologies which have themselves been developed by scientists in partnership with extension professionals and farmers (Röling and van der Fliert 1995).

A clearer focus on the farmer and his or her needs has helped us reconceptualize the relationship between farmers and extension organizations. If we put the farmer at the centre and ask what information he or she exchanges with other individuals and institutions, we find a richness of interactions and a wide diversity among farmers. In a study of farmer information systems in relation to small-scale dairy production in Kerala, India, only two pairs of farmers from a total sample of 120 had identical 'total information systems' (Ramkumar 1994:306). A challenge here for extension organizations is to match their information exchange and delivery systems to the information-seeking systems of farmers (Axinn (Chapter 2), Zijp 1992), and in so doing to redefine the role of the extension worker.

Donor policies and fashions in agricultural extension

The four trends discussed above have influenced, and been influenced by, the major aid donors, particularly the World Bank, FAO, USAID and (more recently) IFAD, with other bilateral donors (for example, GTZ and the UK's Department for International Development (DFID, formerly the Overseas Development Administration)) also playing an important role. The World Bank has pushed the training and visit model with an almost ideological zeal, while USAID, which earlier funded efforts to reproduce the United States extension system based on the land grant colleges, promoted farming systems research and extension in the 1980s. More recently, USAID support has focused on private sector extension, intensifying the use of mass media, and selectively increasing the effectiveness of public-sector institutions (Byrnes 1990).

A review of USAID projects in Africa reveals a number of recurring problems which also occur in other donors' programmes: the high recurrent costs which host governments are left with — leading to unsustainable activities and staffing levels and dependency on donors for funds, compounded by budgetary constraints resulting from structural adjustment programmes; the simplistic measurement of success of training by the number of people trained and the emphasis on training in the USA; insufficient understanding of the local context; imposition of approaches (first the land-grant model and then farming systems); and underestimation of time required for institution-building (e.g., USAID 1989).

Other donors have been less committed to single solutions to the varied circumstances of the countries with which they work, although they have been active in the general search for ways of ensuring more effective farmer involvement in the design and implementation of projects. The shift in emphasis within projects supported by the UK's DFID since 1980, for example, shows the common disenchantment with efforts based on a simplistic 'transfer of technology' model. The initial design of the Indo-British Fertilizer Education Project, in six states of northern India, incorporated the notion of a hierarchical structure of extension personnel giving farmers specific technical advice on a balanced use of fertilizers based on soil sampling. The limitations of this approach were realized during implementation, and a wider range of technical information and advice was made available to rural households. Equity issues were taken up and reflected in the composition of village committees with which the field-level staff planned demonstrations and other extension activities. More recent DFID-supported agricultural projects in India have been designed explicitly as process projects, with participatory technology development as a key component (see Mosse 1993).

Disenchantment with the public sector

There is a growing feeling among donors that the days of large-scale public-sector involvement in agricultural extension are numbered. There are four main reasons for reducing public expenditure on extension:

- o the view that benefits which accrue to individual farmers from extension advice and support should be paid for, just as any other input
- o the high recurrent costs of national extension organizations (such as training and visit systems) set up initially with donor support
- o the recognition that uniform, hierarchical government bureaucracies are not the best way of providing a flexible service tailored to the needs of different categories of farmer and varied agro-ecological and economic conditions (Garforth 1995)
- o the apparent success of developed countries in moving extension towards a commercial, cost-recovering activity, while at the same time enabling it to become more responsive and accountable to clients (Rivera and Gustafson 1991).

Recent papers by Ameur (1994), Antholt (1994) and Umali and Schwartz (1994) strongly promote the privatization of public extension services. The implication for national governments is that they should devise a clear strategy for extension, which is likely to encompass the adoption of multiple approaches to extension. Cost considerations and the limited success of single-system approaches point to the need for action. In particular, some World Bank staff are proposing that the public sector divests itself of those aspects of extension that the private sector can take over, both service provision and input supply. Therefore the role of the public sector will need redefining.

Natural resource management and 'sustainability'

The discussion so far has assumed that the underlying purpose of extension is to facilitate technological change at farm level, which will enhance the productive capacity of the farm and its operators. As noted earlier, however, reflections on the design and performance of agricultural and natural resource management projects have been influenced since the mid-1980s by the growing concern over sustainability of farming systems and over widespread deterioration of the physical environment on which agriculture depends.

Long-standing concerns over soil conservation, for example, have been brought into focus by recent debates about deforestation, soil erosion, desertification, pollution and over-extraction of surface- and groundwater, dependence on non-renewable petroleum, and the inappropriate use of agrochemicals (Pretty 1995).

Sustainability is not just a question of technology. There are important social, economic and institutional issues as well. From a social perspective, agricultural development must provide sustainable livelihoods for rural households, particularly for those with few resources and little opportunity for off-farm work. An economic perspective points to the need for farming systems to generate sufficient returns to justify the resources used. Institutional issues focus on the ability of the supporting infrastructure to guarantee supplies of necessary inputs to farmers, including land, credit, nutrients and information. In some areas, for example, the sustainability of small-scale farming is hampered because poorer families lack secure land tenure.

Another important part of the institutional structure which supports agriculture is the agricultural knowledge and information system, which includes farmers' existing knowledge and abilities. Even if sustainable technology is available, it may not be widely applied if farmers do not have the necessary knowledge and skills.

In terms of extension approaches, social forestry projects have highlighted the importance of group and community involvement in extension, in contrast to the individual farm orientation of most agricultural extension work. In practice, however, successful group approaches are rare, even (or especially) when dealing with common property resources. In range management programmes such as Botswana's Tribal Grazing Land Policy and Livestock II Project, for instance, individual commercial ranching developed at the expense of the management of communally grazed areas. In a similar way, in social forestry programmes in India, farm forestry on individual holdings has developed faster than community woodlots. Arnold and Stewart (1991) point out that even when planting targets on public land are reached, there has been minimal public involvement or consultation and therefore little prospect of effective community management. More recently, community involvement in management has been a central feature of forest and environment projects in India, Nepal and other countries in Asia; however, the methodology and training implications for extension staff have not yet been fully worked out.

Above all, where sustainability becomes a priority, more decisions about the use of land and other resources must be taken at levels beyond the individual farm family. Often, the necessary decision-making bodies (what Niels Röling (1993) calls 'platforms') do not exist. Extension workers will then find themselves increasingly involved in forming groups, negotiating, reconciling conflicts of interest and working in teams with other professionals, and devoting less time to promoting specific changes in farming practice with individual farmers. Much of the time of front-line forestry staff in Nepal, for example, is taken up with supporting the formation of user groups who can eventually take over the management of local forests. Experiences with integrated pest management in Indonesia and the Philippines, rat-control campaigns in Bangladesh, and watershed planning by the National Wastelands Development Board in India, all confirm the need for new approaches to extension when long-term sustainability highlights the interdependence of individual farm decision-makers.

The organizational structure of extension agencies also needs rethinking. The problem of soil erosion, for example, cuts across the areas of responsibility of different sectoral agencies. In Sri Lanka, responsibility for soil conservation is spread among a dozen ministries and nearly 40 government agencies (Belshaw *et al.* 1991). At the very least, effective co-ordination mechanisms are needed to allow specialists to work together without being constrained by their own agencies' priorities. Some projects have found considerable scope for partnership between government and NGOs in combating the degradation of renewable natural resources. Similarly, experience in Bangladesh shows the potential for new forms of co-operation between government and NGOs in developing and promoting sustainable livelihoods for resource-poor rural households. Röling and van der Fliert

28

(1995: 46) observe that in Indonesia, integrated pest management 'seems to require decentralized teams of trained staff, capable of autonomous, locally-specific decision making, based on local monitoring and experimentation, and rooted in active farmer participation and control'.

Issues

The experience reviewed above suggests a number of issues to consider in seeking more appropriate ways of organizing extension support for agriculture and natural resource management.

Who pays for what?

A key issue for the future is how extension services are to be paid for. Moves to shift at least some services to the private sector and introduce partial cost recovery from clients could be an important part of the mechanism by which extension becomes more farmer-led. If farmers are paying directly for the service they receive they, in theory at least, have a measure of control over those providing it. There are two conditions for this to become a reality: farmers must be able to choose whether to pay, and there must be alternative providers — i.e., a market in the provision of extension services. Government should continue to finance extension in two areas: 'public interest' issues, such as environmental protection and management, and as a safety net for those households who simply cannot afford to pay. Governments would also need to ensure the environment is suitable for private-sector provision, including liberalization of input markets, physical and social infrastructure, and functioning legal systems (Umali and Schwartz 1994).

Welcoming diversity

The idea of having a variety of providers of extension services, with different approaches and methods, possibly working with different categories of client, is not a recipe for anarchy and inefficiency. Rather it is a sensible response to the diversity within the farming sector. Farms differ in size and resources, farmers differ in their degrees of reliance on agriculture for their livelihoods, farming systems vary from one agro-ecological zone to another. A farmer-led extension system needs to be able to respond to these differences.

Even within the public sector there is a range of possible organizational forms and means of provision. Decentralization, as has taken place in the Philippines, offers the possibility of local responsiveness to client needs and demands. In China, extension reform has allowed different models to emerge, with local extension personnel and agencies supplementing their central government finance by a range of income-generating measures (Yinghui 1993). In Vietnam, where the government has few resources to invest in setting up an extension service, provincial administrations are co-operating with existing organizations and networks in rural areas to provide extension services to

29

farmers (Christoplos and Nitsch 1994). Governments can also continue to fund extension without themselves managing or directly providing the service, by (for example) contracting out the task of running services to commercial agencies or NGOs.

Relationships between governments and NGOs vary from cool and formal, to warm and active. In the Philippines, municipal agricultural offices have an explicit mandate to work alongside and complement the many NGOs active in rural areas. In some other countries in Asia, there is often mutual reserve or even distrust. However, government extension agencies are now realizing that the NGOs have expertise, and in particular a facility for working with disadvantaged groups, from which they can learn and which can complement their own strengths. In a project in north-west Bangladesh, for example, a major NGO (RDRS) and the Department of Agricultural Extension are pooling their resources to offer a much fuller and more accessible service to farmers than either could provide separately. RDRS works with landless and marginal farmers, while the DAE provides technical support to RDRS and works directly with farmers with more than 0.6 hectare of land.

Another example of complementarity is in the Western Ghats Forest and Environment Project in Karnataka, southern India. Here an NGO with considerable experience in participatory approaches has been contracted by the state Forest Department to train forestry personnel in participatory rural appraisal and joint forest planning and management.

Training extension personnel

A re-thinking of extension approaches necessarily has implications for the training of extension workers. Sustainable agricultural development and a move to farmer-led approaches require extension personnel to have a deep understanding of farming systems and the interaction between agriculture and the physical and socio-economic environment. This is essential if they are to adapt technical advice to the specific circumstances of individual farms and local environments. At the same time, their analytical skills must be developed so that they can help farmers identify the complex web of factors that underlie production problems and the potential for improvement. They need to be able to work closely with groups and communities: to facilitate community analyses of the local environment, to support the development or strengthening of groups which can take and implement decisions about the use of common property resources, to act as intermediaries between farmer groups and government institutions. Training in communication skills (particularly with groups, but also in dialogue with individual farmers), in participatory rural appraisal and in problem-solving becomes increasingly important.

This is not only a question of the content of training: the learning and teaching methods used in training institutions also need to be brought into line with the requirements of 'extension for sustainability'. Communication skills are learned by trying them out and then reflecting, with the critical help of peers and trainer, on the outcome. An appreciation of the variability and complexity of farming systems comes as much from interviewing farmers about their farms as it does from textbooks and lectures. The role of the trainer becomes one of facilitating learning rather than imparting information. These training requirements do not diminish the need for a sound knowledge of agricultural science and technology: indeed, extension for sustainable agriculture requires extension personnel to have more, not less, confidence in their scientific understanding of agriculture.

Equity and targeting

As for the targeting of extension programmes, recent experience continues to highlight gender issues and the needs of the rural poor. It has been suggested that women have a particularly important role as 'environmental managers' (Davidson 1991). They also often use common property resources such as forests and water supplies in very different ways from men. The acknowledged gender bias of much agricultural extension work should warn us of the need to take account of these differences, and to develop approaches that build on women's environmental knowledge and tasks within the rural economy. Considerably more is needed than merely providing gender training for male extensionists. Projects that have provided pre-service and in-service training for female extensionists, group training of farm women and follow-up have successfully reached farm women from small and marginal farms.

It is the rural poor who suffer most from the degradation of natural resources, particularly in marginal areas. They are more likely than their resource-rich neighbours to be dependent on vulnerable common property resources, and less likely to have any reserves to protect them from environmental or economic catastrophe. Many environmental problems, such as the scarcity of firewood or degradation of common grazing, affect the poorest households particularly severely. By definition, resource-poor households are least able to invest in technologies that conserve or enhance resources: the need for low-cost, low-risk technology is particularly acute for them. In the Indonesia integrated pest management training programme, it has been noted that the farmer field schools have reached 'mainly the better informed and more affluent farmers' (Röling and van der Fliert 1995).

Role of farmers' organizations

A strong structure of farmers' organizations has many potential advantages for extension. They offer the opportunity for greater efficiency, effectiveness and equity of provision and access. They can also be a vehicle through which farmers can pay a contribution for services, become actively involved in the planning and management of extension, and act as a voice for their members in 'pulling down' services which meet their needs. Experience in Thailand (Garforth 1994), the Philippines (Campilan 1995) and Nepal (Basnyat 1995:192–7), however, suggests that a policy of working exclusively through farmers' organizations may reinforce previous patterns of exclusion from extension services, and that the scope for extension agencies to create conditions conducive to the emergence and survival of farmers' organizations is limited.

31

Effective use of mass media

Mass media are normally thought of as suitable only for one-way communication of information. However, they can also be used to facilitate widespread farmer-to-farmer extension; and where local radio stations exist, there is a lot of scope for innovative use of media to stimulate and sustain change in farming systems and the management of natural resources. A participatory approach to the identification of programme content (Mody 1991) can help to ensure that mass media respond to the expressed information needs of farmers.

Search for effective participatory methods and approaches

The last point is the crux of the matter. Is it possible to develop — and institution-alize within extension services — methods and approaches which allow farmer-clients to dominate the extension process? The last ten years have given us a new vocabulary, a new set of jargon, as researchers and rural development practitioners have moved from one level of participation, where rural people are invited to take part in outsider-led activities of research and appraisal, to attempts to engage in processes which are (or can be) controlled and led to a greater extent by the local people. We have moved from farmer participatory research (FPR) to participatory technology development (PTD), and from rapid rural appraisal (RRA) to partici-patory rural appraisal (PRA). The principles behind FPR and PTD are clear enough: research done by scientists in partnership with farmers is likely to produce much more appropriate and better-adapted technology, because it allows local knowl-edge and the normal experimental capacity of farmers to influence and guide the research process. Similarly with PRA: the information needed for local-level plan-ning can be collected and analysed much more effectively if local people play a full and active part, while at the same time the PRA process helps them to recog-nize and enhance their own abilities to analyse, plan and work together for their own development.

Attempts to apply these principles in practice, however, have encountered a number of difficulties and criticisms. We mention four below.

o First, in their most extreme forms, arguments for participatory methods imply that all the knowledge needed for agricultural development is already avail-able within the rural population: the role of 'outsider' researchers and exten-sion personnel is to help make that knowledge explicit so that it can be refined and shared more widely. It is more realistic to accept that 'outside' and 'local' knowledge both have a contribution to make in the understanding of current farming systems and the opportunities for improvement.

o Second, the degree of differentiation within rural communities is often over-looked. These differences may be based on gender, wealth, property rights, political affiliation, dependence on common property resources, or degree of reliance on farming for livelihood. Knowledge is located differentially within communities (Cornwall *et al.* 1993): the information and perspectives which are brought out through participatory activities will be those of the (usually) small proportion of the residents of an area who are directly involved. Even among those involved, it is likely that the views of a few — those with positions of power and influence — will dominate. We need participatory methods which make explicit different perspectives, and facilitate processes of negotiation and arbitration (Mosse 1993). This raises the more general question of whether it is possible (and desirable) to prevent 'farmer-led' extension being led primarily by an élite, vociferous and well-off category of farmers.

o Third, the relationship between local people and outside researchers and facilitators can be problematic. The process (of PTD or PRA) is usually prompted by the suggestion or initiative of outsiders who — because they have a preconceived idea of how the process should work — tend, at least in the early stages, to dominate decision-making. Enabling a take-over of ownership and control by the rural participants requires a suppression of normal professional attitudes and behaviour.

o Fourth, the transaction costs of participatory methods are extremely high, raising questions about the feasibility of scaling up from small-scale, intensive activities to large-scale participatory programmes (Farrington 1995).

Looking ahead

The last twenty years have been a learning experience for those involved in extension. As the challenges noted by George Axinn in Chapter 2 have emerged, so too have we recognized the complexity of the process of technological, social and economic change within rural areas. Simplistic, uniform solutions have shown themselves ill-suited to solving complex problems. Extension providers have, almost without exception, come to recognize the need for a partnership between professionals and clients in planning and managing change at farm and community level. Concern over the sustainability of extension organizations[3] is fuelling the view that public sector extension cannot survive at its present level of staffing, and that therefore mechanisms by which farmers take some measure of control of — and help to fund — extension services will have to be found. Many pilot projects and local initiatives by both NGO and public sector agencies have shown that farmers can play a much more active part in the management and control of extension services. This is an appropriate time at which to be sharing our experience of the promise and the pitfalls of farmer-led extension.

---

3. Gustafson (1994) quotes Goldsmith (1992) in defining sustainability of extension institutions as 'the ability of an institution to produce outputs that are sufficiently in demand for enough inputs to be supplied to continue production at a steady or growing rate'.

4 Origins and examples of farmer-to-farmer extension

FARMER-TO-FARMER extension, in which farmers are the primary extension agents, is probably the most common form of farmer-led extension. It involves farmers undertaking extension activities, with or without the support of external agents. Some farmer-to-farmer networks have developed where there were no alternative extension services. However, aside from providing an extension service where otherwise there may be none, farmer-to-farmer extension offers many and varied benefits. The most significant of these include:

o Language: Farmer-extensionists speak the same language as their colleagues, both literally and culturally, easing communication and understanding.
o Relevance: Farmer-extensionists are likely to understand their colleagues' constraints, potentials and aspirations better than more educated, non-farming professional extensionists.
o Availability: Farmer-extensionists can often be available at times more suited to other farmers than professional extensionists find possible.
o Accountability: Farmer-extensionists working in their own communities are more directly accountable to the farmers they serve than is the case with professional extension officers. This is particularly true if farming communities contribute to the costs of farmer-extensionists' work (although the same principles of linking payment and accountability can be applied to professional extension staff).
o Credibility: Farmer-extensionists have the same background, and farm under similar constraints as other farmers. Their demonstrations of new technologies and management practices can therefore be more convincing than those undertaken by professional extensionists.
o Sustainability: At the end of the project, the farmer-extensionists stay in the community and may continue to pursue agricultural or other rural development initiatives.

The management and organization of farmer-to-farmer extension networks varies considerably. For example, farmer-extensionists may receive training from other farmer-extensionists or from an external agent; they may or may not receive remuneration from other farmers or external agencies for their work. The extracts from the papers below illustrate this variety.

Latin America

The *campesino-a-campesino* sustainable agricultural movement in Latin America is the most well-established and best known farmer-to-farmer extension network. It is active in many Latin American countries, as well as in parts of Southeast Asia and Africa. The extracts from papers below describe the evolution and development of these networks.

Holt-Gimenez describes the *campesino-a-campesino* movement; its evolution in Guatemala and subsequent spread to Nicaragua, Mexico and Honduras.

The campesino-a-campesino movement in Latin America (Holt-Gimenez)

'Farmers helping their brothers ... so that they can help themselves ... to find solutions and not be dependent on a technician or on the bank. That is *campesino-a-campesino*'. This is the simple definition provided by a farmer of the grassroots movement in sustainable agriculture which has swept across Mexico and Central America over the last decade – *el movimiento campesino-a-campesino*, or 'farmer-to-farmer movement'. Led by *campesinos*, the subsistence farmers of the ecologically fragile hill sides and forest perimeters of the Mesoamerican tropics, *campesino-a-campesino* engages hundreds of volunteer and part-time *campesino* 'promoters' and the support of dozens of technicians (extension workers), professionals and local development organizations... It is impossible to estimate how many people are involved, because in essence *campesino-a-campesino* is an extensive, expanding and somewhat amorphous cultural process of agricultural transformation. *Campesino-a-campesino* is not so much a programme or a project looking for peasant participation, but a broad-based movement with *campesinos* as the main actors. As protagonists, they are foremost in it and are directly involved in all stages of the generation and transfer of technologies for sustainable agriculture. This includes the adoption and adaption of appropriate modern techniques, as well as traditional practices. Although programmatically elusive, and annoyingly unsystematic, *campesino-a-campesino* has succeeded in regenerating tens of thousands of hectares of exhausted soils in the tropics. While doing so, it has significantly raised and stabilized *campesino* agricultural production, opening the door to crop diversification, marketing, processing, commercialization and other alternatives.

How have *campesinos* helped each other develop sustainable agriculture? On the one hand, by using relatively simple methods of small-scale experimentation, combined with horizontal (farmer-to-farmer) workshops in basic ecology, agronomy, soil and water conservation, soil building, seed selection, crop diversification, integrated pest management, and biological weed control. These have provided *campesinos* with sufficient technical and ecological knowledge to reverse degenerative agro-ecological processes and overcome the basic limiting factors in their production. On the other hand, *campesino* promoters, leading by example, have inspired their peers to innovate and try new alternatives. This has given them the conviction, enthusiasm and pride to teach others, using hands-on learning methods, and to share with others through farmer-to-farmer exchanges. By forging their own sustainable alternatives for agriculture, the promoters have renewed belief in themselves and have formulated a fresh, *campesino* vision for the future of agriculture.

Seen from a *campesino-a-campesino* perspective, the question of how to elicit farmer participation in technology generation and dissemination is turned on its head. Rather, how do professionals in agricultural development programmes identify, foster, support, and participate in farmer-led processes?

Development of the movement. In the mid-1970s, Don Marcos Orozco, a retired soil conservationist employed by World Neighbors in Chimaltenango, Guatemala, had a problem. He had successfully demonstrated the effectiveness of contour ditches and organic soil amendments on his small, backyard plot, but he could not communicate this to surrounding farmers. His experimental corn plants were visibly taller and they had bigger ears than those in the control group, which he grew using the conventional methods of the Mayan farmers in the area. Soil erosion and low fertility were major limiting factors on their steep, eroded hillsides. Yields were low and parcels small. Most farmers had difficulty paying back the credit they had borrowed to purchase hybrid seeds and fertilizers, and were forced to work off their debts as labourers. Many were trapped in a vicious credit-debt cycle. An extensionist, with over 40 years' experience, Don Marcos could easily have explained the new techniques to the surrounding farmers, but he spoke no Cachikel and the Mayans spoke little or no Spanish. Ironically, this was the beginning of a new relationship between *tecnicos* (extensionists) and *campesinos*.

Following the example of promoter-led health services pioneered by the Berhorst Clinic in Guatemala, World Neighbors encouraged Don Marcos to work with a few Spanish-speaking, Cachikel *campesinos* to reduce erosion, improve natural soil fertility, diversify production and improve local seed. Don Marcos helped the small group of farmers to experiment on their own land. When their own experiments demonstrated the value of the alternative practices, the farmers applied them to their entire fields. Because Don Marcos could not speak the local Mayan language, the only way for him effectively to extend information about the new techniques to others was to work closely with the *campesinos*. The Mayan farmers discovered that the best way to convince their neighbours about the benefits of the new techniques was by demonstrating them on their own plots of land, and by helping interested farmers test the alternatives through small-scale experiments on theirs.

Soil and water are major limiting factors in the highlands of Chimaltenango and, consequently, contour ditches, bunds, terraces and heavy applications of compost tended to provide quick and visible results. In addition, yields were extremely low to begin with (less than one tonne per hectare). These two factors led to yield increases of 100–200 per cent within a year or two of implementing the conservation practices commonly being achieved. This resulted in enthusiasm on the part of the participating farmers and widespread interest on the part of neighbours. Soon, the knowledge and skills of the small group of farmers working with Don Marcos were in high demand. The heavy labour requirements of the technologies were assimilated by the Cachikel *kuchubal* mutual assistance groups traditionally used by the Mayans. Groups of three to ten men, working as a group, took turns on each others' land until all had implemented the basic conservation and fertility-enhancing practices.

However, demands upon the small group of innovators soon outstripped their capacity to respond through *kuchubal*. As small-scale experimentation reached higher and higher levels and limiting factors became more complex, there was a need for more theory and a greater understanding of abstract agronomic concepts. Thus the transfer of technology from farmer to farmer began to need more time, effort and different communication techniques for spreading the understanding and sharing what was essentially a locally developed (if embryonic) sustainable agriculture.

World Neighbors and Oxfam–UK must be credited as the first development organizations to recognize the potential of the Chimaltenango experience. By employing technicians to support local farmers in the development of their own agriculture (rather than in technology transfer), they set the guidelines for a new farmer/technician relationship which later came to characterize the *campesino-a-campesino* movement. World Neighbors and Oxfam supported the local efforts by helping to sponsor farmer-to-farmer workshops, technology fairs, further organizational and technical training, and provided seed money for agricultural cooperatives. Eventually, the Cachikeles were able to establish a 900-member cooperative which bought supplies, sold the farmers' basic grains, provided farmer-to-farmer training in basic conservation and fertility techniques and established a farmer-run land bank.

Political events of the early 1980s in Guatemala led to the disbanding of this co-operative, but not before its members had trained visiting *campesinos* from Mexico, Honduras and other areas of Guatemala. The basic knowledge and principles of farmer-led development got passed on orally and experientially from farmer-to-farmer (*de campesino a campesino*) and have continued to grow and spread ever since with the help of local development organizations.

Indonesia

The *campesino-a-campesino* movement and the strategies and methods it uses have been very influential on NGO attempts to initiate extension systems that are responsive to poor and marginalized farmers, particularly in Asia. A number of these are described below.

Sinaga and Wodicka describe the evolution of a farmer-to-farmer extension programme supported by World Neighbors, an international non-governmental organization, in southeastern Indonesia.

Farmer-to-farmer extension in Sumba, SE Indonesia (Sinaga and Wodicka)
In 1981, farmers from several villages in Sumba (an island in the drought-prone province of East Nusa Tenggara) discussed solutions to their problems with World Neighbors. During the first six months of programme development, the World Neighbors area representative visited villages to investigate their farming systems. It became clear early on that the fundamental problems were the poor productivity of the island's dryland farming and the deterioration of the environment through deforestation and soil erosion. Long-term development would require breaking the cycle of poverty and famine caused by destructive patterns of land use.

In 1982, borrowing from experiences gained in Central America, the Philippines, and other parts of Indonesia, and building on some of the more useful traditional practices of local farmers (such as the use of rock walls and leguminous tree species for improving soil fertility), World Neighbors started a small programme in basic soil and water conservation with a few farmers. A basic extension training approach was used, employing informal discussions, evening meetings and slide shows, as well as practical on-farm demonstrations (e.g., building an A-frame, measuring contour lines, and planting hedgerows). During these activities, interested farmers were encouraged to try the new practices in their own fields, test their application, and compare them with traditional practices. Based on the degree of interest they displayed, individual farmers were then selected to be trained more intensively and were encouraged to pass on these technologies to their neighbours. These farmer leaders/extensionists were sent for training to the nearby island of Flores and returned as enthusiastic and competent trainers.

The problems and small successes encountered during the first year of trials led to further improvements in technical practices being promoted and the training approaches employed. At the end of the first year, the results of the trials were evaluated and compared with neighbouring farmers, and suggestions were made about how to continue. It was clear to farmers that the new methods offered important alternatives and the enthusiasm of the first few caught on. By the following planting season, the programme had spread to four neighbouring villages.

After three years of World Neighbors' presence in Sumba, farmer leaders and field extensionists from the resulting dryland farming programme decided to form an autonomous

38

federation under the auspices of the Tananua Foundation. Today, this foundation serves almost 3000 farmers in 30 villages spread throughout the island of Sumba.

The programme has proved in a dramatic way that with proper soil and water conservation methods to protect and improve the land, successful and continuous cropping is possible. However, the real impact of these practices has been in convincing farmers of the opportunities which arise once they have stabilized their land and begun to see hope in the future. This changing attitude has led to long-term investments in planting a range of economic tree crops. Small-scale reforestation (or family forestry) and management of high-value estate crops has become a major element of programme assistance in the last several years. Finally, with access to improved forage for livestock, farmers are beginning to adopt cut-and-carry feeding systems and it is hoped that this activity can be intensified in the future. These practices offer a long-range, comprehensive approach to farm management, which forms the foundation for success in all extension efforts in the marginal uplands of Sumba.

Over the past 15 years, the Tananua Foundation and World Neighbors have developed a number of strategies and approaches to ensure a greater role for, and greater voice from, farmers in identifying problems and needs, selecting and testing new practices, monitoring and evaluating programme development, and in decision-making regarding programme policies and directions. These strategies represent a vast array of experiences, some of which have worked and some of which have been more problematic.

India

Kapoor describes a farmer-based extension project supported by the Aga Khan Rural Support Programme (AKRSP) in India. Although not directly influenced by the *campesino-a-campesino* movement, the AKRSP project is based on similar principles of supporting farmers to provide other farmers with extension services.

Farmer-to-farmer extension in India (Kapoor)

Extension volunteers. In 1987, AKRSP developed the concept of extension volunteers (EVs) — village level functionaries selected jointly by village institutions and AKRSP. EVs are public-spirited, keen learners of new ideas and issues related to putting these ideas into practice. They volunteer to share their skills and knowledge with other villagers and be involved in all the activities undertaken by village institutions in relation to natural resource development. For the time and effort they spend in this regard, they are compensated by incentives partly contributed by AKRSP and partly by the village institutions. Experience shows that these EVs are innovative in both adapting technologies and practices, and in communicating with other farmers. They generally try out an idea themselves first, testing its relevance to local conditions before advocating its adoption by others.

EVs take up different responsibilities, for example motivating people to organize themselves; engaging in soil and water conservation and afforestation works on private and public land; adapting agricultural practices to better suit local conditions; and meeting credit needs and participating in other commercial activities promoted by village institutions, for example constructing biogas plants. They are involved in participatory planning, implementation and management of different interventions. Being local, they not only talk in the language of the communities within which they work, but are also more aware of the context, strengths and limitations of those communities.

Master extension volunteers. The success of the EV model led to the evolution of another cadre of village-level functionaries in 1990 — the master extension volunteers (MEVs) — the objective of which is to expand the implementation of successful interventions. MEVs have generally established their effectiveness in the work, and their skills are used to speed up the expansion of similar programmes in other areas. They are also involved in training the EVs and beneficiaries.

The creation of a cadre of MEVs has resulted in a faster expansion of the programmes, and contributed to building up knowledge and skills at the local level and reducing the costs of service delivery. However, their accountability to the people's institutions is yet to be fully established...

Village institution committees. To avoid skills being monopolized by a few individuals and to equip more local people with extension and supervision skills, AKRSP decided in 1990 to promote the formation of committees at the village level for different programmes. Committee members, trained by AKRSP, supervise the EVs' work and also take the responsibility of motivating other villagers. The three cadres of local people — EVs, MEVs and village committee members — are being trained to interact with other agencies as well, such as concerned government departments, banks, private sector organizations and other local organizations. There are numerous instances in which the three groups have negotiated with outside agencies for better delivery of services to community development activities.

Philippines

Bhuktan, Killough and Basilio describe two farmer-to-farmer extension projects in the Philippines based on information gathered through focus group workshops, key informant panels, household interviews, in-depth interviews with farmer-extensionists and participatory farm exploration techniques.

Farmer-to-farmer extension in the Philippines (Bhuktan, Killough and Basilio)
Soil and Water Conservation Project, Cebu. In the soil and water conservation project of Mag-Uugmad Foundation in Cebu, farmer-extensionists are developed with the support of World Neighbors. Initially World Neighbors staff worked to disseminate various soil and water conservation technologies using the demonstration farm approach and employing some farmers as extension aides. In attempting to expand the project to other villages, World Neighbors developed farmer-extensionists from among the outstanding farmer adopters through a fairly long and systematic process involving graduation through the following phases: adopter; outstanding adopter; farmer instructor trainee; farmer instructor on probation; fully fledged farmer-instructor or farmer-extensionist. Farmer adopters were considered as candidates for farmer-instructors if they:

o had a deep understanding of the principles and practices of soil and water conservation
o applied the soil and water conservation technologies and maintained their farms well
o demonstrated a willingness to share technology-related experiences with other farmers
o had time to engage in sharing with other farmers
o possessed good communication skills
o enjoyed credibility with the community
o were friendly, helpful, hard working and resourceful.

Farmers aspire to become farmer-instructors primarily because the project compensates them financially for the number of days of work forgone on their own farms. Although only about a third of each month is allowed for extension work, the farmer-instructors see the honorarium they receive as an attractive economic incentive. The farmer-instructors are proud to report their years of achievements, but also feel bored in extending the same set of technologies to the same farmers. When adoption of the soil and water conservation technologies has reached saturation in the community, the extensionists feel they have no new information or skills to offer the villagers. As a result, they feel the villagers are not as excited about their work as they were in the past. Nevertheless, since they are paid to carry out extension work, they continue to do so. Many farmer-instructors would not continue this work if the project stopped paying them.

Upland Farm Management Project, Albay. The Upland Farm Management Project is being implemented in the upland rural areas of Santo Domingo municipality in Albay province. It is based on the same principles as the project in Cebu described above; it is supported by the International Institute of Rural Reconstruction with initial support from both Mag-Uugmad and World Neighbors. Similar development stages are pursued in establishing the farmer-based extension system, but there is a greater emphasis on leadership capability development among farmer-instructors.

Following very intensive educational and social preparation among poor upland farmers, the project identified five pioneer farmers who formed a *hunglunan* (mutual-help, labour-sharing) group. These five farmers were encouraged to develop their land into demonstration farms and to form new *hunglunan* groups under their own leadership. Consequently, after a year five *hunglunan* groups emerged with a total of 23 farmer adopters. Some of the pioneer farmers then went on to form more than one *hunglunan*. Their capacity to lead these groups, and the number of groups they formed, were thought to be important criteria for their selection as farmer-instructors in the future.

Initially, each member of a *hunglunan* was required, after establishing his or her demonstration farm, to try to form another *hunglunan* under their leadership. However, after the first generation of *hunglunan*, progress slowed. Most of the second generation of *hunglunan* members just managed to establish their own farms as demonstrations and remain in their original *hunglunan*, but for various reasons were unable to form an additional group. Newly designated farmer-instructors therefore became fully responsible for forming new groups (the 'leapfrog' mechanism for expanding the programme), because the 'cell division' strategy (splitting a *hunglunan* that had grown too large) did not work. In this way, the number of farmer-instructors and *hunglunans* grew over the years. However, as in Cebu, the farmer-instructors experienced problems of 'technology fatigue'. The project responded to this by transferring some farmer-instructors to new villages. This worked fairly well in the beginning, but adoption saturation levels were reached faster in the new villages than previously, mainly due to the increased experience and expertise of the farmer-instructors.

Vietnam

Pham Xuan Du describes a farmer-to-farmer extension programme in Vietnam supported by VACVINA, a national NGO. Bhuktan, Killough and Basilio also describe the same programme. The following section about VACVINA's activities is made up of the editors' amalgamation of extracts from both these papers.

Farmer-to-farmer extension in Vietnam (Pham Xuan Du, and Bhuktan, Killough and Basilio)

The National Association of Vietnamese Gardeners (VACVINA) was established in 1986 as a national, membership NGO to help resuscitate a traditional system of integrated household garden production system, known as VAC. Such gardening had been neglected when farm co-operatives became the main actors in rural areas. VAC is an acronym which stems from the Vietnamese words for 'garden' or 'orchard', 'fishpond' and 'livestock building' — cattle shed, pigsty or poultry coop. The VAC production system involves the integration of horticulture, fish rearing and animal husbandry aimed at sustainable agricultural development. With the changes in government policies in Vietnam aimed at encouraging the development of the family economy, VAC activities were revived. VACVINA, which now operates in all provinces of Vietnam, has three objectives:

o Developing nationwide campaigns for promoting eco-VAC gardening
o Introducing appropriate techniques to enhance the effectiveness of VAC systems
o Promoting exchanges of experience and skills with national and international organizations in rural development and between farmers in building up the family economy.

It gives emphasis to the development of poor rural areas, in particular those affected by catastrophic natural calamities; located in remote mountainous areas or inhabited by ethnic minorities, thus focusing on the poorest, disabled people and women and children.

Its extension activities are based upon the principles of democracy and self-motivation. They are dependent on farmers volunteering their services and engaging in self-help and the mutual exchange of information. Active, voluntary, self-motivated participation of local farmers has remained the pivot of all of VACVINA's extension projects.

Due to Vietnam's historical background, public sector agricultural extension units were set up only in 1993. Prior to this, public extension services focused on the cultivation of irrigated rice, cash crops such as tea, coffee and rubber, and the rearing of pigs and cattle on state farms or large co-operative farms. Assistance in the development of individual family farms has been been provided only since 1993 and is based on the provision of technologies deemed relevant.

Consequently, VACVINA had to rely on its own extension network for VAC development. It has done this through a membership system, which now incorporates about 160 000 families. An integral part of the diffusion process is that, when farmers become VACVINA members, they accept responsibility for helping to transfer knowledge about the techniques being used. The diffusion techniques used vary from one area to another, ranging from merely distributing VAC documents and organizing the occasional training course, to the application of a whole range of gardening techniques on the farmer's own land. VACVINA staff are trained to support extension based upon the enthusiasm and involvement of dedicated and experienced members. VACVINA and its branches have therefore been engaged in development of the strengths of VAC promoters and encouraging new promoters to share their experiences, as well as produce improved seeds, planting materials, animal breeds and even create credit funds in some provinces.

In developing this extension network, VACVINA has collaborated with a number of research centres, institutes, universities, high schools, the Farmers' Association and the Women's League. The main impetus has, however, come from VACVINA members at all levels. They have been engaged, first, in establishing their own VAC systems and, secondly, in helping to solve their country-fellows' problems through their examples. This extension by 'insiders', based on technologies well tailored to local farming conditions, has had a strong persuasive power on farmers, since farming models have been created by farmers

42

from their own communities. Naturally, assistance in the choice of technologies may come from 'outside', through discussions with district or provincial VACVINA members, but everything is then 'carved' in the farmers' village, through the labour of local VACVINA members. The fact that local VACVINA members are the main actors in their own communities provides for solid extension work.

The first obstacle encountered by VACVINA after its establishment was the fact that gardening systems had been neglected for decades. Therefore, there were no research findings available from universities or other institutes about the establishment and management of small-scale, bio-intensive land farming systems. Most of the technologies available in the public sphere in the 1980s had been developed for large-scale farming. VACVINA therefore began its activities by collecting local knowledge on the VAC system. Specialists were fielded to various ecological zones throughout the country to undertake surveys; discuss with local farmers their gardening experience and know-how; test out various VAC systems and identify the most appropriate techniques for effective management. These activities were carried out with close collaboration between technicians, scientists and interested farmers, especially members of VACVINA. Cross-visits between households in different villages and communes were supported in the effort to gradually improve the VAC systems designed.

VACVINA has developed into a national enterprise and the NGO has branches at all levels. VACVINA central headquarters provides a training centre and also undertakes experimentation and multiplication activities. VACVINA provincial centres provide training courses and workshops; conducts pilot activities and support communes and schools in implementing the VAC gardening system. They also do experiments and multiply planting materials. At the district level, training courses and workshops are provided, pilot activities implemented and villages and schools interested in VAC gardening are supported. Demonstration VAC gardens are built and planting material multiplication is undertaken. At the commune or village level, training courses and workshops are offered, families are supported to pilot VAC gardening activities, and model VAC gardens and nurseries are established. VACVINA would like to be regarded as part of the national agricultural extension network, with support from the public sector. Its national structure is complementary to that of the ministries of agriculture and food industries, forestry and fisheries.

43

5 Principles and methods in farmer-to-farmer extension

Latin America

FARMER-TO-FARMER extension employs a wide variety of methods. Holt-Gimenez describes some of those deployed by the *campesino-a-campesino* movement in Central and South America. Many subsequent farmer-to-farmer extension networks and projects have adopted and adapted various aspects of these. Since the *campesino-a-campesino* movement is among the oldest of the farmer-to-farmer extension networks, these field methods are likely to be the most tried and tested. They therefore provide us with a rich source of experience on which to draw.

Methods used by the campesino-a-campesino movement (Holt-Gimenez)
Farmer innovation and farmer solidarity are the two pillars of the *campesino-a-campesino* methodology. These primary aspects are encouraged and reinforced by small-scale experimentation and farmer-to-farmer training. In turn, such experimentation and training are implemented through and complemented with promoter-led workshops, field visits and farmer-to-farmer seminars, gatherings and symposiums. Farmers do not just share information, they share culture. This is the basis for sharing knowledge (which can be shared but not taught).

While professionals may support this process with technical information, methodological training and organizational capacity building, it is still primarily a farmers' activity based on and in their own culture. Put simply, there can be no farmer-led extension if one of the parties is not a farmer.

The basic methodological principles of *campesino-a-campesino* have not changed significantly since they were detailed by Roland Bunch in *Two Ears of Corn* (1982). They are:

o obtain rapid and recognizable results
o start small, go slowly
o limit the introduction of technology
o use small-scale experimentation
o develop a multiplier effect.

Similarly, the basic components of farmer experimentation, theoretical and practical instruction, and teaching others remain central to *campesino-a-campesino*. The advantage of these basic principles is their flexibility. This allows for *campesino* (and extension worker) creativity, which over time has resulted in a myriad of methodological and technical techniques which are constantly being invented, adopted and adapted by *campesinos* and promoters. It has also given rise to constantly-evolving changes in organization at village, national and international levels. Likewise, the technical, methodological and organizational flexibility of *campesino-a-campesino* has allowed the movement to extend from the exhausted soils of the dry and semi-humid hillsides to the lowlands and humid tropics of

45

the agricultural frontier. As *campesino-a-campesino* spreads, the original practices have been adapted and complemented with new techniques. Exchanges between farmers from different ecological zones sometimes result in an inappropriate application of a particular technique at first. However, experimentation allows errors to be corrected and technologies to be adapted. As a result, the technical basket of sustainable agricultural practices is now quite large and diverse.

Although the *campesino-a-campesino* movement did not begin as part of a pre-designed programme, it has been used by many others as a basis on which to develop support projects. Holt-Gimenez draws out some of the insights from the movement that can and have been used in the design of farmer-to-farmer extension projects or programmes.

Programme steps from the campesino-a-campesino experiences (Holt-Gimenez)
The development of the *campesino-a-campesino* technological basket has been unsystematic, evolving as *campesinos* from different areas become interested and begin experimenting with and sharing their innovations. None the less, NGOs that support the movement with technical assistance and sustainable agricultural projects have developed some programmatic guidelines. Table 5.1 is meant to be descriptive rather than normative and illustrates how this methodology can be organized and implemented on a project level.

Table 5.1: Steps in farmer-to-farmer extension programmes

Stages	Activities
Getting started	Diagnostic, site selection, identification of key farmers Visits to *campesino-a-campesino* promoters' fields Promoter-led workshops, promoter-led field surveys First problem assessment Extensionist support
Identifying useful small-scale elements	Promoter-led workshops on conservation and farmer experimentation
Design of experiments	Promoter-led workshops and group site visits for experiment selection and design based on farmer-identified problems and possible solutions
Sharing experiments	*Campesino-a-campesino* group visits to field experiments; follow-up by promoters and/or extensionists
Sharing results	Local and national group and community field visits Local seminar (*encuentro*) for farmer-experimenters Publication of results in local and national farmer newsletters and magazines, radio and TV
Spreading and consolidating the movement	National and international *encuentros* Local transects Community workshops

Adapted from Holt-Gimenez and Cruz (1993)

The canasta metodológica. Within the parameters of the above basic principles and programme steps, an impressive and ever-changing body of knowledge about how to teach and promote sustainable agriculture has been developed by the *campesino-a-campesino* movement. A rich basket of didactic techniques has proven very effective in teaching the complex, diverse and abstract agro-ecological concepts basic to sustainable agriculture. Functional illiteracy among the majority of *campesinos* has demanded both creativity and a tremendous attention to detail in teaching and learning. Despite the introduction of television, *campesinos* continue to relate events, information, values and ideas through oral, visual and physical expression. Thus, *campesino* methods for learning sustainable agriculture usually employ several techniques for introducing, understanding, learning and remembering a new concept or practice. These may include a site visit and a hands-on trial of the practice, as well as a game, a related physical demonstration or experiment to enhance understanding and a song, story, poem or play to help relate the experience to others. A wide collection of such learning methods (SIMAS 1995), called the '*canasta metodológica*' (methodological basket), groups different methods into the following pedagogical categories:

Problem analysis

o   basic concepts of ecology, equilibrium and synergy
o   activities for group agro-ecological appraisals of farms and watersheds, including record-
    ing ecological histories, identifying weak links in the ecological chain and limiting
    factors in production, selecting principal problems, understanding their causes and
    proposing possible solutions.

Experimentation

o   experimentation based on overcoming limiting factors, controlling variables
o   making valid comparisons and accurate measurements within the group
o   developing working hypothesis and designing experiments to test these
o   methods for recording observations and results.

Promotion

o   horizontal communication
o   developing watershed models
o   spreading general agronomic knowledge on concepts related to soil pH levels, water
    stress, evapotranspiration, erosion, soil texture, soil absorption, soil organic matter,
    average slopes and tillage.

Examples from the canasta metodológica. The *campesino* learning methods documented in the *canasta metodológica* are deductive, hands-on and frequently laced with humour and local folklore. For example, a problem analysis activity to help define ecological equilib-rium and sustainability, begins by pitting two contestants against each other. One contestant is given two chairs, the other one chair. Bets are taken to see who can hold the chair(s) in the air longest. Most bet on the person with one chair. But the person with two chairs gets them placed carefully on each shoulder, balancing the load. The other, with one chair, holds it out, poorly balanced on an extended arm. When it falls first, the question asked is 'why'. The ensuing discussion revolves around the importance of equilibrium for sustainability. These concepts are later applied directly to help analyse the agro-ecological equilibrium (or lack of it) in the farmer's field.

Ecology itself is defined by throwing a ball of string between participants in the workshop. Each person holds on to the string with one hand and throws the ball to another participant with the other hand while calling out the name of something in 'nature', for example, 'trees', 'river', 'grass', 'birds', etc. When the string is used up and the group is all connected by a spider's web of string, the group reflects on the metaphor of ecology as 'everything in nature and the connections and relationships between them'. The string is held taut, but allowed to run freely across each participant's hand or finger. When one person drops the string ('What happens if we lose the birds?'), everyone connected to the string feels the slack. Discussion ensues about the local environment and the effect that changes in one aspect of the agro-ecosystem has impacted other aspects.

Another technique which illustrates the necessity of controlling variables in experiments is a simple story. In it, a grandmother with a nagging backache takes three different sets of advice and three different remedies, all in the same day. When her pain vanishes the next day, she does not know which of the remedies has done the trick.

One good promotion technique in the repertoire consists of submersing two bags filled with equal weights of compost and sandy soil in a bucket of water for a minute. Then the bags are taken from the bucket and allowed to drain. When they are weighed again, the bag with compost outweighs the bag with sandy soil, helping to illustrate the importance of organic matter for water retention.

A review of the *canasta* methodologies reveals a strong emphasis not simply on skills acquisition, but also on knowledge acquisition. *Campesinos* want to know not only the 'how' of sustainable agriculture, they want to know the 'why'. And not only do they want to know, they want to teach.

The basket of methods has broad applicability. The games, activities and demonstrations have been used in elementary school gardening programmes (Mexico); eco-tourism training guides (Nicaragua), and orienting extensionists, agronomists and college students throughout Mesoamerica. The *canasta* also demonstrates that it is possible to learn sustainable agriculture on a practical and conceptual level *from* farmers.

The deductive and experiential nature of the *canasta* is well suited for teaching the basic concepts of ecology and sustainable agriculture, and is a refreshing change from the rather ineffective learning by rote which dominates teaching in Central America. Also, learning agriculture from *campesinos* helps overcome the conventionally paternalistic (and frequently antagonistic) relationship between extensionists and *campesinos* and it builds self-confidence among *campesinos* as a group.

Indonesia

Sinaga and Wodicka describe in some detail the strategies and methods used in the World Neighbors-supported farmer-led extension programme in the uplands of Sumba. It can be seen from the following extract that, although some elements of the *campesino-a-campesino* approach have been adopted, they have been adapted to the Sumbanese farmers' preferences and, also, some additional methods have been added to the repertoire.

Methods used by Tananua in Sumba (Sinaga and Wodicka)
Farmers as trainers. While the informal approaches to training offer the most appropriate method of training local farmers, a number of requests from other agencies (NGOs and government) has necessitated the formalization of some of the training. Modules have been

48

developed in collaboration with agricultural and forestry services and agroforestry training courses, and are now being offered on demand. Farmer-leaders with many years of experience participate in these training sessions as trainers, often side-by-side with more educated extension officers from both the public sector and NGOs. The practical orientation of these farmer-leaders stands out next to the more theoretical approaches of extension officers. While formal training provides more opportunities for leadership development and more interaction with extension officers, its frequency can draw participating farmer-leaders away from the more immediate task of training and following-up with local farmers.

Participatory, on-farm research. Farming systems require continual experimentation and responsiveness if they are to meet the economic and environmental changes taking place. In the uplands, location-specific research, based on agro-ecosystems analysis which reflects the local farmers' priorities, is essential to address these evolving needs. The World Neighbors programme supports research which is conducted in close partnership with farmers, predicated on their natural inclination towards experimentation. On-farm research linked to the broader network of farmers provides an excellent mechanism for involving a wider segment of the communities in the planning process, assessing results and disseminating experiences to a larger audience. The role of on-farm research is also important in creating capable and innovative farmer-leaders who form the core of farmer-based extension systems.

Model farms. Trials of new ideas are undertaken on the farms of Tananua extensionists and farmer-advisers, which become places for learning and sharing experiences. Extension staff work intensively with a few farmers (farmer-advisers and ordinary farmers) who are pioneers in the process and possess long-term vision. This process is significant in planning and developing model farms that can be replicated by other farmers. Extension activities will generally succeed if farmers start from their own farms: methods which have already been tried by a few farmers are more easily transferred and accepted by other farmers.

Field workers and farmer-advisers are required to develop and maintain model farms. It is through these examples that they can become more effective extensionists. In fact, the neglect of their farms leads to their dismissal as extensionists.

Field workers. Field workers hired by the Tananua Foundation also play an important role in the extension process. Although field workers should possess sound technical and practical experience, their main role is to facilitate dialogue among farmers. In some circumstances, the field worker may provide some technical advice and backstopping. Field workers must live in the community they are assigned to serve, and they are also required to develop a model farm. Their role is to assist in the development of local farmer leadership, while working with farmers on testing the various practices available to them.

Field workers generally possess a secondary education in the field of agronomy. Before they are hired they must undergo an intensive three-month orientation in the field. During this time they learn from farmers the practices that have been tested so far, and they familiarize themselves with the approaches of Tananua. At the end of this period, they are evaluated in an open forum (usually during a quarterly meeting) by their peers and by community members. The evaluation consists of a set of questions pertaining to technical and social aspects, as well as the principles and approaches of Tananua. Some questions involve simple verbal answers, while others require simulation of events where meeting participants take part in playing out roles. Candidate field workers are scored on their answers by a panel of farmers and other field workers. Should the field worker get a mark below seven out of ten, they are considered to have failed the evaluation. The panel will then make a recommendation to Tananua either to find a replacement or extend the orientation period of the candidate.

This rather long and arduous process has discouraged many field workers, but those who have endured it have usually lasted. This process also applies to farmer-advisers. The involvement of the community in selecting field workers and farmer-advisers ensures greater accountability to the farmers.

Extension media. Filmstrips and slides, which were used early on in the programme, have proved an effective tool for motivating farmers and facilitating discussions on potential solutions to their problems. The programme continues to make use of visual materials and has developed a number of titles on the various practices developed so far. Slide presentations are usually done in the evening and followed up with field practicals the following day. Tananua, in collaboration with another NGO (Studio Driya Media), has developed a series of extension media to support farmer-to-farmer extension. These include a series of booklets on soil and water conservation, integrated farming, planting tree crops, goat raising, soil fertility management and fish ponds, as well as posters and flipcharts.

These learning materials undergo a lengthy process of development before being disseminated. The instruction booklets are based on technologies tested by farmers themselves, and the scripts and drawings are field-tested by farmers and field extensionists to ensure that their contents are relevant to farmers' needs. Although many farmers are illiterate, they generally use the booklets for group discussions where some of the farmers are able to read. The drawings, based on local culture, enhance the learning process. These simple booklets have so far been used by many different programmes throughout the region, and represent a significant contribution to the programme. These materials are, however, best used in combination with practical demonstrations on the farms.

There is no doubt that good quality learning materials based on farmer needs, even if kept simple, are costly to produce both in terms of financial and time resources. A recent evaluation of the effectiveness and impact of the booklets has tried to determine whether the impact outweighs the costs, but the results of this evaluation are not yet available.

Cross-visits. Cross-visits are visits organized between farmers of the same village, farmers of different villages, or farmers from different islands. These visits are intended to improve the skills and knowledge of the farmers, as well as broaden their perspectives in further developing their farms. For those farmers living in remote areas, contact with outside villages seems to generate much enthusiasm towards farm improvement, and experimenting with their own ideas.

Cross-visits can be costly due to the difficult geography of the Nusa Tenggara area (which consists of many small islands) and the small number of farmers who can participate in such cross-visits. However, programme leaders unanimously stress the tremendous impact such visits can have on farmer leadership and the adoption of technical innovations. The key to successful cross-visits is threefold. First, participating farmers need to be selected very carefully, usually by both farmers and the programme staff, based on their willingness to work with other farmers and to test new practices. The selection of participants must avoid influences by élitist or government elements. Second, the group should be accompanied by a facilitator (field worker or farmer-leader) who will ensure effective learning among participants. Finally, after the cross-visit, participating farmers must sit down together to plan follow-up activities on their farms or with other farmers. These plans form the basis for monitoring the impact of the cross-visits. It is estimated that cross-visits have had 90 per cent success rates, i.e., that if they are well-planned, with careful selection of farmers and facilitators, nine out of ten farmers participating will return to their farms with clear follow-up plans, which they will go on to implement.

Relay field visits. An encouraging trend has been a number of requests from new villages, where farmers have taken the initiative to contact programme leaders or neighbouring farmers, because they have heard about or witnessed the progress of farmers served by the Tananua programme. Sometimes these requests come from a few farmers in a village, from a farmer group, or as an official request from the village head and farmers. If possible, the approach is to invite interested farmers to visit villages with on-going activities and to take part in farmers' quarterly meetings (see below). This approach is locally referred to as 'relay field visits'. A relay field visit is a period of approximately one month of travelling from village to village, spending a few days in each, where new participating farmers are introduced to the concepts and practices of the programme by farmer-leaders along the way.

Training. The experience of the programme in its early phases proved that the more informal and practical the training, the more effective the results. Therefore, the programme has resisted efforts to organize set courses or workshops until more recently. Experienced farmer-leaders and programme supervisors generally take the initiative to promote the practices in new communities, facilitate training, and follow up on participants as they implement them. The basic approach pursued is to work with farmers, individually or in their work groups, and to demonstrate the improved practices while working together on farms.

Farmer field days. Another important aspect of programme training involves 'farmer field days', which are collective walking tours of farmers' fields where the new practices being adopted are shown. During these sessions, farmers discuss the strengths and weaknesses of the respective farms, provide insights and suggestions to their neighbours, and stimulate a great number of ideas on improved farming practices. These sessions are often led and facilitated by programme supervisors or experienced farmer-leaders.

Quarterly meetings. Given the rugged terrain and relative isolation of many participating villages, a key aspect of programme management involves regular attendance at the quarterly meetings. These meetings are rotated between communities so that they are accessible to different regions of the island each quarter. Given the seasonal variations in the demands of agricultural activities, the highest attendance at these meetings occurs during the dry season. Farmers learn about the time and venue of these meetings through public radio messages transmitted in advance. The meetings are open to all farmers who wish to attend. Tananua usually organizes transportation and provides meals. The host village is responsible for preparing food and putting up farmers in their homes for four to five days. These meetings are now attracting between 70 and 100 farmers at each. Increasing attendance has resulted in splitting the meetings into two areas (east and west) to allow for more farmer participation.

The main objective of these meetings is to give greater voice to farmers in setting the agenda, and to allow farmers to share their experiences in adopting the improved practices. Every farmer is given the opportunity to report on his or her farm activities and plans, or on the farmer group's progress. In addition, field staff and supervisors are required to report on their activities as a way of building in more accountability to the communities. These meetings also serve as a means to develop farmer leadership by rotating the role of moderator among farmers and by encouraging critical analysis of presentations.

The meetings are usually designed to focus on the activities of the host village, so that visiting farmers can work with local families in evaluating their activities. For this reason, the meetings tend to alternate between villages which have been relatively successful and those which are having specific problems. The meetings also serve as an important forum for the evolution of Tananua's policies and basic philosophy, as well as practical concerns related to farming technologies, programme expansion, budget issues, etc. A basic tenet of

51

Tananua is that all decisions should be made collectively and all active farmers have the right to participate in policy formation.

More recently, farmers have suggested many new ideas to enhance the effectiveness of these meetings. Some of these suggestions include organizing special training during the course of the meeting, encouraging contributions in money or in kind to reduce the costs of the meetings, bringing seeds and seedlings of local tree species for exchange among farmers, etc. There is no doubt that this type of regular forum is one of the key mechanisms for facilitating more farmer-to-farmer communication and farmer solidarity. In addition, these meetings are relatively inexpensive (between US$300 and US$400 per meeting).

Quarterly farmer meetings, however, also need to be critically assessed in terms of encouraging wider farmer participation. Attendance is hampered by the rugged terrain and poor roads. Farmers often have to travel for several days just to attend the meetings. Their regular attendance is probably a sign of their enthusiasm, but the meetings also present a real drain on their time off the farm and away from their families. Another weakness has been the poor attendance of women farmers. The present structure, time and place of the meetings does not allow for greater participation by women. Even women farmers from the host village are rarely able to attend because they are kept busy preparing food for their guests.

Farm planning. With increased confidence in more sedentary farm management practices, farmers in selected areas have recently begun the regionally unique initiative of farm planning. Farm planning helps farmers look to the future and make the systematic investments necessary to create a more sustainable farming system. Farmers make sketch maps of their farms and draw up calendars of activities. These sketches are used as planning, monitoring and evaluation tools.

Equally importantly, these farm plans serve as excellent extension tools. During quarterly meetings, farmers present their farm plans and report on their progress. The visualization of the farm on paper facilitates discussion among farmers and generates many new insights and suggestions from which all farmers can learn.

Historically, technologies have been extended only one at a time. This has facilitated communication with farmers who often have limited formal education. However, recent experiences with farmer training has shown that even farmers who have not yet adapted any of the soil and water conservation technologies are able to develop farm plans based on their needs. Farm planning actually provides a means by which farmers can exercise a greater voice in determining their priority needs and the technologies they require to address those needs.

Philippines

Bhuktan, Killough and Basilio describe the important components of the farmer-based extension system in the Mag-Uugmad Foundation/World Neighbors-supported Soil and Water Conservation Project in Cebu.

Methods used by Mag-Uugmad in the Philippines (Bhuktan, Killough and Basilio)
Demonstration and model farms. The demonstration farms showcase the ideal recommended technologies so that farmers visiting them can see the various technology options from which to choose. The model farm displays the various technology components that are appropriate to the particular locality. A model farm is not just a showcase of the range of technological options available, but the product of a long process of local technology adaptation by the farmers themselves. All farmer-extensionists are required to conduct their own

experiments to ascertain the appropriateness of new technologies to their own farms, prior to disseminating them to other farmers. These experimental plots provide living proof to other farmers that the technology works in their locality and thus hastens adoption. Model farms serve as a living example of the technologies promoted by the farmer instructors, thus making other farmers' training and cross-visits genuine learning exercises. Having a model farm also reinforces the owner's credibility as an extensionist, since it exemplifies consistency between their words and deeds.

Labour-exchange groups. Given the laborious nature of installing soil and water conservation structures, the formation of *alayon* labour-exchange groups is encouraged among the adopter farmers. This enables farmers to establish and maintain contour farms through a mutual sharing of labour within groups of 5–8 farmers. The *alayon* also serves as an avenue for group learning and problem solving among the members. *Alayon* also became the major vehicle for spreading the soil and water conservation technologies to other groups of farmers. When an *alayon* gets sufficiently large, it is divided into two. This mechanism of technology spread is called 'cell division'. In addition, years of sustained participation in an *alayon* leads to the honing of farmers' social and technical skills. This assists in producing more farmer instructors, who are then able to lead new *alayons*. This is referred to as the 'leapfrog' type of technology spread. Usually, over time, both mechanisms take place within each *alayon*.

Farm planning, training and cross-visits. Individual farmers, together with their families, make their own farm plans, keeping in mind the future model of their farm. Training and cross-visits are arranged, mainly for would-be adopters. These usually involve visits to model farms and comprise a lot of practical exercises and sharing of experiences with farmers who already have experience of the technologies.

Baile, a farmer-extensionist in Albay, Philippines, describes some approaches that worked, as well as some that did not.

Methods used by the IIRR-supported Upland Farm Management Project (Baile)
As farmer-extensionists, we tried out various strategies to encourage our co-farmers to try to adopt the technologies we are promoting. More of the strategies or approaches that we tried worked than failed. Some of the ones that work are as follows:

o In starting in a new village, a courtesy call, co-ordination and constant updating of village officials on the status of the project are very important. This not only gains their support in the promotion of the technologies, but also gives them a high regard for the interventions made in their area.

o Selection of pioneer farmer co-operators in certain village is critical. The first farmer co-operators should always possess the basic criteria we follow in selecting new farmer co-operators: they must show community leadership potential and be able to be trained as the main promoters of the technology at the community level; they must have a sloping or hilly farmlot which can be developed as a demonstration site; they must be interested in testing the technology, willing to share the technology with other interested farmers, and willing to attend regular meetings and comply with what have been agreed upon during meetings.

o Taking pictures during *hunglunan* activities (slides or prints), distributing these pictures, and presenting slides during project/technology orientations, encourages other farmers to take part, join *hunglunan* groups and try the technology.

53

o Facilitating cross-visits to farms successfully demonstrating the technology being promoted is important. Through this strategy, farmers learn from each other's experiences and gain more information on the benefits of adopting the technology.

o Teaching while demonstrating is a very effective strategy, especially when starting to establish a demonstration farm owned by a farmer. This strategy will be adopted by the farmer once he or she becomes a farmer-extensionist.

o Distributing planting materials, cuttings or seeds not common to the area (e.g., fruit-tree seedlings, hedgerow seeds, cuttings, etc.) encourages farmers to try new technologies. Once a farmer receives seedlings or seeds he or she is also required to disperse the same number to other interested farmers.

o Goat and cattle dispersal projects and the introduction of technologies that will give them additional fodder or forage, also encourages farmers to adopt these activities.

o Sharing of a hunglunan's experience on *hunglunan* savings, (a capital build-up/revolving fund scheme for emergency use, where each member contributes one peso per *hunglunan* day, or a sum agreed upon by a majority of members), also encourages members to form *hunglunan* groups and adopt the technology.

o Sharing by experienced farmers during informal gatherings of farmers (near a village store, etc.) slowly encourages other farmers to try the technology and later seek support from the farmer-extensionist.

o Booklets on soil and water conservation technology and goat management also help promote the technology. Sometimes these booklets are neglected, because farmers have no time to read, or they do not know how to read. Sometimes, however, these booklets are read by farmers' children, who relate the contents to their parents.

o Providing honoraria to farmer-extensionists, at a rate equivalent to the income they could lose by foregoing their farm work in the service of their fellow farmers, not only inspires them to do extension work, but also encourages other interested farmers to double their effort in order to pass the criteria and become a farmer-extensionist.

o Assigning farmer-extensionists to different villages rather than their home village, makes them more credible and effective in doing community extension work.

The strategies that we tried but which did not work were as follows:

o Co-ordination with village co-operative officials to gain their support in the promotion of the technology. This strategy did not work because it was not the officials' priority. At that time they were concentrating on production loan projects, credit programmes and other activities not related to sustainable agriculture.

o Co-ordination with local (municipal) government units. This did not help in the technology promotion process within the locality or municipality. Municipal government staff sometimes co-ordinated with us so their visitors could visit some of the farms which had adopted the technology.

o Assigning a farmer-extensionist in his or her own village. This strategy works only for maximum of one year. After that, the commitment of the farmer-extensionists declines, possibly because they are no longer challenged if they have already tried encouraging almost all farmers in their village to adopt the technology.

Vietnam

Pham Xuan Du and Bhuktan, Killough and Basilio describe the details used by VACVINA to promote the VAC system of gardening in Vietnam. Extracts from both these papers are used below to describe these.

Methods used by VACVINA in Vietnam (Pham Xuan Du, and Bhuktan, Killough and Basilio)

After designing a VAC system suited to a specific locality, VACVINA's extension efforts begin. Interested and experienced VACVINA members are encouraged to improve their old gardens through using and adapting the VAC model that has been developed for their locality. The objectives of the adaptation tests or trials are well defined through carefully conducted discussions between specialists and the farmers who are undertaking them. While the trials are going on, 'training workshops' are conducted in the area to inform other VACVINA members and other farmers about the technologies being tried. These training workshops are more aptly described as seminars or discussion groups. Instructors who lead them do not give lectures, but make suggestions about new approaches and measures to which all attendees are invited to respond. They could be called 'training courses without trainers' in which all attendees collaborate with each other in a free discussion about the strengths and weaknesses of existing local gardening practices, and 'instructors' suggest ways to improve older systems and to adopt and adapt new techniques. To conduct such workshops well, instructors have to have been previously involved for some time in mapping the social and physical characteristics of locality and in farmer interviews and discussions. They should also be familiar with good examples of household VAC systems established in neighbouring villages and be able to base their suggestion for improvements on comparisons of the results of VAC gardening with conventional gardening.

Following the training workshops, participants are divided into groups of five to seven farmers or farm households facing similar gardening conditions and living near to each other. They are asked to:

o discuss, on an individual basis, with their household members, means of improving their own garden
o make plans to implement such improvements
o draw up layouts and work calendars to include activities they can carry out by themselves and identify those in which they will require technical assistance from local VACVINA teams.

Household VAC plans are then brought to a group meeting for discussion about their feasibility. The group helps individual households to improve and implement their plan by providing advice, engaging in labour exchanges for various activities (e.g., pond digging, pigsty maintenance or repair; farmyard manure composting), or providing seeds or planting materials. There have also been cases where VACVINA members pool their financial resources to provide seasonal credit to the poorest among them, thus enabling them to purchase planting materials.

Once a VAC project has been started, there is a continuous exchange of experience and skills between households in the same group through monthly meetings. VACVINA members play a pivotal role in these meetings and help other farmers evaluate the results they have obtained from their garden trials and sum up their field experience. Some village-level VACVINA branches or groups also organize field trips and visits within their locality to obtain a better overall view of the progress gained in VAC gardening.

Every six months there is also a meeting at which team leaders and member households review what has been done in the past half-year and plan the operations to be undertaken over the next six months. Corrective measures to individual household practices can be suggested during these meetings. At the end of the first year of a group's activities, a more exhaustive evaluation is undertaken, facilitated by delegates from the district, provincial or even central branches of VACVINA. Awards to, and citations of the best local gardeners are given during these evaluation meetings.

The processes of establishing contacts with farmers and of technology dissemination through the VACVINA extension network are illustrated by Bhuktan, Killough and Basilio below.

Technology dissemination in Vietnam (Bhuktan, Killough and Basilio)

In Hop Nhat village (Ba Vi commune, Ha Tai province), VACVINA first contacted Mr Tam, the village leader, through its provincial VAC branch. It sent him some VAC magazines that featured various kinds of VAC technologies used by farmers in different parts of the country. Mr Tam thought the VAC system offered something new that could solve some of the problems faced by his fellow villagers, who had recently been brought down from the mountains and resettled to engage in settled farming. A VACVINA staff member was then sent to Hop Nhat. Mr Tam organized a villagers' meeting with the VACVINA staff member that night. This was attended by 85 household representatives, who, during the meeting, were introduced to the VAC system technology.

The Dao people are an ethnic minority who lived from shifting, slash and burn, cultivation and hunting and gathering on the mountain slopes. During the meeting they realized that they had learned how to search for fertile land for cultivation, but not how to enhance and maintain soil fertility in a fixed place for settled cultivation. The VACVINA member of staff stressed the important potential of improving livelihoods through using the VAC system technology and explained the way in which the technology worked to ensure household food and income supplying from a fixed piece of land. The meeting raised considerable interest in the VAC system. It was very timely, because the newly settled people were facing difficulties in adopting fixed farming.

About two months later, the first VAC system training workshop was conducted in Hop Nhat, which was attended by 200 farmers, 50 per cent of whom were female. The training was conducted at the people's committee meeting hall over the course of two days. Three resource persons from VACVINA's central office in Hanoi attended. During the first day, the advantages of the VAC gardening system were discussed. During the second day, the training focused on the component parts of the VAC technology — not the detail, but the principles behind the system, for example growing crops and fruit trees, as well as raising livestock and engaging in aquaculture, while maintaining soil tilth and fertility. Although the training was like a classroom session, the participating farmers learned much, which they were then expected to put into practice. Realizing that they would need support in internalizing and implementing the techniques, Mr Tam facilitated the formation of 25 working groups (similar to the Philippine *alayons* or *hunglunans*), each composed of five farmers. These groups met frequently and discussed the VAC system technology as applied to their own farms. They also helped to establish VAC systems in each others' gardens.

No restrictions on the use of technologies were imposed. Farmers were encouraged to adapt the technologies to their own land conditions and household needs. Many farmers soon registered as VAC members. In addition, some of the poorer members were given an in-kind loan package worth US$70 — comprising seeds, seedlings, fertilizers, pesticides and cash for purchasing pigs and chickens — to enable them to establish a VAC system in their gardens. Apart from the initial training workshop, Mr Tam and the other farmers continued to learn about the VAC system through reading the VAC handbook and VAC magazines, their own farm experiences and sharing their practical experiences with other farmers.

A few months after the initial workshop, a national seven-day course for VAC trainers was conducted for over 100 village leaders, in which three farmers from Hop Nhat (including Mr Tam) participated. In this fairly advanced course, the principles behind the 'how to' aspects of the VAC system were covered in detail. The participants were then expected to disseminate the technology, provide technical advice to, and monitor the gardening activities among 90 farmers in their villages. Mr Tam and the two other leaders from Hop Nhat worked in their respective areas of the village to disseminate VAC technologies through periodic meetings with farmers (usually at night) and broadcasts over the village loudspeaker network, but mostly through informally visiting farmers and their gardens. They did not follow the recommended monthly monitoring schedule, because it was practically impossible, given the multiple responsibilities that village leaders hold. However, the leaders found that although their village was ethnically mixed, farmers freely shared experiences and material resources among themselves. Technical consultations were mainly held among neighbours. Farmers seldom requested technical assistance from the village leaders, although they often asked them for planting materials.

Within two years, almost the entire village was covered with VAC gardening technology. Each farm or garden was established differently according to the topography of the land and sources of water — there were numerous cropping patterns; trees and crops were organized differently, as were the shape, size and location of fish ponds and pig pens. It was clear from interviews and discussions with farmers and casual observation of the way male and female farmers were working on their farms that, within a short span of time, farmers had internalized and put into practice the VAC system technologies, and that each was confident in doing so. Many trials and tests of the different components of the technology and their various adaptations were being undertaken. The village leaders said that all these improvements in the VAC technology were taking place at the hands of farmers. VACVINA staff at all levels encouraged farmers to innovate and those innovations which brought about remarkable production improvements were featured in the monthly VAC magazines — the most widely read of VACVINA's print media. Coverage in this popular magazine encouraged farmers to try further innovations and test more adaptations.

VACVINA's farmer-based extension approach is a simple one. The NGO supplies a 'model' of a good VAC garden through its published media. However, it does not prescribe the implementation of exact copies of such a model. Rather, information about a range of technologies is disseminated through its handbooks, magazines and mass training exercises, and farmers are encouraged to adapt these to suit their own farms and households. The entire VAC technology and its principles are introduced to farmers in training courses of only two or three days' duration, through keeping the emphasis on the principles of the system, rather than specific technological inputs. Farmers are then encouraged to experiment with these principles and to do so in collaboration with other farmers. Hence, VACVINA's approach to farmer-to-farmer extension is organized around 'extension for adaptation' rather than 'extension for adoption'.

Nepal

Pandit describes how the Nepal Agroforestry Foundation's strategies and methods in its farmer-to-farmer extension programme in Nepal fit in within a range of other conventional extension techniques.

Methods used by the Nepal Agroforestry Foundation (Pandit)

Steps in farmer-to-farmer extension

The following five steps show how the farmer-to-farmer extension strategy used by the Nepal Agroforestry Foundation (NAF) works.

Orientation and contracts. NAF provides technical and material support to grass-roots NGOs. Regular monitoring and evaluation are undertaken by NAF using participatory rural appraisal tools. An orientation programme, including strategic planning meetings, is held with grassroots NGOs and farmers at the beginning of programme support. The role of each co-operating agency and farmers is discussed. If both parties agree, a contract is signed.

Cross-visits. NAF facilitates cross-visits for interested farmers to nearby on-farm agricultural and forestry demonstrations. The objective of these visits is to motivate farmers to plant fodder, fuelwood or timber trees, and cash crops on their farms, and to share their experiences with each other.

Training of home nursery farmers. Interested and motivated farmers are given one day's training in running a home nursery. In order to make the programme self-supporting and sustainable, training is organized at the local NGO's headquarters either by a NAF agroforestry trainer or by a grassroots farmer-trainer who lives nearby. Home nursery farmers produce seedlings required for both themselves and community plantations. NAF pays for the seedlings required for the community plantation.

Farmer group formation. If a farmer group does not already exist in the community in which the local NGO is working, NAF will facilitate the formation of one. Every month group meetings are held, during which members help each other to produce plants and protect their fodder trees, grasses and fruit trees, and discuss problems. Interested farmers in adjoining communities are also encouraged to attend these meetings to share their experiences.

Ensuring sustainability. The central goal of NAF's programme is to raise individual household incomes beyond the subsistence level. In order to achieve this, farm communities must make full use of all the farm and forestry resources to them on a sustainable basis. The following points are therefore kept in mind:

o Locally managed community forests can provide farmers with a continuous supply of fuelwood, fodder and grasses.
o Farm produce (fruit, seeds, cuttings, livestock, etc.) can help farmers increase their income. NAF has been assisting farmers to identify and develop their products, markets and selling decisions.

In addition, NAF operates on the basis that, if farmers serviced by an NGO and supported by NAF are motivated through the provision of resources and skills to adopt sustainable agroforestry technology for one year, they will be able to continue such activities from the second year with minimal, or no, external support. Within this framework, farmer-promoters operate as facilitators in the following specific extension methods.

Individual extension methods

Farm visits. These visits are made to establish a friendly working relationship with the farmers; supply general information on agricultural and forestry practices (e.g., nursery techniques, farm plan preparation) and to follow up and observe results.

Office calls and enquiries. Since NAF is short of time and personnel, some farmers and NGO staff are invited to come to its offices to obtain necessary information and support. Seeds, training resource kits, nursery materials, household survey formats and so on are usually provided during such visits.

Letters and telephone calls. NGOs and farmers are often contacted by letter, or telephone calls where appropriate. These forms of communication are usually used to arrange board meetings, strategic planning meetings, nursery planning workshops, etc.

Informal contacts. When formal contacts are not possible, farmers may be contacted in public places such as tea shops and marketplaces.

Group extension methods

Group meetings. NAF facilitates group meetings in many communities to encourage community members to take decisions collectively; obtain community members' opinions; introduce and discuss new ideas and practices; and encourage collective problem-solving. Group meetings, though the oldest method of extension, are popular and provide an efficient means of contacting and communicating with farmers. Each farmer group holds a meeting every month to review their past work, discuss on-going trials and problems, and plan for the future. These meetings are held at one of the demonstration farms. Currently there are 78 farmer groups, which NAF supports through grassroots NGOs. Most NGOs have their own focus community, and each community has its own user committee. Farmer groups are formed under this committee, as interested and motivated farmers join groups formed around specific needs and priorities. Initial meetings of the groups focus on farmers' problems and needs, which then serve as a focal point for group discussions. Recently NAF has also begun to work with community forestry groups.

Training and follow-up visits. NAF trainers arrange to meet a number of participating farmers and staff at regular intervals to assist them in implementing the tasks already commenced. Participating farmers and NGO staff are advised and shown skills to improve farm performance.

Demonstrations. Both result and method demonstrations are used by NAF as a means of expanding the impact of its programmes. 'Method demonstrations' (e.g., how to make a sunken bed, fill polypots, prepare trays for small seeds, prick out small seedlings, etc.) are used most during training, while 'result demonstrations' are used to see the results of certain agricultural or forestry practices after a certain period of time. Result demonstrations are becoming an important tool in motivating farmers.

Cross-visits and study tours. These are very important extension methods which offer people the opportunity to see for themselves evidence of improved practices in different places. Most cross-visits supported by NAF are to demonstration plots near the local NGO site.

Mass extension methods

Circular letters. NAF seldom uses these methods to inform farmers, but last year it sent circular letters to many NGO and government project personnel enquiring about psyllid damage to *Leucaena leucocephala*. The response was satisfactory.

Wall newspapers. NAF publishes occasional wall newspapers to be distributed to a large number of people. These contain successful stories of some farmers' exploits. Local people have shown great interest in reading such papers.

59

Flipcharts, posters and booklets. These materials have been most frequently used by NAF as a means of motivating farmers. A series of improved practices has been presented as a flipchart, called 'terrace planting of fodder trees and grasses'. Posters on 'homestead agroforestry' and 'how soil fertility is gained and lost' have also been published by NAF and used over a long period of time. In addition, NAF has supported photographic displays, radio interviews, exhibitions and cultural shows.

Summary

It can be seen from the extracts above that all the farmer-to-farmer extension networks described share some field methods. Common ones include:

o training of farmers and farmer-extensionists by external agents and other farmers in technological developments and in communication, extension and training skills
o cross-visits among farmers and exposure of farmers to other institutions of interest, such as research organizations
o facilitation of farmers' research into, and testing and adaptation of, new technologies and management practices
o farmer group formation and development, and regular group meetings for planning, learning, sharing experiences and problems, evaluation, etc.

These four sets of methods appear to constitute a core of activities in all the farmer-to-farmer extension efforts described in the papers quoted here. However, there are also many additional ones, some more commonly deployed than others. These include: conscientization; leadership training; facilitation of farmers' research, mass mobilization; forming and actively managing linkages among farmers, NGOs and government; and developing conflict-resolution skills. Some of these methods will be discussed in later chapters. Ultimately each farmer-to-farmer extension network has to decide upon the field methods best suited to its own objectives, resources, demography, agro-ecology and social and economic situation.

6 Roles and responsibilities in farmer-to-farmer extension

WE NOW TURN to more detailed analyses of the role farmer-extensionists and professional extensionists play in implementing the methods discussed in the previous chapter. Since in any farmer-to-farmer extension network, the farmer-extensionists or promoters are going to be the most critical elements for success, a clear understanding of what has been tried and what does and does not work is important.

Farmer-extensionists

Holt-Gimenez and Selener, Chenier and Zelaya paint a broad-brush picture of the roles farmer-extensionists or promoters have assumed in the *campesino-a-campesino* movement in Central and South America. The movement's longevity suggests that much can be learned from it.

Promoters in the campesino-a-campesino movement in Central America (Holt-Gimenez)
The primary actors in *campesino-a-campesino* are of course, the *campesinos* themselves, who as protagonists of their own movement, are at once potential executors, beneficiaries and sponsors of farmer-led experimentation, training and extension. Among the *campesinos*, the promoters are clearly the catalysts.

Promoters are frequently the first to formally experiment with alternatives and are the primary training providers. They often organize local workshops, provide formal and informal follow-up, and prepare future promoters. The salient characteristic of the promoter is the fact that he or she does not abandon agricultural activities in order to provide 'extension' services. Rather, it is his or her farm itself which is at once a laboratory, workshop, and living proof of the viability of sustainable agriculture for *campesinos*. As one Mexican participant remarked:

> With the extensionists, if the practice is good or bad, they always get their pay cheque. Whatever they do, they always eat, whether their [demonstration] farm makes money or not. But a promoter has to live off his land. I know whatever works for him and his family, will work for me and mine. That's how it is between *campesinos*.

Experience has shown, however, that several things can put the relationship between promoters and other *campesinos* in jeopardy. If the promoters are perceived as receiving too many special advantages, (salaries, perks, etc.) they will be considered as 'different' and the alternative technologies implemented by them may be considered (rightly or wrongly) as beyond the reach of the 'average' or 'ordinary' *campesino*. Likewise, if the promoters advance too far ahead of their neighbours technologically, their farming system will appear too complex for the latter to adopt. Finally, if promoters work alone, they may be ridiculed by the community for breaking with convention or tradition. This can produce a certain cultural introversion on the part of the promoter, who may come to depend on professionals and programme officers rather than the local population for acceptance and support.

Lopez, a farmer-promoter and programme manager in the *campesino-a-campesino* movement for nearly two decades, first in Guatemala and later in Honduras, describes several broad roles that farmer-promoters assume. He highlights the fact that farmer-extensionists play critical roles in the communities they serve and can often access important external resources.

Role of the farmer-extensionist in Central America (Lopez)

First, we should be clear about the purpose of villager-extensionists or promoters. We do not see villager-extensionists as some sort of second-class extension workers — people with the same role as extension workers, but with less education. They are not substitute extension workers, sometimes preferred because they cost less. Nor should the objective of their training be that of teaching them everything about agriculture. The role of village agricultural extensionists, like that of village health workers before them, is not one of having a general, over-all knowledge of their particular subject area — of becoming village doctors or extension workers. Their role is, rather, to learn the solutions to the most common problems in the village, and then know when they should refer to professionals or other sources of information for additional knowledge. Although villager-extensionists may consequently have less technical knowledge than extension workers, they have a number of additional abilities and characteristics that make them equally valuable in the extension process. The villager-extensionist can take advantage of his or her knowledge of the local ecological and social environment and of local agricultural and economic conditions; personal relations with the people; role and perceptions as a villager; experience as a farmer, and ability to understand and communicate with the people. These qualities are complementary to those possessed by the extension worker. Therefore villager-extensionists should complement the role of the extension worker, not replace it or, even less desirable, compete with it.

Thus, the technical knowledge of the villager-extensionist is often narrower, but deeper than that of the extension worker. Whereas the extension worker knows about all sorts of crops, the promoter knows about the crops locally grown, how they fit into the traditional farming systems, what local varieties are used, etc. Whereas the extension worker knows the solutions to local problems in theory, the promoter has spent days and days working with these solutions in practice, understanding how much effort and labour they take, what problems they present, and in what ways they might be modified or improved. Through this experience, the village extensionist comes to understand how these solutions interact with local weed populations, soil conditions, moisture conditions, seasonal labour availability, cultural factors in the village, economic forces inside and outside the village, etc. Thus the villager-extensionist becomes a specialist in a limited, but highly relevant technology for local use. This knowledge base will, of course, widen little by little as the village's ability to assimilate new technologies grows, and as the diversity of technologies and crops in the village expands. It is because of this limited but relevant and practical knowledge, as well as the villager-extensionist's role as a member of a village, that he or she can be particularly valuable in fulfilling the tasks or roles described below.

It should also be mentioned that villager-extensionists are not and should not be merely extension workers' helpers or aids, nor should they just become the extension worker's representative in the community, to do errands and bring the people together to listen to the extension worker. Such a role, all too frequently observed in the field, is far too limiting. Much of the potential that villager-extensionists can have in moving the development process along is thereby lost. And the possibility that the villager-extensionist will come to lead the process in the village, to take the reins and to carry on the process after the extension worker has left, is eliminated. Below, some of the main functions and roles that villager-extensionists fulfil are described.

Liaison and motivation. Most communities already have leaders. When development agencies arrive in communities, one of the first things they usually do is make contact with these leaders. These leaders can often call together the community for classes or meetings, and help explain the purpose of new programmes to the other villagers. Such leaders are also often the first people to try out new technologies in small plots in their fields. Generally, these first plots, if successful, are the factor most responsible for stirring the interest of the remaining farmers. Frequently this process itself becomes an important part of the training of villager-extensionists. The success of their initial experimental plots often attracts a large number of other farmers. As these leaders begin to explain to their visitors what they did, how they did it, and what the results were, they are unconsciously developing the skills of a good extensionist. They are learning to talk in front of a group and express themselves, experiment and learn constantly, teach by example, teach in the fields rather than in a classroom, talk about practical issues, and allow the people's concerns to be expressed in a very participatory atmosphere. Whether the programme personnel realize it or not, the training of the village extensionist has already begun.

Of course, the communication achieved by the villager-extensionist goes both ways. They also serve as a link between the extension worker and the community by letting the extension worker know what the people in the community are thinking, what their needs are, etc. Even though many groups and agencies now use participatory rural appraisal or some other method of gathering information about the community, the feedback provided by villager-extensionists can be ongoing and constant. It can deal with factors the extension worker would never think to ask. And it can be quite candid.

Most villagers are extremely reluctant to tell a professional of any kind when the latter has made a mistake. The 'conspiracy of courtesy' is alive and well in much of the world. Nevertheless, if the relationship between the extension worker and the villager-extensionist is what it should be, the latter will be able to mention problems and snags to the extension worker before they become too serious. After all, the villager-extensionist has laboured long and hard to make a success of the innovations, and he or she has a vested interest in helping the extension worker avoid major problems.

Facilitating development and conservation. Villager-extensionists have special advantages in facilitating the development process in general. Much of this role is already widely recognized and described in the literature. Less widely recognized is the role village leaders can play with regard to environmental protection or conservation. Villagers often contribute to the destruction of natural resources. In the case of forests, for instance, they harvest forest resources needed for their own use or to sell, or they cut down the forest in order to use the land for other purposes. Thus, villagers can play a special role in consciousness-raising about the sustainable use or protection of these resources.

Farmer leaders can do more than talk about the problem. They can provide a personal example of how a villager can use these resources more sparingly or less destructively, use them sustainably, or even stop using them altogether. In the Guatemalan Petén, for instance, farmers use velvet bean to avoid slash-and-burn or swidden agriculture, providing tremendous impetus toward more sustainable use of the rainforest through their own example.

Simplifying and interpreting information. Generally, professional extensionists are accustomed to using technical language, making it difficult for villagers to understand them. In other cases, the language of the professionals may be understandable, but is much less graphic, less laced with humour and less pertinent to the practical needs of the farmers, making their lessons much less interesting. In still other cases, the extension workers simply cannot speak the language of the villagers. In these cases, villager-extensionists often understand technical terms better than the other villagers, are able to read somewhat, or may speak the national language or language of the universities. They may also make an effort to assimilate new knowledge, and try out the innovations on their own land. Thus, they can serve as communicators of information from more technical, nation-wide sources, and make it understandable to farmers in the villages, through the language they use and practical examples provided by their experiments. The latter method of communication is usually the most effective.

From the moment that the volunteer extensionists try something out in their fields, friends and neighbours will often become curious and begin debating among themselves the merits and problems of the innovation. Of course, sometimes these debates may involve a good deal of merited or unmerited criticism of the innovator, but another part of the villager-extensionists' role is to take this criticism and gradually, through example and a willingness to suffer a certain amount of initial criticism, make the climate for future adopters a bit more favourable.

Villager-extensionists can also take advantage of a large number of opportune moments for talking about innovations that are not normally open to professional extensionists. They can teach their neighbours about innovations being tried when these neighbours walk past the extensionist's fields, when the crops are growing, and during harvest work, which in some cultures is done in groups. They can also discuss farming techniques during family and social gatherings. Furthermore, villager-extensionists need not be rigid in terms of working hours. They are in the village early in the morning, late in the evening, and on weekends. Much, if not most, of farmers' social interaction occurs at these times. In addition, what farmers learn during informal conversations with friends often has more impact on their future actions than what they learn in formal classes. In part, this greater impact may be because they are much less likely to perceive the information as being motivated or skewed by the particular interests of some outside institution.

Another advantage of the villager-extensionists is their constant presence in the village. They can repeat the ideas taught much more often than a professional. They will also be available, and will probably be informed very quickly, when problems crop up, thereby having some chance of solving them in a timely manner.

Villager-extensionists can also simplify the message by focusing on just a very few innovations. Focusing on specific, limited knowledge allows them to narrow, or simplify, the message. They can spend a good deal more time explaining one single technology, dealing with all the practical issues of interest to the farmers, and explaining at length the advantages. By doing this, the farmers understand better and are not confused by the welter of other technologies or issues not immediately relevant to their situation.

The methods of communication generally used by these extensionists are very practical. This factor also improves communication. They tend to do their teaching right in the fields, sometimes while they are actually working. For example, they teach in-row tillage by actually doing a few metres of it, and show people how to incorporate organic matter by actually incorporating some. And, of course, they will usually get the participants to do some of the work. That this work is being done in the extensionists' own fields is fairly convincing proof that they believe the practice will be beneficial to their own crops. Even when only talking about new ideas, villagers' knowledge of local experience and history can be valuable. For example, when broaching the subject of environmental decay, they often know precisely which signs of environmental deterioration have been most noticeable in the village, or which ones have most affected local life or made an impression on people. Thus they can get their neighbours to reflect on the consequences of some of their actions — on the evidence of decreases in their soil fertility, the gradual disappearance of their forests, and the resulting disappearance of animals they can hunt and eat.

Another factor that is more important than most people realize is that teaching villagers and convincing them to try out new ideas, especially when done in a participatory manner, requires a good deal of patience. Not all professional extension workers have the patience, or are able or willing to dedicate the needed amounts of time to the process. On the other hand, villager-extensionists are accustomed to the slower pace of village life. Furthermore, they know personally how hard it is to risk one's livelihood — and local reputation — on new ideas. They went through the same process themselves, so they realize that they must walk at the same slow pace as their friends.

Of course, the villager-extensionists must know more than just practical ideas. They must also understand, and teach, a certain minimum of theory. They must understand the different ways organic matter acts to improve the soil, the importance of biological diversity, the role forests play in regulating the water cycle and maintaining environmental balance. They must know the reasons behind each of the practices they use. Without theory, the villager-extensionists might, once again, just become extension workers' helpers.

Experimenting with innovations. Villager-extensionists are usually the first to experiment with new innovations. They therefore make it easier for others to follow in their tracks. They also often work out a few of the problems, looking for local kinds of solutions (appropriate technologies) to those problems. Villager-extensionists may try out new ideas that they hear from sources other than visiting extension workers, such as those they have heard on the radio, are told by commercial input suppliers, or have thought up themselves. These experiments may improve the innovations taught by the extension worker, or may solve some of the problems associated with new innovations. In all cases, this experimentation will result in better recommendations for other farmers. Such experimentation ensures that the villager-extensionists avoid the problem that is all too frequent among agricultural development programmes: they will not be teaching others technologies that do not work in village conditions or that are not appropriate to local conditions.

Villager-extensionists' own experiments and successful fields are the most important arm in their fight for local improvement. A great deal of credibility is afforded them by these tools. Any time there is any doubt on the part of the participants as to whether the technologies being taught are useful, the extensionist can merely say, 'Well, next week you can come and see my crops, and see what you think. That way you can see for yourselves the reality: whether these technologies work or not.' When the participants see the fields of the extensionist, which normally are producing more than their own fields produce, they know that the extensionist not only knows the technology in theory, but knows how to apply it, and can afford to apply it (which means they, too, can afford it, a factor farmers are seldom convinced of even in those cases when extension workers do manage successful plots). In the same way, they know the extensionist truly believes in the technology. Such 'educational field visits' are not only motivational. They also provide a very good context for new questions to arise. When villagers really understand what things will look like with the application of the technology, a whole new set of doubts, worries, and wonders begins to come forth.

Continuing to experiment after the programme has ended. Such experimentation will continue, always, to be an important way for villager-extensionists to continue to learn, progress and have new ideas to spread, so the music they sing will always be fresh and lively. If the extensionists quit learning, their students will quit showing up for classes. But if they continue to harvest more, learn about new and more profitable crops, and improve the quality of their soil and water, villagers will continue to know that there is more to do, progress to enjoy, and more ideas they need to learn from their extensionist. That this process of constant innovation and improvement can be sustained is evidenced clearly in the results of a study done five and 15 years after we had terminated our work in some areas. In San Martin Jilotepeque, for instance, where we worked during the 1970s, many of the villager-extensionists are still active in experimenting and sharing ideas 15 years after external support ceased. Some of the extensionists from this programme are working with other development programmes in other areas of Guatemala, and even outside the country (as in my case). However, a number remain in the area. Very few of those still in the village give formal classes, but they are heavily involved in experimenting, sharing ideas, providing advice and motivating others to begin or continue the process. Similarly, in Guinope and Cantarranas, townships in Honduras in which we worked in the 1980s, the villager-extensionists have gone far beyond the soil conservation and basic grain work learned during the programme's tenure. They are now leading a move to acquire irrigation systems, developing commercial vegetable production and establishing fruit orchards. The beneficial results of these processes are obvious. In San Martin Jilotepeque, villages where average yields reached more than 2 t/ha of maize at programme termination, have now reached 4.8 t/ha, with lower levels of chemical fertilizer use than when the programme existed (Bunch and López 1994).

Providing a role model. Another, often ignored, but extremely important role of villager-extensionists is the positive influence their example can have on the people in the villages. Here is a person whose family has plenty to eat; who harvests three or four times as much as others do; who seems to enjoy farming as a way of life; who teaches dozens, if not hundreds, of other villagers how to improve their harvests and their land; who earns a salary (however modest that might be); whose work is visited by important officials; who can talk in front of anyone, no matter how important — in short, who economically, intellectually and socially has made it beyond what many thought possible.

When young farmers or children see a person who has achieved so much, yet is the son or daughter of another villager just like them, it often adds a new dimension to what they feel they can realistically strive for. It gives them a new role model, a new objective to aim towards and a new source of hope and personal motivation. They realize that development may not have to be as seemingly unattainable as they had thought. Such factors are subtle — seldom mentioned — but they can be powerful stimuli for positive change within a village, especially among the poorest people in the most isolated villages.

In their review of farmer-to-farmer extension networks in the Philippines and Vietnam, Bhuktan, Killough and Basilio stress the importance of farmer-extensionists' responding to other farmers' ideas and suggestions. They highlight the importance of this role for effectiveness and self-motivation, particularly after programme or project support for the extension system is withdrawn.

Role of farmer-extensionists in the Philippines and Vietnam (Bhuktan, Killough and Basilio)
'Will you continue serving your fellow farmers even after the project stops paying your honorarium?' Some, but not the majority of the farmer-instructors from both the Soil and Water Conservation Project in Cebu and the Upland Farm Management Project in Albay answered that they would. They were not prepared to continue regular monitoring visits to

adopters' farms, but they would entertain farmers coming to their own homes for advice. Interestingly, this small number of farmer-instructors did not have a strong feeling of technology fatigue, as did others.

In addition, these farmer-instructors were disseminating the recommended technologies using different approaches, and some of them were found to be emphasizing farmer testing, experimentation and adaptation. They discussed with the farmers how they were using the technologies and the types of adaptations they were making. They were doing this independently; project staff had not even noticed this variation in their approach. In both projects, the sponsors had focused only on farmer-instructors in encouraging trials in order to cut down the farmers' technology testing and adaptation process and to hasten adoption. However, the farmer-instructors concerned received more and more questions from farmers visiting their demonstration farms about testing and experimenting with technologies. This told them that other farmers had not stopped testing the technologies even after they had seen them tested on the model farms. Sometimes a good deal of discussion ensued between the farmer-instructors and farmers about the findings of their respective technology trials.

The farmer-instructors soon found that farmers were interested in trying some components of the recommended technologies, but not necessarily for regular use or immediate adoption. Farmers also often asked how a given component of the technology worked and about the ideas behind it. In response, the farmer-instructors began promoting the technologies by saying 'why don't you try...'. In this manner, the farmers would ask questions which gave the farmer-instructor a chance to explain the technologies more fully. It also allowed continued adaptation of the technologies.

The most successful farmer-instructors enjoyed continued acceptance among their fellow farmers. Unfortunately, many farmer-instructors emphasized only certain technologies, and they and the farmers they dealt with got bored due to technology fatigue. Most of the farmer-instructors had taken the technology recommended by the project as prescribed; they thought that altering it might aggravate soil erosion. Moreover, evaluations of the farmer-instructors' demonstration and model farms stressed the recommended technologies. The farmer-instructors did not think that encouraging alternative applications of the principles behind the technologies would bring them high scores when they were evaluated — and a low score could lead to their being suspended. So farmer-instructors never discussed with project staff their support of farmers' adapting the technologies. When a farmer adopted a different technology, the farmer-instructor reported him or her as having dropped out from using the recommended technology, even if the new technology was adapted from the recommendation or based on its principles.

Despite this, numerous farmers were able to use the ideas and principles behind the introduced technologies in minimizing soil erosion and addressing low soil fertility problems and, thus, increase their farm productivity and diversity in a sustainable way. Since these farmers increasingly used the introduced technologies in controlling their production processes and environment, it can be said that they were empowered by the farmer-to-farmer extension approach.

The same types of role are reflected in others' descriptions of farmer-extensionists' activities and responsibilities. For example, Selener, Chenier and Zelaya summarize the roles and activities of farmer extensionists identified during two participatory workshops in Honduras and Ecuador and attended by 75 farmer promoters, all with at least five years of experience as such.

67

Roles and activities of farmer-extensionists in Latin America (Selener, Chenier and Zelaya)

In relation to the community:
o facilitate problem identification
o plan and organize activities
o provide technical assistance and training by disseminating useful knowledge
o look for resources to be used by the community
o facilitate participatory technology development and evaluation
o look for information needed by the community
o support community leadership in different local development initiatives
o facilitate monitoring, evaluation and follow-up of community projects
o promote grassroots development.

In relation to NGOs and farmer associations:
o participate in planning activities with NGO staff
o achieve institutional objectives
o participate as facilitator in training activities and field trips
o facilitate the systematization of activities and elaboration of progress reports
o estimate needed resources for project activities
o be aware of existing local knowledge and resources to be considered in project activities
o conscientize NGO staff of real needs of the community and make sure that those are used as a basis for project activities
o co-ordinate activities with organizations working in the same community
o promote linkages and networking with other projects
o facilitate communication in local languages
o provide a channel of communication, information and interpretation between NGO, farmers' association and community
o support farmers' associations to integrate and co-ordinate activities in different communities
o avoid paternalism and promote sustainability of development projects.

Baile lists his main roles at different stages in his career as a farmer-extensionist in the Philippines.

Roles of different levels of farmer-extensionists in the Philippines (Baile)
In the Upland Farm Management Project, there are three levels of farmer-extensionist: farmer-leader, farmer-technician and senior farmer-technician. A farmer-leader is a leader of one or two *hunglunan* (labour-sharing) groups with four to five members each. A farmer-technician provides technical support to farmer-leaders and their *hunglunan* members, and a senior farmer-technician provides technical support to farmer-technicians, farmer-leaders and farmer-cooperators.

Farmer-leader
o being in charge of the *hunglunan* (labour sharing) group's activities
o encouraging other farmers to form *hunglunan* groups
o providing technical support to farmer co-operators on soil and water conservation technologies
o Monitoring the development of group members' farms.

Farmer-technician
o organizing, re-organizing and strengthening *hunglunan* groups
o promoting improved cropping system
o training and providing technical assistance to interested farmer co-operators
o conducting trials on alternative agricultural technologies
o promoting all project components.

Senior farmer-technician
o assisting farmer-technicians in organizing/re-organizing and strengthening *hunglunan* groups
o promoting the conduct of trials and alternative agricultural technologies
o providing guidance to the farmer-technicians in the implementation and promotion of project components
o assisting NGO staff in training and strengthening the capabilities of farmer-technicians, farmer-leaders and farmer co-operators.

Extension workers and support agencies

With all the above functions being undertaken by farmers, one is led to wonder what, if any, role extension workers have to play? If farmers are to become extensionists, what is the role of professionally trained extension officers or agents? Both Holt-Gimenez and Lopez argue that such individuals have an important part to play in supporting farmer-to-farmer extension, although they stress that this is likely to be very different from their former, more traditional roles.

Extension workers in Central America (Holt-Gimenez)
It has not been easy for extension workers trained to extend Green Revolution technologies to participate in the *campesino-a-campesino* movement. In Nicaragua, there are still less than a dozen (out of several hundred in the public sector) supporting over 300 promoters. Why is this so?

In the first place, few have any training or practical experience in the skills required. For example, farming systems research notwithstanding, the majority of mid- and lower-level extensionists in Mesoamerica are not trained to analyse systems or detect agro-ecological problems. Few have much practical experience of experimentation. Most have been primarily concerned with distributing pre-determined recipes or messages to farmers. These extension methods, when applied to the complex and dynamic agro-ecological problems and opportunities of sustainable agriculture, have proven ineffective. Second, conventional extension, while providing solutions to production problems, does little to promote an innovative process among farmers. Centre stage is occupied by the extensionist as solution provider and expert, which not only discourages farmer autonomy and technological independence, but it also acts as a barrier to the development of more horizontal relationships between the two parties. The traditional role of the extensionist contradicts the notion of farmer as protagonist.

During the earlier years of the movement, these differences resulted in conflicts between promoters and extension workers (particularly those who felt their technical territory was being infringed upon). More recently, with the privatization of agricultural services, public-sector extension services have in effect disappeared. Nevertheless, from the very beginning, the movement has benefited from the support of a few key professionals, who have helped train and guide the promoters technically, methodologically and organizationally, through recognizing problems and opportunities, bringing in new information, making contacts, providing institutional back-up and documentation. In general, these few professionals have supported *campesino-a-campesino* by standing next to (or behind) the promoter in their role as protagonist in their own movement.

What is the future role of extension workers in farmer-led extension? Partnership, the easy answer, is not as easy as it sounds. Social and cultural conventions are not easily changed, particularly if there is no visible incentive. While it may be easy to convince farmers that their technical and cultural protagonism will result in more stability and control over their own agriculture, why should an extension worker change roles? There are a number of reasons emerging. For example, given the present socio-economic panorama, extension workers may soon have little choice. If they are not able to redefine their relationship with the majority of Central America's farmers, they will be stuck extending 'what is already known well in ways which are poorly understood'. Whatever the reasons they choose to change, those extension workers who do, may need some assistance if they are to acquire the skills necessary to support farmer-led research and extension. For example, training in the *campesino-a-campesino* approach and agro-ecology is essential, especially if they can be trained by *campesino* promoters. But this in itself is not enough. Clear programme guidelines and support for their new role, in the form of coherent goals and objectives, are also important. Finally, extension workers must be trained to share project management (including the use of resources) with promoters themselves. The professional success of the extension workers must be measured by the quality of their participation in the farmers' processes and the extent to which this actually empowers farmers.

Above all, in terms of farmer-led extension, care must be taken to ensure that farmers are not simply seen as substitutes for professional extensionists. This would effectively deprive the extension worker of his or her legitimate counterpart with whom to develop sustainable agriculture. On the contrary, such substitution not only ignores the farmer's comparative cultural advantage, it places them in a false, competitive position with the few practising extensionists still active in agriculture.

Future of the extension worker in Central America (Lopez)
When villager-extensionists take over many of the roles that were previously thought to be those of extension workers, many extension workers begin to fear that their importance will diminish. Nevertheless, experience has shown the opposite to be the case. The role of the agronomist has become more important, varied, and productive. Basically, this new role includes initiating the innovative process in the communities; identifying and training villager-extensionists; managing and supporting these extensionists; providing technical back-stopping for them, and providing a liaison between them and other development programmes and sources of information. These extension workers also provide a general sense of direction to programmes and initiate the process of programme termination when it is appropriate.

Two factors have emerged that have increased the demand for extension workers where farmer-led extension is being used. First of all, the newly acquired innovative activities of the people, and the success of their innovations, have dramatically increased the demand for more technical information. Villagers begin actively to search out new ideas. Thus the demand for extension workers and their knowledge also increases dramatically. Second, when development institutions realize the potential that farmer-led extension has, when they realize the tremendous influence this process can have for empowering and improving the life-styles of thousands upon thousands of villagers, they tend to dedicate more of their time and budgets to agricultural improvement. Donors are also willing to spend more money on these endeavours. Therefore, the number of jobs open to extension workers also generally increases.

Role of other support agencies in Central America (Holt-Gimenez)

The first major lesson to be learned from the *campesino-a-campesino* experience for 'outsiders' interested in promoting farmer-led extension might be that for it to take place, farmers must be genuinely involved in the entire process of agricultural development, from analysis of the problems to the generation of alternatives, their validation, diffusion, evaluation and back again. There are probably no quick fixes for extension in this sense. The bottom line is sharing the development process with farmers, which means sharing power with them: power to set experimental agendas, use extension resources, determine diffusion strategies, plan and execute production and conservation strategies, etc. The question then, is not are farmers capable of farmer-led extension, but are we?

If we accept the notion that today's *campesinos* have more social, scientific and intellectual resources at their disposal than they did a generation ago (illiteracy notwithstanding), and if we accept the legitimacy of farmer's endogenous development processes, then we may be able to conceive honestly of participating in a partnership, rather than a 'patronship', for agricultural development. Participation in this context means our participation in their process. Can we help? Can we open lines of communication, clear up conceptual voids, provide methods to facilitate the discovery and generation of knowledge? Can we support farmer organization for developing and sharing innovations? Can we stand back and allow *campesinos* to become the protagonists in agricultural development? If we are interested in a partnership with farmers, what does this mean, institutionally and programmatically? The *campesino-a-campesino* experience suggests the following guidelines may be helpful:

o Promote small-scale experimentation and farmer-to-farmer training and exchanges through local development and farmers' organizations.
o Provide local, regional and national opportunities for farmer gatherings, symposiums and conferences.
o Actively promote the development of sustainable, low-external input agriculture.
o Provide direct and indirect technical and financial support for groups of farmer-promoters.
o Train and orientate technicians technically and methodologically in their new support roles.
o Provide formal and informal opportunities for farmers and promoters to share their experiences, share their doubts and express their demands to formal research and extension systems.
o Document farmers' experiences and testimonies in sustainable agriculture and make them available as videos, radio programmes and pictorial articles.

Are 'outsiders' capable of promoting farmer-led extension? Clearly, some of us are, although it implies fundamental changes in our development paradigms. But as agricultural development turns toward sustainable agriculture for solutions to the agro-ecological crisis, and as peasants continue to exert their influence in the countryside, one wonders what will happen to those institutions not capable of making the change. The future of agriculture extension may depend not on whether the state ministries, agricultural universities, technical training schools and agricultural centres can convince farmers to adopt technologies, but whether these institutions can change their traditional role of providers to that of facilitators. Seen from a *campesino-a-campesino* perspective, the question of how to elicit farmer participation in technology generation and dissemination is turned on its head. Rather, how do professionals in agricultural development programmes identify, foster, support, and participate in farmer-led processes?

71

Farmer-extensionists' training and relationships with supporting organizations. There is no fixed set of rules regarding the relationship between the promoters and outside agencies, but a total lack of rules tends to be counterproductive. If training and extension activities are carried out under a nebulous or tenuous set of agreements, or if agreements are non-existent, the lack of clear ground rules will allow opportunists to take advantage of the programme and their motivation may well be economic compensation, power or prestige. Worse, if projects begin by offering even the hope of salaries and perks, instead of plain hard work, they run the risk of training people interested in gaining advantages over their neighbours, rather than in working with them. Becoming a promoter then becomes seen as an end in itself, rather than a means to increasing living standards by improving agriculture.

The importance of training a solid group of promoters cannot be over-emphasized. Groups allow innovations to be generated rapidly and diffused broadly through existing, extended family communication networks. In groups, there is also more of an opportunity to specialize — some promoters may be better at giving workshops, others at experimenting, others at providing follow-up. In addition, the promotional work load itself is shared, thus promoters can work as little as a day a week away from their farms, eliminating in large part the problem of salaries. Having groups of promoters also allows for the necessary rotation and training of promoters without undue disruption of the work. Finally, having groups affords the 'pioneers' of new innovations some support for what may appear as strange or even crazy ideas to the local farmers. A group can help defend fledgling promoters from unnecessary and demoralizing ridicule (from both farmers and jealous technicians), especially at the start of the process.

Putting monetary remuneration aside for the moment, what motivates a farmer to become a promoter? Self-development as a farmer, the satisfaction of helping others, the prestige and respect of the community are all aspects mentioned by Bunch (1982) and certainly continue to be important factors. However, with the growth of the *campesino-a-campesino* movement, another important factor has come into play, namely a profound sense of contributing and belonging to the future of agriculture. This is admittedly a romantic notion, but none the less important.

Campesino-a-campesino is, in part, a belief in the fact that *campesinos* are not simply poor people with problems to be solved (through self-help or otherwise), but legitimate, social actors, capable of generating solutions, not only for themselves, but for agriculture and the environment in general.

7 Issues and problems in farmer-to-farmer extension

THE OPERATION OF farmer-to-farmer extension networks and programmes raises a number of issues for those interested in initiating and improving such activities. Selener, Chenier and Zelaya succinctly summarize the main issues identified by 75 farmer-extensionists during two workshops in Honduras and Ecuador. All the participants in these workshops had been farmer-extensionists or agricultural promoters for at least five years. The main issues they identified are listed in Table 7.1. The first two issues (roles and methods) are discussed in Chapters 5 and 6

Table 7.1: Issues in farmer-to-farmer extension (Selener, Chenier and Zelaya)

Roles	What are farmer-extensionists' precise roles—in relation to the communities they serve and, where applicable, to farmer associations or organizations and the development institutions supporting their activities?
Methods	What learning and extension methods should farmer-extensionists use and how should these be decided upon?
Selection	How should farmer-extensionists be selected: by the community, the programme supporter, farmers' organizations, etc? Should specific criteria be used in their selection or should they be allowed to emerge over time; be voted into office, etc? If explicit selection criteria are to be used, what should these be and how should they be defined?
Payment	Should farmer-extensionists be paid a salary or expenses? If so, how much should they be paid, and what expenses should be covered?
Time allocation	How much time should farmer-extensionists devote to extension; should they operate on a volunteer basis; on a demand basis; allocate specific proportions of their working time to extension or become full-time extensionists?
Work	Should farmer-extensionists work in their own communities or in others?
Specialization	Should farmer-extensionists be specialists in particular commodities or commodity systems, or should they be generalists?
Gender	Should women, as well as men, be farmer-extensionists?
Incentives for communities	What incentives can farmer-extensionists offer communities?

above. This chapter deals with each of the remaining issues in turn (except the last, 'incentives for communities', which was not discussed in the Philippines workshop on which this book is based).

Selener, Chenier and Zelaya argue that decisions on these issues can be made only in relation to specific networks or programmes. The decisions will depend on:

o the organizational philosophy of the supporting agency or agencies
o the level or function expected of the farmer-promoters in the extension system, for example whether they operate in the community, as co-ordinators or trainers and the degree of leadership expected
o farmer-extensionists' accountability to the community, NGO, farmer organization or government
o the characteristics of the project — its type, topics of focus, objectives, sources of funding, geographical scope and transportation resources.

However, the workshops in Honduras and Ecuador drew up some instructive lists of the pros and cons, from a farmer-extensionist's point of view, of doing things in a particular way. These lists are given in the relevant sections below.

Selection of farmer-extensionists

How should farmer-extensionists be selected, by whom and when? The answers to these three questions have been heavily debated and, frustratingly, no 'best practices' have been developed — or are likely to be. Nevertheless, experimentation has revealed some benefits and disadvantages of undertaking selection in particular ways, as described by Lopez below. In Table 7.2, Selener, Chenier and Zelaya summarize the pros and cons of gradual selection.

Timing of selection (Lopez)
Early selection. Many programmes select villager-extensionists, or have the villagers select them, right after work in the village has begun. Long experience has lead us to believe this is a mistake. Frequently the very best leaders in a village do not begin participating in a new programme until it has proven itself. Often the first people to show up are those most interested in getting something for free or those who are most excited about any new idea that comes along. These individuals may lose interest just as soon as the next new idea comes along. Villager-extensionists selected at the beginning that do not follow through by experimenting or teaching others often cause a number of problems. First, they provide a very bad example of the programme's effectiveness and impact. Some programmes try to push them, or pay them, to fulfil these roles, but such practices almost always backfire, and if the programme tries to select another leader, the first one frequently reacts with jealousy or opposition. The individuals with persistence, who really stick with an idea, are frequently those who, at first, are persistent with their traditional ideas. It may take a year or two for them to become convinced of the technologies, but once convinced, they will often become the best leaders one could have. Thus, an early selection process will completely miss many of the best leaders.

Selection after two or three years. Waiting for two or three years to select future extensionists really does not cause any problems for the programme. Since the activities that the programme

Table 7.2: Selection of farmer-extensionists through a gradual process (Selener, Chenier and Zelaya)

Pro	Con
· The performance and effectiveness of the farmer-promoter is demonstrated before a formal selection is made. · There are more opportunities for more farmers to be trained and given opportunities to demonstrate their interest and capacity to be farmer-promoters. · More farmers can be selected. · There are more possibilities for the NGO and community to evaluate together the job done by the candidates and choose them more objectively. · Since usually there is no salary paid yet, the farmers' commitment as a promoter is tested in advance. · Natural selection of the 'best fit' occurs.	· The selection process takes a longer time. · More human and economic resources are required. · It is more difficult to achieve immediate results.

uses to initiate the whole development process in the villages are exactly the same ones that are used to train villager-extensionists, the programme can wait two or three years to select the extensionists without wasting any time. By waiting two or three years before selecting extensionists or leaders, a programme will have a good deal more information on which to base the selection. It knows who has tried out the technology, who is managing it best, and who continues to use it. It can see who has shown the most interest in learning about the technology and who has become most enthused about its value or has worked hardest to apply it. Even more importantly, the programme can begin to see who is most willing and able to teach the technology to others and the degree of impact they can achieve. This is the most important criterion we can use. Furthermore, after two or three years, the emerging extensionists are likely to have already increased their farm productivity and therefore begun to establish their credibility in the communities, and their willingness and ability to help others will have become general knowledge. That is, they will have begun paving their own way to becoming effective extensionists.

Who should select farmer-extensionists?

Who should select the farmer-extensionists? The answer is not as simple as it may at first seem. For example, if the community selects those to be trained as farmer-extensionists, this may lead to élite bias. Alternatively, if an external agency does the selecting, this will be necessarily based on partial knowledge and may raise questions about the farmer-extensionists' accountability.

In Table 7.3, Selener, Chenier and Zelaya weigh up the pros and cons of selection by the community or an NGO or farmers' organization.

Table 7.3: Selection of farmer-extensionists by the community or an NGO? (Selener, Chenier and Zelaya)

Selection by the community

Pro	Con
• Community members trust and support promoters they choose themselves.	• The community may choose a promoter only to find favour with the NGO and to assure the start of the project.
• Participation by community members is enhanced if they elect their own leaders.	
• Selection by the community respects its organization and dynamics.	• Promoters could be chosen for their economic status, power, friendship and contacts, but without being the most appropriate persons for the job.
• Community selection can gather and reproduce locally generated knowledge and experiences.	• The community may always choose the same persons without giving others a chance.
• Community selection facilitates planning and co-ordination of activities with the community leadership.	• If a community leader is chosen, he or she may be too overworked to perform both leader and promoter functions well.
	• In many cases, a promoter may be elected by a few individuals who do not represent the majority's desires or interests; later the promoter may not be supported by the community.

Selection by the NGO or farmer organization

Pro	Con
• This works when the organization does a good job in identifying the best farmers who have demonstrated capacities in previous work.	• If the organization pays a salary, this may become the farmer-promoter's main source of motivation.
• The selection process is quicker and less expensive.	• The organization may not know the chosen farmer, who may be the wrong person for the job.
• The organization has more resources for selection.	• The community may not want to collaborate with a farmer-promoter chosen without its participation or concurrence.
• It can choose promoters who help it achieve its institutional objectives.	• Envy and divisions in the community may occur if the farmer-promoter receives a salary.
	• The farmer-promoter may prioritize institutional objectives over the community's real needs.

Selection by whom? (Lopez)

Increasingly, programmes allow the villagers themselves to select their villager-extensionists. However, by the second or third year of the process, the selection has already largely been made. When villagers are selected early on, the process can be totally subverted by personal interests, the influence of wealthier or more powerful community members, a lack of any idea on the part of villagers as to what qualifications an extensionist should have (e.g., selecting youths with a good education, when these are precisely those who most wish to leave the village), or even just the lack of importance they give to the process (e.g., frequently just selecting the youth with the most free time). However, if the selection process occurs two or three years after programme activities begin, and the overall process is functioning well, the people understand quite well what is required and, most important, have already 'voted with their feet'. Everyone, programme and villagers, can usually already see very clearly who is best prepared and willing to teach others and who the others are most desirous and willing to learn from. The people's choice is so obvious in most cases that a village election, if held, is often a mere formality. Jealousy and infighting are kept to a minimum, because the reasons for the selection, whether by village or programme, are apparent to all.

Obviously, when villager-extensionists are being chosen to work in villages other than their own, it makes little sense for their own neighbours to choose them, as their work will be with other people. In this case, it usually makes more sense for the programme to choose the extensionists.

Using selection criteria

In some cases, clearly defined and explicit selection criteria are used to choose farmer-extensionists. Holt-Gimenez describes some criteria used in such a process. He also reviews attempts to identify innovative farmers.

Using selection criteria for farmer-promoters (Holt-Gimenez)

Ideal qualities of promoters. The training of promoters is at least a medium-term investment. Within the *campesino-a-campesino* movement quite a bit of effort has been spent defining the preferred qualities of promoters. Bunch (1982) describes the ideal promoter as possessing the following qualities:

o the motivation to help others
o good technical knowledge
o an ability to teach
o enthusiasm
o conviction
o prestige.

Promoters and villagers frequently emphasize the following qualities. Promoters must:

o be motivated to experiment, share, learn and teach
o be willing to donate time and be capable of interpreting and responding to local felt needs
o have a deep love of the land and for other *campesinos*
o be honest and responsible
o should practise what they preach
o understand both theory and practice
o not have an alcohol problem.

Many efforts have been made to establish an effective means of promoter selection. Clearly, imposing promoters selected by outsiders on other farmers runs at cross-purposes to the objective of empowering local populations to develop their own agriculture. However, attempts at democratic election of promoters by local communities has met with limited success. What appears to be most effective in the final selection are the results the promoter obtains in his or her field and their willingness to share their knowledge with others. As one experienced and biblically oriented promoter said 'One recognizes a tree by its fruits and a promoter by his or her actions'.

The process by which promoters are trained and the agreements through which they relate to outside development partners will also contribute to this 'natural selection'. This places a tremendous responsibility on the supporting organization.

Characterizing innovators. Socio-economic, agro-ecological and even cultural profiles of the *campesino* innovator have been developed in an attempt to define and isolate those special qualities which set him or her apart from the rest. This is a somewhat futile exercise, in part because *campesinos* often change their social and economic profile significantly after working as promoters. Quiet, shy men and women who may never have held any socially responsible position in their lives have become eloquent teachers and tireless advocates of sustainable agriculture. Loners can become stalwart group organizers, sedentary farmers begin to travel, semi-migrant agricultural workers can shift their focus to family farming. Also, misconceptions about literacy, levels of schooling and prior leadership experience have been shattered by the weight of experience. If anything, the typical promoter distinguishes himself or herself by being a typical *campesino*.

Despite the problems raised by using explicit selection criteria, some farmer-to-farmer extension networks do abide by this practice. For example, Pandit describes the use of such criteria in NAF projects in Nepal.

Criteria for selecting farmer-extensionists in Nepal (Pandit)
One or two farmers from each group are chosen by their group to be farmer-promoters. Groups select farmer-trainers according to their own criteria. Some of the criteria that have been used are that the farmer-leader should:

o be interested and enthusiastic
o be a successful demonstrator of the new technology and have a home tree nursery
o have adequate time to give four to five days' training support to the group
o develop a farm plan of his or her farm
o be willing to produce some seedlings or raise mother plants
o be willing to attend quarterly farmer-trainers' review meetings
o be willing to lead a farmer-to-farmer cross-visit to another community
o live on the land.

Payment and time allocation

It is hotly debated whether to pay farmer-extensionists for their expenses — let alone a fee. This, and the choice of selection mechanisms, are probably the most controversial issues surrounding the implementation of farmer-to-farmer extension. Debates about paying fees or expenses are closely related to those about how much time promoters should devote to extension work, so we deal with these two questions together.

It is commonly accepted that voluntary farmer-extensionists can devote only a small portion of their time to extension, whereas paid ones can be part- or full-time. The farmer-extensionists who participated in the workshops in Honduras and Ecuador described by Selener, Chenier and Zelaya summarize the pros and cons of paying farmer-extensionists transportation costs and salaries in Table 7.4.

Lopez links the payment issue with the amount of time a farmer spends on extension activities. This is how the issue often manifests itself in practice. He explains that programmes may go through a series of approaches to payment, from relying on unpaid volunteers at the start, to increasingly relying on part- and full-time paid farmer-extensionists.

Different kinds of villager-extensionist (Lopez)

Generally, the best of programmes allow villagers gradually to work their way into becoming extensionists. In this manner, they gradually learn, through their own experiences, the skills needed at each stage, in the time-honoured process of 'learning by doing'. Normally, this process begins when certain villagers who have tried out a new technology decide other people really need to learn about it too, and they feel they want to teach it to their family members, friends, neighbours, or larger community. At this point, and hopefully with the encouragement and active support of a programme, they begin teaching others, formally or informally. At this point, they become, in a largely self-selective manner, 'volunteer extensionists'. Eventually, the programme needs more extensionists because of expanding demand from the villages to learn the technology, or a programme-initiated decision to expand its area of impact. At this point, the programme may hire some of these already experienced, somewhat proven volunteers to work part-time for the programme. After they have had several years of experience in a part-time position, the programme or some other agency may want to hire one or more of these extensionists full time. Each of these stages is different, and often exhibits a different dynamic and a different set of needs that the programme should plan to meet.

Volunteer farmer-extensionists

Lopez goes on to discuss the roles of unpaid volunteers, part-time and full-time paid farmer-extensionists. The 75 farmer-extensionists at the workshops in Honduras and Ecuador also considered the pros and cons of each. For each of the three types we give below Lopez's discussion; Tables 7.5 to 7.7 show Selener, Chenier and Zelaya's summaries of the Honduras and Ecuador workshop outcomes.

Volunteer extensionists (Lopez)

Almost always, if the initial technology taught in a community is truly successful, according to local cultural values and economic conditions, a handful of farmers (perhaps one in every 30 or 40) will begin doing some sort of voluntary teaching. This can range in intensity and formality from just helping a family member to trace a contour line when asked, to walking 10–15km to a neighbouring village to give classes once a week for a year or two. The initial motivation is usually that of a desire to serve friends, family, and the community (out of either solidarity and personal concern, or out of religious motivation), although the desire to have a more prominent role in the community, and gain respect, may also play a

Table 7.4: Payment of farmer-extensionists' transport costs and salaries (Selener, Chenier and Zelaya)

Payment of transportation costs

Pro	Con
• An important factor influencing farmer-extensionists' personal motivation and thus the quality of their job. • Permits efficient mobilization between communities and within a community, which greatly facilitates the work. • More time is dedicated to work in a community, instead of spending time walking or waiting for public transport. • Transport is a status symbol and motivates the farmer-promoter. • It is less tiring for the farmer-promoter if transport is provided. • There are inexpensive alternative forms of transportation.	• Providing transport is an additional cost for the organization. • Transportation may be abused. • Lots of accidents occur with motorcycles. • Maintenance and repair costs can be high. • A vehicle may create a social distance between the farmer-promoter and the community. • The farmer-promoter may get tired of travelling. • Dependency may be created. • If insufficient funds are available to support transport costs, the number of visits may fall.

Payment of salaries

Pro	Con
• Paying salaries allows concrete activities to be planned and specific objectives to be set. • Salaries provide stable and secure income for the farmer-promoters. • They provide opportunities for personal and professional advancement for the farmer-promoters. • It is legitimate to pay a salary as compensation for the time farmer-promoters invest in serving the communities and miss working in their own fields. • Salaries improve the quality of life of the farmer-promoters and their families. • Promoters become more responsible in doing their job. • The community and supporting organizations can demand punctuality and responsibility in the job. • Salaries discourage farmer-promoters from migrating to the cities. • Salaries allow expenditures to be planned and the use of money to be optimized.	• Because salaries are generally low, farmer-promoters may feel disadvantaged since NGOs do not recognize their efforts and the quality of their work. • Promoters have less time to attend to their own farms. • They can become dependent on a salary. • Salaries may create jealousy in the community. • Paying salaries may make the project less sustainable if it is not planned who will continue with the project when funds end. • Promoters may work only if money is available. No money—no work • Salaries hinder the voluntary spirit of the community, since they may create a feeling that if there is no money, nothing can be done. • Salaries may diminish the 'mystique' of community voluntary mobilization. • Farmer-promoters may feel they are better than others.

role. The time a volunteer extensionist can dedicate to this work is often limited to a maximum of a half-day per week, and is usually less. After all, it is not easy for people living close to the edge of subsistence to dedicate much time to unpaid activities, even when they are highly motivated. Frequently those who have dedicated the most time to such voluntarism have heard complaints from their families about their work, because of the loss of income it represents.

It is interesting that the highest levels of voluntarism are often shown by those who are very religious. In some areas of Central America, for instance, virtually all the volunteer extensionists have also previously done volunteer work as catechists or religious leaders in their communities. Of course, the desire to fulfil religious teachings about caring for others, common to most of the world's major religions, can be another powerful motivation to become involved in voluntary agricultural training. In such cases, if the family in general is also deeply religious, the volunteer's family may sympathize more with his or her activities. Thus, we have found that it is often a good idea to work especially closely with village religious leaders. Frequently they will also turn out to be the best villager-extensionists.

The lack of time villagers can dedicate to voluntarism is one major shortcoming of volunteer extensionists. Another shortcoming is that, sooner or later, they begin to feel they have done their fair share for the community. Only under very rare circumstances has a volunteer extensionist, in the early stages of a programme, continued to work more than five years, and two or three is frequently the limit. A third shortcoming of volunteer extensionists is that they are not easy to manage. Programmes totally dependent on voluntarism find even medium-term planning almost impossible, because volunteers are only willing to make short-term commitments. Asking such volunteers to cover certain villages, regularly attend programme meetings etc., is frequently impossible. A well-run programme, even with a minimum of short- to medium-term planning, is virtually impossible using only volunteer extensionists. Attempts on the part of some programmes to get villagers to motivate the volunteers to do more, or work more systematically, have frequently backfired; the extensionists often react by abandoning their volunteer activities altogether.

Despite the shortcomings of volunteer extensionists, they have a crucial role to play in the development of agricultural programmes, especially during two phases: the first few years of work in a community and after the formal programme leaves the area. In the first case, it is extremely important in providing experience for future extensionists. Even more important, early voluntarism is by far the most reliable indicator of which villagers will be the best extensionists later on. First and foremost, the programme can observe which of the volunteer extensionists has the most motivation to work for the well-being of others. This is the most important single factor in choosing future paid extensionists. The programme can also watch the effectiveness of these volunteers in terms of the quantity and quality of adoption and agricultural improvement they achieve. Early voluntarism also provides an important, undeniable testimony to the importance of what is happening, and makes the villagers feel that the process is much more 'theirs' than if it is led entirely by professionals.

The second phase at which voluntarism is extremely important is during and after programme phase-out. In this case, the objective is for the extensionists (many of them having been paid extensionists of one kind or another) to continue working for the development of their communities indefinitely. There are often three or four such extensionists in a community, so the burden is shared. Furthermore, they are all much better off economically, with a healthy economic distance between them and mere subsistence. Thirdly, their agriculture is much more diverse and non-traditional-knowledge-dependent. Thus they are very aware that their continuing prosperity depends heavily on continuing to acquire new knowledge. They therefore see the sharing (both giving and receiving) of knowledge throughout the village and beyond as a necessary support activity for their own well-being. And, lastly, by this time, experimenting, if not sharing information from their experiments, has become a way of life. At this point, the method of sharing information is likely to be informal — no one is likely to go to the trouble of giving formal classes. The activities in question will consist much more of sharing information during village meetings or social occasions, visiting each others' fields to observe and discuss innovations, etc. Nevertheless, we have seen from long experience in a number of nations that at this point in the process and in this informal manner, permanent involvement of villager-extensionists in originating, searching out, and sharing new ideas and innovations can be expected, assuming the programme has done a good job. In San Martin Jilotepeque, Guatemala, volunteer extensionists continued developing new systems of production and spreading them 15 years after programme termination. Systems of intensive cattle-raising, coffee growing using fruit trees as shade, and even a system of sustainable forest management, totally different from anything the programme had ever done, had been created and disseminated long after the formal programme had left the area. The introduction and village-wide spread of totally new commercial vegetable crops occurred in the Cantarranas and Guinope areas of Honduras within only five years of programme termination (Bunch and López 1994).

Table 7.5: Volunteer farmer-extensionists (Selener, Chenier and Zelaya)

Pro	Con
• Volunteers invest their own time with little personal interest or reward in return.	• The NGO cannot impose the achievement of certain objectives.
• Volunteers are more autonomous than paid workers.	• Volunteers may not be available when the NGO or the community needs them.
• Volunteers teach using concrete examples proved in their own farms.	• The project's goals and objectives may be harder to achieve in a reasonable time.
• Their work is motivated by the advancement of the community.	• Information may be shared very slowly.
• There are no additional costs for the development organization.	• After being trained by one NGO, volunteers might be hired for a salary by other NGO.
• The work of the farmer-promoter is in one community and is more concentrated.	• Since they do not receive a salary, volunteers lose motivation quickly and do not continue serving the community.
• Through their exemplary work, the volunteers serve as models for the community.	• Volunteers may have problems with their families because they work without being paid.
• Volunteers get in frequent contact with outsiders and acquire new knowledge and experiences which they share with the community.	
• They become a link between the community and the development agency.	

Part-time paid farmer-extensionists

Lopez also analyses the implications of relying on part-time paid farmer-extensionists, a compromise which often heightens the weaknesses of both the volunteer and full-time options, without being able to take advantage of the strengths of either.

Part-time paid extensionists (Lopez)

Sooner or later, almost any good-quality programme will have enough volunteer extensionists that it will be able to expand its activities. In order to do this it will probably need to plan the villager-extensionists' actions over several years, set goals and monitor their achievement, send them to new villages kilometres from their homes, and have them attend meetings and receive systematic training. For most of these activities, at least some of the extensionists must receive some sort of a regular stipend. Thus, it is argued that the programme must hire some of the volunteer extensionists. There has, however, been much debate about whether villager-extensionists should be paid, and if so, how much.

Many organizations have serious doubts about the advisability of paying salaries or stipends to villagers. Reasons given for not paying them include the need for voluntarism to remain high, and the feeling that if people are paid, voluntarism will end. Other reasons arise from past negative experiences, which include watching villagers battle over who will be paid and severe problems of jealousy and envy erupting when some people begin receiving pay. Corruption, manipulation, and favouritism have, in some cases, destroyed the relationship between volunteer extensionists and other members of the villages when pay for extension work was introduced. In a few larger programmes, the stipends were attractive enough that the process of choosing the villager-extensionists became politicized. Much more commonly, organizations have noticed that, almost universally, when the stipends end, so does the work.

It is true that voluntarism is negatively affected by paying villagers. Often, when the salary ends, the work ends too. But we must remember that voluntarism in the early stages of a development programme will not last very long, anyway. The most important reason for paying volunteer extensionists is that, if we don't, their learning process will be cut short before it has really got very far. If we want to train truly competent villager-extensionists, ones whose role in the villages can become permanent, and ones who can do a really high-quality job, they will have to be paid so they can work at it long enough to acquire the experience needed to become such quality extensionists. Lastly, there exists the issue of equity. How can we justify paying extension workers all the time, but refuse to pay villagers when they do much the same sort of work? Is this not, in fact, another form of discrimination against village people?

A number of different ways of resolving the difficulties of paying villager-extensionists have been tried. Some programmes have established a policy of never paying villagers to work in their own village. The new employees are told that they are being paid to work in other villages, but they will be expected to continue doing volunteer work in their own villages, to show their voluntarism, and because such work also benefits them. This procedure has generally worked out quite well, and helped maintain a spirit of voluntarism. In addition, experience has shown that most of the above problems can be solved by avoiding overly attractive stipends. In Central America, World Neighbors, COSECHA, and many other groups have paid new villager-extensionists approximately twice the going rate paid by small farmers to agricultural day-labourers. The justification for this is that the villager can earn a day's wage and have another daily wage to pay someone who will attend his or her crops. This standard results in wages low enough that most of the above problems are avoided. It also avoids constant bad feelings over wage raises — if inflation is high, the local daily wage rates will reflect that fact, and wages can be reset periodically according to the going rates among local farmers.

Some programmes have proceeded directly to hiring villagers to work as full-time extensionists. For various reasons we feel it is far better, if it is necessary to hire villager-extensionists, to do so part time.

It is generally better to employ two villagers half time than one full time. Half-time employment allows twice as many villagers to have the experience of working in the programme and of participating in decision-making. The extensionists in the programme can represent more of the villages in the programme area. Extensionists who work half-time still have the time to tend their crops and animals, thereby keeping up their own experience at farming and at trying out innovations. By farming half time, extensionists also avoid becoming too economically dependent on the programme.

Furthermore, extensionists who continue to be part-time farmers maintain their identify as small farmers, continue to be members in full standing of their communities, and have less tendency to feel superior to other villagers (Bunch 1982:178).

One additional reason for preferring part-time villager-extensionists is the fact that full-time ones can only rarely maintain good quality farms of their own. Even when they try to pay hired labour to keep up their farms, they find the labourers do not fully understand what they are trying to do, or do not have the motivation to do it well. Thus the extensionists become frustrated watching their own farms deteriorate, and they lose credibility with their students. They also lose, to a large extent, one of their most important sources of information about the innovations they are teaching: their own experience with the technology. While maintaining their own farms, part-time extensionists, as opposed to volunteers, will be able to greatly enrich their learning. They can learn to conduct meetings and help make decisions in a democratic manner by attending programme planning and personnel meetings. They can spend more time learning (by doing) to plan classes and make audiovisual aids, visiting the work of other extensionists, and writing reports on their activities. They will also have a chance to learn more about the theory behind the agricultural technologies being taught.

Table 7.6: Part-time farmer-extensionists (Selener, Chenier and Zelaya)

Pro	Con
• Part-timers can effectively combine work in their own fields with spending time on their family needs and serving the interests of the community and the NGO.	• The promoter is sometimes not available when needed.
• Part-time payment allows optional use of time and resources.	• A salary or compensation can make the community envious or make them withdraw their support or collaboration.
• Part-time payment allows the NGO to assess the promoters' effectiveness before hiring them full time.	• Short-term and part-time commitments can hinder project continuity.
• Promoters can continue giving examples based on their own work.	• The promoter may be seen as an NGO employee.
• They can be accountable to both the community and the NGO.	
• Part-time payment can be part of the process of personal and professional growth of the promoter.	

Full-time farmer-extensionists

Finally, Lopez weighs up the benefits and disadvantages of having full-time, paid farmer-extensionists — generally the most controversial of the three options for compensating farmer-extensionists.

Full-time paid extensionists (Lopez)

The major use of full-time villager-extensionists occurs when some institution wishes to employ them a long distance from their homes. Then, obviously, they must be paid more generously, because they have to rent a home, buy all of their food, and travel back to their own village on occasion. In some countries (e.g., Mexico, Guatemala, and Honduras), the hiring of the very best villager-extensionists to work in other parts of the country, as a means of spreading the activities the programme is supporting, is common practice. It has, in most cases, produced exceptionally good results.

However, the hiring of villager-extensionists to work away from their homes has both advantages and disadvantages. The chief disadvantage is that it often weakens the development process occurring in their own villages. It also raises the costs of using villager-extensionists. And, of course, these extensionists will no longer have the personal ties that often aid their work in their own villages. Nevertheless, significant advantages exist, too. First of all, more than one very good extensionist often emerges in the same village. Thus the leadership abilities of one of them is often wasted, or at least under-utilized. Secondly, even when only one extensionist has emerged in a village, the momentum of agricultural improvement often pushes others to take over his or her role and develop their own leadership skills if that leader moves away. A third, less frequent occurrence is that an extensionist who made an early mistake or is from the wrong faction in one village may blossom when allowed to move somewhere else. Perhaps most important, when villager-extensionists begin working with new organizations, they can often serve to show whole new organizations how the process works. They just naturally take the technology and methodology with

Table 7.7: Full-time farmer-extensionists (Selener, Chenier and Zelaya)

Pro	Con
• The salary of a full-time promoter provides a secure income.	• The salary can become the main source of motivation.
• Full-timers can serve more communities, ideally five to eight.	• The promoters may neglect their families.
• The NGO can better plan and establish goals and objectives and can request the promoter to achieve them.	• They may abandon their fields, losing the capacity to teach through their own example.
• The farmer-promoters become permanent partners or employees in the project or NGO.	• The salary is low compared to the extension agent's.
• The promoters have well-defined roles and objectives to achieve.	• Paying a salary involves costs for the NGO.
• Their work can be improved through ongoing monitoring and evaluation.	• Promoters may be considered as outsiders.
	• Project sustainability and sustained effort of farmer-promoters depend on the availability of funds.

them. If the new organizations genuinely wish to learn from them (and that can be an important 'if'), such a move is often the very best way of transplanting the entire process from one organization or area to another. Lastly, moving such extensionists to new areas can promote social justice: even if it does slow the development process in the previous community, it can help the new communities to begin to catch up to the previous ones.

Sinaga and Wodicka discuss their experiences and problems in addressing the issue of whether to pay farmer-extensionists in the World Neighbors-supported project in Sumba, Indonesia.

Payment of farmer-extensionists (Sinaga and Wodicka)
The use of financial incentives to encourage farmer leaders to contribute more time to the development of the extension programme has provided many benefits, but has also created problems that were unforeseen in the beginning. The decision whether to pay farmer-extensionists or work through volunteers is not an easy one. Paid farmer-advisers are able to ensure more quality control, with regular follow-up and clear reporting of activities. They are also able to develop their leadership skills much quicker than volunteer farmers, since they are required to attend more meetings and take on more leadership and decision-making roles. Leadership development is a long-term investment for the Tananua Foundation, as some of these farmers eventually decide to become full-time field staff or even supervisors, and some of them take on important leadership roles within the wider community. Given that most farmers have limited formal education, the process of forming farmer leaders can take many years. Paid farmer-advisers are also more cost-effective and often have a greater impact than both government and Tananua extension staff, who are generally paid higher salaries and require long adaptation periods.

On the other hand, paying farmer-extensionists can also create problems for the farmers and for the programme. Farmer-advisers have often complained that they spend too much time away from their farms, which have suffered as a result. In addition to serving their neighbours, farmer-advisers are often expected to accompany the numerous visitors coming to learn about the programme. Often they are also expected to help organize local village events and activities. While many of these activities fall outside the programme, these expectations are closely tied to their status as farmer-advisers and make high demands on their time.

Another problem that has arisen is that financial compensation tends to undermine the development of voluntarism throughout the programme. Jealousies over status and incentives enjoyed by farmer-advisers have often discouraged the development of more farmer-leaders within the communities. On the other hand, farmer-advisers have often complained that their wages are unfair given their levels of responsibilities and those of Tananua field staff who receive higher wages. These are perhaps management and policy problems that can be dealt with by limiting service terms, for example; however, they have far-reaching implications. Starting in 1995, the Tananua Foundation has decided to stop compensating farmer-advisers. As such, these farmers will become volunteers and will no longer bear the obligations of the programme. It remains to be seen what impact this decision will have on programme development.

There are also problems of sustainability in considering whether a project, as opposed to communities, should pay farmer-extensionists. This was clearly illustrated in the two Philippine projects described by Bhuktan, Killough and Basilio (excerpts from their paper are not included here). In his report on the AKSPR project in India, Kapoor comments on the possibility of asking communities to pay for the services they receive from extension volunteers (EVs).

Extension volunteer compensation by communities (Kapoor)
Experience has demonstrated that communities can be motivated, without much difficulty, to contribute towards the honoraria paid to EVs for the services they provide in 'hardware interventions' — for example, soil and water conservation works, wasteland development, and biogas production. However, motivating beneficiaries to contribute for the 'software components' of the EVs' work, such as agricultural extension and group building, requires a lot more effort, time and patience. Currently AKRSP is considering the possibility of asking communities to contribute to EVs' honoraria on the basis of paying for the totality of the services provided by them and the village institutions.

In weighing up the pros and cons of paying farmer-extensionists salaries and expenses, it may be useful to assess the issue within the context of the totality of incentives and disincentives faced by such actors. In Table 7.8, Selener, Chenier and Zelaya summarize those identified by the 75 experienced farmer-extensionists who participated in two workshops in Ecuador and Honduras.

Table 7.8: Incentives and disincentives for farmer-extensionists
(Selener, Chenier and Zelaya)

Incentives	Disincentives
• Appropriate salary	• Low salaries — much less than other NGO staff who do the same job
• Allowance for transportation and food	
• Training and field visits to other projects	• Lack of training
• Promotion	• Lack of transportation and food allowance
• Participation in planning, evaluation and decision-making	• Lack of promotion or equal opportunity
• Recognition of good quality work from NGO and community	• Lack of decision-making power within the NGO
• Fringe benefits and perks (medical insurance, bonus)	• Lack of responsibility or motivation by the community
• Visits to the project area with outsiders	• Unjustified complaints from the NGO or community
• Provision of technical books, pamphlets, etc. and other resources	• Lack of trust and disrespectful treatment from NGO field staff
• Certificates when attending courses, seminars, etc.	• Racial and class discrimination
• Replication of work in other communities	
• Opportunity to be hired on a full-time basis with a salary	
• Respect from extension agents, NGO staff, etc.	
• Work with motivated communities	

Work location

Should extensionists work in their own villages or be assigned elsewhere? Table 7.9 summarizes the 75 Latin American farmer-extensionists' assessment of this.

Table 7.9: Where should farmer-extensionists work? (Selener, Chenier and Zelaya)

In other communities

Pro	Con
• Promoters may be accepted better than in their own communities	• Working elsewhere requires more time and money for mobilization.
• Outsiders can motivate initially without their own example, just with words.	• Promoters spend less time in each community.
• They can work with different groups within the community, without being identified with one in particular.	• They can be manipulated or misled by bad leaders, since they do not know the details of community dynamics.
• Since they work in different communities, promoters learn form other experiences.	• They are not always available.
• Promoters have more privacy.	• They may see work as an obligation.
• Promoters have potential to become leaders of a farmer association or federation.	• Promoters sometimes do not know where to eat.

In own community

Pro	Con
• Time and money is not used for travelling to other communities.	• Promoters' work may not always be recognized or respected. 'Nobody is a prophet in their own land.'
• Promoters have more time to work in the community and be with their families.	• The community may demand the promoters' support at any time since they are always available.
• The community has more access to the promoter.	• The promoters have limited privacy.
• Promoters have their own plots in the community, which serve as examples.	• Their private life is open to scrutiny, possibly affecting their work quality.
• They understand better the community's history, problems and situation.	• The community may pressure the promoters to conduct certain tasks (or view them as 'worker-peons'), so take on less responsibility itself.
• They can have flexible working hours.	
• They know when people are available for training demonstrations or community work.	• Promoters may serve mostly their own relatives and friends.
• There is potential for the promoters to emerge as community leaders.	• They have fewer opportunities to visit other sites.
• They know the people better.	• Community members may feel envious, especially if promoters are paid.
• They become examples for their communities.	• Promoters may feel they are more important than community leaders.

Specialization

Should farmer-extensionists specialize in one set of topics, or should they be generalists? The 75 farmer-extensionists in Ecuador and Honduras listed the pros and cons of each approach (Table 7.10).

Table 7.10: Specialists or generalists? (Selener, Chenier and Zelaya)

Generalists

Pro	Con
• A generalist approach is very effective and useful when few farmers want to serve as promoters.	• Generalists cannot provide in-depth information on any subject.
• It is desirable for potential leaders to be generalists since they learn problems in a holistic way.	• They find it hard to solve very specific problems.
• Generalists can try to solve several kinds of problems.	• Working on several topics, they get too busy and do not do the job well.
• They can help design and initiate projects on different topics.	• They acquire many responsibilities, so may not find it easy to implement planned activities.

Specialists

Pro	Con
• Specialists can be assigned to and responsible for one specific component of a project.	• Specialists have a limited scope of work, especially since many problems are holistic in nature.
• They are trusted more by NGO staff than are generalists.	• They may be less creative in solving problems.
• They receive training and acquire specialized knowledge.	• They may come to feel part of the NGO staff, rather than as a member of the community.
• They can solve specific problems more easily.	• They usually expect a salary.
• They achieve results more easily since they focus on one topic.	

Gender issues

As with traditional extension approaches, farmer-led extension has found it difficult to incorporate women — both as farmer-extensionists and as members of the groups they serve. The excerpts below discuss some of the difficulties encountered and ways that have been tried of overcoming them. In Table 7.11, Selener, Chenier and Zelaya list some pros and cons of women promoters.

89

Role of women in VACVINA's extension activities (Pham Xuan Du, and Bhuktan, Killough and Basilio)

Women have played a very important role in VACVINA's extension projects and in the family farming economy. They are involved in all activities — cattle and pig rearing, vegetable production, soil dressing and processing of produce. VACVINA's extension efforts would fail without their active participation. However, as a rule, women in rural areas cannot often attend social meetings and they rarely voice their opinions in group meetings in which men are the main participants. VACVINA has attempted to motivate women's participation in its VAC extension programmes through collaboration with Women's Leagues. Through this institution, which is well established in Vietnam, women have been encouraged to participate with their husbands in all village VAC extension meetings. In addition, small focus-group discussions are held at appropriate times of day and on appropriate dates to specifically match women's needs. This too has helped to get women involved in all VAC projects.

Women's involvement in AKRSP programmes in India (Kapoor)

AKRSP-supported interventions related to animal husbandry programmes were carried out through women's groups between 1989 and 1992. Some women became extension volunteers (EVs). However, in 1992, the animal husbandry programmes had to be abandoned, due to an absence of linkage agencies which could have provided marketing, veterinary health care support, etc. AKRSP has since been endeavouring to involve women in other types of programme intervention, and there has been an encouraging response in biogas and forestry programmes. For example, there are 35 female EVs and 1 female master extension volunteer (MEV) working in the biogas programme, and 7 female EVs and 2 MEVs in the development of public wastelands programme. In addition, all nurseries under the forestry programme are raised by women, and all EVs concerned with agro-forestry extension activities are women.

Table 7.11: Women promoters (Selener, Chenier and Zelaya)

Pro	Con
• Women promoters can work in any kind of project, not only in those traditionally considered as 'women's projects'.	• Women promoters can take on a 'triple burden' of family, agricultural production and promotion work.
• They are more interested in maintaining and respecting cultural and ethical values.	• They may have problems with their husbands because they are out of the house.
• They understand better women's and family problems.	• When they marry, they quit.
• They conduct specific projects and activities more efficiently than men.	• They are susceptible to harassment.
• Their work boosts their self-esteem.	• They may neglect their family duties.
• They serve as examples to other women.	• Sometimes men don't take them seriously.

8 Farmer field schools

FARMER FIELD SCHOOLS offer another approach to farmer-led extension. These schools grew out of projects supported by FAO in Southeast Asia, and have been used mainly in integrated pest management (IPM) programmes. They involve farmers in learning and discovering for themselves relationships between crops, pests, predators, soil and water in their fields. There is thus a strong element of research in the field schools. Indeed, the division between extension and experimentation is somewhat arbitrary in all types of farmer-led extension.

Farmer field schools can be complementary to farmer-to-farmer extension; indeed, field school projects often encourage their participants to share their methods and results through farmer-to-farmer extension.

This chapter is structured in a similar way to the discussion on farmer-to-farmer extension in previous chapters. First, we describe the origins and principles of farmer field schools. Then we discuss methods and strategies used in this approach, including ways in which the farmer field schools can interface with farmer-to-farmer extension. We then turn to such aspects as the role of professionals, training needs and participant selection before discussing some of the lessons learned.

Origins and principles

Dilts and Hate describe the origins and the principles behind farmer field schools. As they point out, their main thrust is to facilitate farmers to become experts in developing technologies and managerial practices to solve their specific problems, within the agro-ecological context of their own farms. The aim is to ensure that technologies developed are appropriate to local agro-ecological and economic conditions, and that the process of technology generation is continuous and sustainable. Indeed, the approach was developed following the failure of 'blanket recommendation' extension efforts. Farmer field schools also require that professional researchers and extension officers become experts both in farming and in facilitating farmers to undertake their own research.

FAO-supported farmer field schools in Indonesia (Dilts and Hate)
The phrase 'farmer field school' began to be heard in Indonesia in 1990. For most, this was a strange, if not alien, juxtaposition of the disorderliness of the paddy field mud with the orthodox orderliness of the classroom. Five years later IPM farmer field schools have been conducted in more than 15 000 villages in Indonesia, and in thousands in Vietnam, India, Bangladesh, the Philippines, China, Korea and Sri Lanka. In Indonesia the sight of these

91

'schools without walls' is no longer strange: they involve farmers gathering together on a weekly basis throughout a crop season to go into the mud to analyse the progress of their crops; learn of the biotic interactions between soil, plants, and insects; and bring this knowledge together to make a locally responsive field management decision.

Perhaps, to environmental and democratic activists, the most amazing thing is to see the farmers recapturing their rights and their abilities to learn, speak, and make their own decisions — while being able to back up their positions with scientific evidence which they themselves own and control. To NGO personnel and extensionists, the remarkable part of this story is not that farmers are capable decision-makers, but that the process of learning is facilitated on a broad scale through the medium of 'normal' government extension workers; 'people's theatre' conducted in thousands of villages; 'farmer research' going on in every province; thousands of 'farmer technical seminars' and 'farmer planning meetings' taking place, in which farmers are the planners and implementers and government personnel are consigned to a listening role. Currently, over half of all IPM farmer field schools are being run by farmer-trainers, with no diminution of process quality.

Origins of the farmer field schools. The field school approach for IPM was developed in response to two challenges:

o the ecology of tropical rice, which is locally specific, resisting generalizations and blanket recommendations; and therefore
o the need for farmers to generate their own scientific processes in their own fields as a basis for crop management decisions for IPM to be effective and sustainable.

The farmer field school approach represents an attempt to get away from centralized extension practices and return the locus of interaction to the farmers' fields. It is at heart a process that brings people and ecology into direct interaction. If agricultural extension is defined as the practice of 'extending' packages and information developed from centralized research to farmer 'target groups' (Freire 1989), the field school approach, with its emphasis on decentralized educational processes and *in situ* discovery and learning by farmers, represents a radical departure from established practice. Many have described this departure as a 'paradigm shift', because many of the previous articles of faith and basic assumptions of extension have been called into question. In short, the field school approach for IPM seeks to replace 19th century, top-down, input technologies with 21st century, knowledge-intensive technologies.

The demands of an ecological approach. Much of the technical basis for IPM, especially for tropical rice, has long been known. In Indonesia, for example, national scientists enunciated the basics of IPM for rice in the early 1970s. However, early attempts at IPM seldom gained a foothold. In Indonesia and in other neighbouring Asian countries a range of approaches were tried with little success, including 'strategic information campaigns' in Malaysia, training and visit in the Philippines, and 'demonstration plots' in Thailand and Bangladesh. Even where these had some success, the spread of the technology was extremely limited.

Counter-intuitive concepts, such as pest resurgence (the more you spray, the more pests you get) or plant compensation (30 per cent leaf/tiller loss early in the season makes no difference to crop yields), only make sense when farmers can directly observe and manipulate, and hence clearly understand, the ecological interactions between plant, pest, predator and pesticide. In IPM training, via the field school, an article of faith is that all principles can be learned directly — concepts and theories are discovered and drawn from the field and linked to previous conceptions and experiences. In this way 'the book' becomes readable, and farmers regain control.

The IPM programme's belief in farmers' capabilities is not based on naive populism. The last 25 years of agricultural extension have been ruled by an assumption that the main 'gap', scientifically and practically, was that which existed between the high yields attained on the research station by trained scientists and the low yields obtained, even by 'good' farmers on their own fields. This situation has changed. Recent research at IRRI (Rola and Pingali 1993) shows that the yields of these same 'good' farmers now outstrip those on research station fields run by 'experts'. Currently, the main gap is that between different farmers. Hence, if our interest is in improving both national production and individual farm viability, do we wait for the next 'breakthrough' in research which may or may not be widely applicable for years to come? Or do we base our efforts upon the proven capabilities of farmers, and work to spread this tested and effective knowledge to as many as possible? This approach does not negate the value of research, but it does propose that research and learning are not the exclusive domains of trained experts. Further, widespread capability at the farmer level will help ensure that any useful new knowledge or technology can be quickly and effectively tested, adapted, transformed and integrated into viable practices within actual farming systems by farmers themselves.

Following from this, IPM is not a technology package researched by experts, extended by field workers, and adopted by farmer 'target groups'. Instead, the goal of the IPM farmer field school approach is to strengthen the process of knowledge generation and knowledge dissemination within and amongst the farm community. When this context of the field school programme is understood, then many of the activities involved, such as 'farmer technical workshops', 'farmer seminars', 'farmer planning workshops' and 'farmer-to-farmer media', begin to make sense.

Education vs extension

> I never teach my students, I merely create opportunities so that they can discover and learn by themselves. — *Albert Einstein*

The high variability of tropical ecology is a major constraint upon these 'blanket' approaches. For example, two plots within a few metres of each other may comprise insect populations varying by a factor of 1000 depending upon a wide range of variables. In one set of such fields in Karawang District, West Java in 1994, the brown planthopper density in adjoining plots was 5 vs 900 insects per plant; despite the fact that the plots utilized the same variety and were planted at the same time in the same season. If these two plots were observed several weeks later, the situation might change drastically. Facing this dynamic, an effective and accurate centralized 'forecasting' system would therefore require the stationing of a full-time field staff member permanently in each and every field across the 10 000 000 harvested hectares of rice fields in Indonesia.

The complexity of rice field ecology is a challenge, but also a driving force. Field ecology studies in the Yogyakarta area of Java identified more than 700 species of insects in a single hectare of rice field, making it one of the most complex ecological systems on the planet. Rice is a unique monocrop in the sense that its complex ecology is the result of 3000 years of co-evolution. In the field school approach, the rice field is seen as a 'book' and the goal of the educational process is to provide farmers with the language of field ecology that will allow them to read and understand the book. As in any educational endeavour, simple books quickly prove boring. The complexity of rice field ecology provides an endless text of interactions that challenges enquiry.

Farmers as experts: IPM by farmers. As with ecology, the field school approach requires a radical shift in our attitudes towards, and perceptions of, farmers. For too long we have heard farmers described as 'conservative', 'risk averse', 'lacking in formal education', 'tradition-minded', 'under-resourced', 'closed-minded' and so on, all suggesting that farmers are reluctant to accept our messages and change their behaviour in the way prescribed by outsiders. Farmers are often seen as the difficult 'factor X' impeding development.

In the IPM field school approach, farmers are seen as the fundamental resource — strong agriculture will only be created and sustained through strong farmers and strengthened farmer organizations. Unless farmers can master the process of creating knowledge for decision-making on their own, in their own fields, IPM will not work and future gains in agricultural development will not be realized.

The learning process within the field school programme is not value-free and is strongly linked to our perception of human nature. People are viewed as intrinsically curious and creative, as having a strong desire to gain control over their lives through an understanding of the forces and patterns affecting them. For farmers, gaining an understanding of how the ecology of their fields operates, and being able to manage the complex processes occurring, is a form of empowerment which reduces insecurity and replaces it with self-confidence.

What is learned is a process, not pieces of information. This process allows farmers to face new challenges and the ever-changing dynamics of their fields. Education is seen as a process that takes place in the learner, not in the teacher/facilitator. Therefore, at a field school, it is farmers who gather data, discuss, analyse, present and experiment. A farmer who masters a process can also 'teach' the process to other farmers, also allowing them to discover for themselves.

World Education, an international NGO, has also had considerable experience in farmer field schools and IPM in Indonesia. It supports local NGOs and farmers' organizations in developing activities which promote farmer research, but it also stresses co-operative exchange among farmers, NGOs, government and researchers for the development of community-based sustainable agriculture programmes. As Kingsley and Musante point out, in these efforts, the initial focus was on IPM.

World Education's support for farmer field schools in Indonesia (Kingsley and Musante)

Policy and programme context. Chemical pesticide use as the dominant component of crop protection strategy has a dubious foundation, given the capacity of pest populations to develop resistance and the destruction of beneficial insects (pest predators and parasitoids) that check the growth of pest populations. In Southeast Asia, the use of pesticides threatens the sustainability of crop production, takes a toll on farmers' health, results in the poisoning of non-target species and is an expensive input that reduces farmers' incomes (Rola and Pingali 1993). Furthermore, alternatives to chemical pesticides are readily available, particularly for rice farmers, through a more complete understanding of rice paddy agro-ecosystems and careful management of indigenous natural enemy insect populations.

In 1986, after linking the brown planthopper pest outbreaks of 1985 and 1986 to escalating increases in pesticide use, the government of Indonesia banned 57 broad-spectrum pesticides for rice, gradually eliminated state subsidies on pesticides, and instituted IPM as the national pest-control strategy for rice. The Indonesian National IPM Training Programme, with the assistance of the FAO Rice Integrated Pest Control Programme, then developed the IPM farmer field school as the model for government extension agents and pest observers to train farmers in IPM. Since 1986, total pesticide production in Indonesia and imports have been reduced by more than 50 per cent (Kenmore 1991). In addition, studies have shown that rice farmers reduce pesticide applications by 40–80 per cent after participating in National IPM Training Programme farmer field schools (Pincus 1991).

The farmer field school extension approach signals a move away from the conventional promotion and for provision of a packet of technologies, towards 'making farmers experts in their own fields' through non-formal education methods and a field-based, experiential learning process. Basic IPM principles are learned in farmer field school training, such as:

o grow a healthy crop
o conserve natural enemies
o monitor fields weekly.

By applying these ecological principles, farmers can make their own decisions about crop management based on their own experience and local field and market conditions.

The World Education IPM project. In late 1990, World Education, a private voluntary agency based in Boston which provides training and technical assistance in adult non-formal education, started a parallel NGO IPM project with support from USAID and the FAO Rice Integrated Pest Control Programme. Known as the Improved Environmental Management and Advocacy project, it now has collaborative programmes with ten local NGOs and farmers' organizations, involving over 2500 smallholder farmers in lowland rice and highland vegetable-producing regions of North Sumatra, Lampung and Central Java. It has strong ties to the National IPM Training Programme, drawing on their resource persons, training and technical materials. The National IPM Programme encourages the development of NGO IPM programmes and recognizes their role in further developing field school activities, designing new training components, developing farmer networks and advocating for policy change on pesticide issues.

The goal of the World Education project is to assist Indonesian farm families to develop critical ecological, decision-making and leadership skills which can be used to reduce environmental degradation and increase productivity in their farming systems. It provides technical and managerial assistance, on a monthly basis, to NGOs and farmers' organizations; manages a small grant fund for specific NGO/farmers' organization activities; offers specialized training on programme design, management and non-formal education methods for NGO/farmers' organization staff, and develops mechanisms for sharing and exchange among collaborating groups.

Virtually all IPM programme participants are from relatively resource-poor farming communities, working small plots that they own or rent. In Brastagi, North Sumatra, vegetable growers sell most of their produce to traders for export to Malaysia and Singapore. Some of these vegetable growers use hired labour on an irregular basis. The lowland rice farmers in North Sumatra, Lampung and Central Java are part of a national market economy and either rent or own their small plots of land (usually less than 0.75 hectares). In lowland rice growing communities over the last 25 years farmers have had less and less say in the management of their own fields — decisions about agricultural production have been increasingly determined by government agencies and officials.

Due to their apparent success, IPM farmer field schools have spread through both public-sector and NGO efforts to many countries in Southeast Asia. For example, Maningding describes the origins and principles of a public sector IPM farmer field school project in Benguet province in the Philippines. He stresses the centrality of supporting farmers in their own learning efforts and processes, which provides for both relevance and sustainability.

95

Farmer field schools in Benguet, Philippines (Maningding)

A pilot was established for vegetables in Atok, Benguet province, in response to a cyanide scare besetting farmers at that time. In early 1993, local leaders in Atok sought assistance to resolve this problem. Staff of the National Crop Protection Centre, based at the University of the Philippines at Los Baños, came to Atok to convince the local government to establish a demonstration area. The mayor of Atok took up the idea and began convincing farmers to try experimenting with introducing diadegma wasps through the conduct of farmer field schools. Some farmers agreed to try this approach. At the first two meetings only a few farmers came. In part this was probably due to the earlier introduction of diadegma, through conventional means, by another project. At that time farmers continued to use chemical pesticides and rejected the introduction of diadegma. However, after a month of activity under the new pilot project, when they noticed the tremendous decrease in the pest population, more farmers became interested.

During the same month, a 10-day crash course was run for technicians to enable them to become IPM trainers at farmer field schools. Evaluations showed that farmers involved in the pilot used significantly less pesticides, attained equal or better yields and earned higher incomes from their crops than others. Farmers involved in the project have reduced their spraying from 18 times a season to twice, and some have ceased using chemicals altogether Moreover, there was an awakening of farmers' interest in crop ecology, which made them quick to seize upon and adapt the IPM ideas to their local conditions. Some of the farmers involved in the pilot project willingly became farmer-facilitators in the conduct of other farmer field schools. They were accompanied by one of the trained IPM technicians in this. As a result of their activities, IPM farmer field schools have now radiated to eight other municipalities in Benguet and five municipalities in Mountain Province. Each field school consists of 25 farmers, meeting for one day each week throughout a crop season — i.e., from 14 to 16 weeks. The field school has a 1 000m^2 'learning field', containing a farmer-run comparative study of IPM and other relevant field experiments. The field schools bring farmers together to undertake an intensive training process on IPM methods and issues over the life cycle of a crop. The IPM training team is assisted by the public sector agricultural technician assigned to the area in which the field school is being conducted. Mobilizing local government to provide counterpart funding, and the support of local leaders in terms of funding, have contributed to the efficient implementation of field schools.

The following guiding principles have also contributed to the effectiveness of the IPM farmer field school approach:

o The field is the primary learning resource. All learning activities take place in the field and are based on what is happening in the field.

o Experience from the basis for learning. The activities that take place in the field and on farmers' farms form the basis for discussions and analyses by farmers, who arrive at concepts which they test and improve upon through further field activities.

o Decision-making guides the learning process. Training focuses on the analysis of the agro-ecosystem of the crop. The combination in farmers' training of analytical methods, ecological principles and basic IPM methods helps farmers gain insights into the ecological interactions in the field and provides them with greater confidence in making crop management decisions.

o Training lasts the entire cropping season. Farmers acquire a firm understanding of the relevant IPM concepts for each stage of growth the crop goes through, as well as the factors that influence pest control decision-making at all stages of the plants' growth.

o   The training curriculum is based on local conditions. The field school curriculum and
    materials are based on their appropriateness to a particular set of farmers their prob-
    lems, needs and local conditions.

Methods and strategies

Working in collaboration, the Indonesian government/FAO and World Education
programmes use similar strategies and methods in their farmer field schools. These
approaches have been adopted and adapted in other countries. As a result, they are
now quite widespread in Southeast and South Asia. They are described in the following two excerpts.

IPM farmer field schools facilitated by farmer-trainers (Kingsley and Musante)
Over the course of a growing season, farmers learn an ecological approach to crop management through weekly observations, experiments, analysis and discussions about crop health,
pest populations and populations of natural controls of pests. Two main objectives of the
field school are for farmers to gain the knowledge, critical skills and self-confidence to
make decisions about farm management based on their own observations and experience,
and for farmers to work together on pest control and other farm management issues.

Main characteristics of farmer field schools
A field school generally consists of 15 to 30 farmers divided into subgroups of five or six
for most of the field activities. Sessions usually take place on a weekly basis, each session
lasting three to four hours. Field schools are conducted throughout the entire growing season of the crop so that farmers can study all the stages of plant development, as well as pest
and natural enemy life-cycles over the cropping season.

The field plots used are offered to the group by one of the participating farmers. Farmer-
trainers are now using participatory learning methods, such as mapping, transect walks and
seasonal analysis, to plan, with farmers, the most appropriate time and place to begin field
schools and identify major crop problems and available resources. Typically, two plots are
planted: the control plot, which is managed according to conventional local practice (e.g.,
applying fertilizers, pesticides, etc.) and the IPM-managed plot. If needed, field schools
also make additional study plots to test varieties, crop compensation after pest damage, etc.

The usual process in each session is as follows:

1. The first activity is field observation (agro-ecosystem analysis), in small groups, of a
    sample of 10 plants marked at various points in the field. Participants make notes on
    weather conditions, plant growth, types and numbers of pests and natural enemies,
    weeds and plant diseases. Insects of interest, damaged leaves and other items are put in
    small plastic bags for further observation and discussion.
2. In a shaded area close to the field, farmers then analyse and discuss the agro-ecosystem
    in their subgroup. This entails drawing the plant at its present state of growth, sun or
    clouds to symbolize weather conditions, the pests and natural enemies observed and
    other relevant information. Comparisons are made between the number and type of
    pests and the number of natural controls, and whether the ratio between the two will
    prevent significant crop damage and yield loss is discussed. Each small group then
    notes its conclusions on the status of the field (agro-ecosystem) and decides what, if
    any, pest control measures or other crop management operations (weeding, fertilizing,
    etc.) are necessary.

97

3. Small groups then present their findings and conclusions to the larger group. Farmers discuss what they have observed and present their conclusions for critique by others. On the basis of these discussions, a decision is made, as a group, about what measures to take in the field school plots.
4. During each session, special topics and activities are introduced by the farmer-trainers. Topic selections are based on local agricultural problems and conditions. These might include pest and plant biology, the role of natural enemies, the impact of pesticides on the local agro-ecosystem, types of chemical, biological and mechanical controls and/or plant diseases prevalent in the area. Simple experiments are often set up. For example, the use of 'insect zoos' is very popular, in which plastic screening is placed over two or three plants to facilitate observation of insect-crop relationships, determine the role of each species, and gauge the relative strength of natural controls.
5. The farmer-trainer's role is to facilitate the learning process, not to lecture. The main concern is to encourage participation, group cohesiveness and to provide opportunities for self-discovery. For example, participants' questions about pests are seldom answered directly, rather questions are returned with further questions, such as 'What do you think?', 'Where did you find it?', 'What was it doing?', etc.

The field school approach must distinguish itself from those of agricultural input entrepreneurs and some extension personnel who simply tell farmers what to do — and usually which product to buy. In the field school process, distinctions are made between what a farmer has been told, a farmer's own opinion or guess, and what has actually been observed in the field or experienced in the past by the farmer. 'Buktikan sendiri', prove it yourself, is a common phrase heard in field school exchanges. Rather than accept IPM on the basis of someone else's word, farmers are asked to prove for themselves, in their own fields or on the field school plot, whether the principles and practices are effective or not. Taking up this challenge develops self-confidence and critical skills which enable farmers to make decisions based on their own observations and experiences. This becomes the basis for crop management, farmer experimentation, and adoption and adaptation of new practices following the first field school.

Dilts and Hate describe the similar field methods and activities supported by the Indonesian government and FAO.

Methods used in farmer field schools (Dilts and Hate)
Self-generated materials. At the field school level the main educational materials do not comprise posters, leaflets, slides, videos and other conventional extension tools usually used to present information. The main learning material is the living rice field. Fortunately, this is widely available and usually free. Other materials include blank newsprint, markers or crayons, plastic bags, bamboo and string. Field activities and experiments are organized according to 'field guides' which outline the steps in a learning process (e.g., 'creating an insect zoo' or 'testing the effects of pesticides on natural enemies'). In small teams of five persons, farmers themselves develop their own materials, undertake their own experiments and write up their results based on direct interaction with the field. At the end of a season, each farmer has a living record of the evolution of a crop over a 12-week season, from seedbed to harvest.

Analysis and decision-making. The 'trademark' of the IPM farmer field school is the agroecosystem analysis undertaken at each of the field school sessions. Each week, in small groups farmer participants examine the environment in which they farm, recording water conditions, plant growth stage, and insect populations. These data are visually arrayed on a large drawing created by each team of farmers. Based on this array each group makes a crop management decision for the coming week. The results from each group's analysis are then presented and discussed with other groups. During the course of the programme, over 1 000 000 agro-ecosystem diagrams have been produced by farmers themselves.

As participants become skilled in discussion and analysis, more complex technical and social tools are introduced. Special sessions produce 'energy-flow diagrams' and 'insect life-cycle interactions', and field trials (fertilizer optimization, pesticide impacts, etc.) are plotted graphically across the season. By the end of the season farmers are undertaking supposedly difficult social analysis techniques such as SWOT (strength, weakness, opportunities, threats) analysis and ZOPP (goal-oriented project planning) to underpin their follow-up programmes. From our experience these so-called 'complex management methods' present few problems for farmers despite (or because of) their lack of formal education. If such methods are focused upon real issues, based on meaningful data and use graphic-based, open-discussion modes of communication, then they are easily mastered by farmers.

Season-long training. The local crop season determines the timing of the field school. This puts a strain on many extension systems which often require the farmers to align themselves with an extension programme, and not vice versa. The field school programme begins with several sessions held with a farmer group to map out the local rice fields and rice-field problems, explain the field school programme, select participants for the field school, and develop a 'learning contract' for the programme. Subsequently the field school meets once per week for four to five hours for a period of 12 weeks. In this way participants are able to follow their crop across all the crucial stages of development, while directly observing the effects of their field management decisions. In addition, the same analytical methods are repeatedly applied to an evolving and changing crop; further building farmer confidence and an understanding of the entire crop cycle. At the end of the season, after final yield and financial analysis, farmers often feel sure that they 'learned from their own fields', not from outside provided information.

Role of professionals

Once again we are left with the question of the role professionals can play in supporting farmers' own research. As was the case with farmer-to-farmer extension, this role is best seen as one of facilitation — in practice a huge range of professional activities, depending on the constraints farmers meet. Dilts and Hate summarize this role.

Role of the facilitator (Dilts and Hate)
The role of the field worker in the IPM farmer field school is to organize a structure for learning. When observing a field school, it should be difficult to identify the field worker except that he or she should be the first one into the mud and the last one to talk. The role of the field worker by the end of the school should be minimal indeed, as most of the facilitation should have been taken over by the farmer themselves, including planning any follow-up activities. If outside facilitators are too active in answering questions, prodding participants, co-opting analysis, etc., they not only compromise the learning process, but in effect steal and insult the pride and honour of the participants. Fortunately, many examples of good facilitation exist. As one of the programme's most successful field workers from Central Java states, '(as) an IPM field school facilitator, my job beginning in week 5 is to 'sleep' at the back of the group.'

Linking farmers

Aside from the field schools themselves, many, if not all farmer field school programmes also encourage a sharing of ideas and experiences between farmers — often some form of farmer-to-farmer training or extension. In both the government/FAO and World Education programmes in Indonesia there is an emphasis on building networks or organizations among farmers. Kingsley and Musante describe below various networking activities supported by World Education. As was the case with farmer-to-farmer extension activities, much emphasis is placed on supporting farmers to visit each other and supporting farmers' meetings.

Linking activities supported by World Education in Indonesia (Kingsley and Musante)

Two central strategies of World Education's work with local NGOs and farmers' organizations on community-based IPM programmes are:

o Begin a group learning process among farmers through IPM field schools and continue to support and monitor group activities and experimentation over several growing seasons.
o Link these field school groups together in active local networks of farmers, NGOs, government organizations and researchers to further enrich and build on field programmes.

Four key activities which have been applied and further developed to put these strategies into action are:

o IPM farmer field schools, facilitated by farmer-trainers
o cross-visits and quarterly programme forums
o the establishment of collaborative linkages with researchers
o training of farmer-trainers.

These activities have been effective in initiating and establishing a group learning process among farmers in their communities, and in linking farmer field school groups together in active local networks. Results to date from approximately 40 project sites include significant reductions and often the elimination of pesticide use in irrigated rice crops; stable or increased yields; farmer testing and development of new IPM practices; and the establishment of farmer-trainers in local communities who facilitate these processes. Networks among IPM field school groups have been developed which consist of regular, end-of-season forums rotating among field sites in a region, as well as exchanges among regions related to agricultural technologies and seed material, participatory approaches and programme management. This networking has resulted in a wide exchange of ideas and resources, the spread of IPM farmer field schools from community to community, the further development of farmer-leaders and field activities through access to role models and model programmes and local enthusiasm and political legitimization by virtue of belonging to a larger IPM movement.

The World Education project's quarterly programme forums are based on the quarterly meetings used by Tananua in Sumba (see Chapter 5). The project adopted the idea of such meetings after a visit to the Tananua project area by World Education programme managers and field-level extension staff in 1992. Kingsley and Musante describe these meetings below.

Quarterly programme forums (Kingsley and Musante)

Quarterly programme forums allow interested farmers and IPM programme leaders within a geographical region to jointly evaluate and plan IPM farmer training and field activities. Participants come together at the end of a growing season to evaluate field school progress, exchange information on innovative farming practices, analyse results of farmer-to-farmer approaches and outline training or research activities for the following growing season.

In lowland rice IPM programmes, these three-day meetings usually involve 60–100 farmers and IPM trainers primarily from field school locations and neighbouring villages. Quarterly forums among highland vegetable growers only last one day, but the content is similar to those in the lowlands. The meetings are hosted by different project villages on each occasion and are planned, organized and facilitated by IPM trainers and farmers from the host village. Representatives from other NGOs, government extension agencies and research institutions are also invited to provide technical input on specific topics identified by the organizers and to contribute to the planning process. This tends to keep visitors, even senior officials, focused on the forum objectives and not on their own research or extension programmes, which may not be immediately relevant to the local communities.

The responsibility for hosting and facilitating the meeting, and the responsibility of farmer representatives from neighbouring villages to stand up and present their group's experiences and plans, helps to develop local leadership. Conclusions and plans are critiqued and improved by the other forum participants through basic meeting procedures with the assistance of a designated moderator.

By early 1994, quarterly forums in North Sumatra had become too big to manage well. With 100 participants or more, the large number of people caused too many distractions. Accordingly, the structure was adjusted to the following framework:

Day 1 – Programme presentations by representative farmers from each group/village attending, with the number of total participants limited to 35–40 persons. These presentations cover field activities, numbers of participants, experiments and results and they review local maps of participants' fields and other media, such as insect or plant collections. Questions and discussion follow each presentation.

Day 2 – Fields are visited to see local agricultural problems and farmers' experiments. Participatory rural appraisal-type methods (e.g., mapping or seasonality analysis) might be used in small groups to start a problem-solving process with farmers from different hamlets. On this day, all interested locals, including local government officials, are invited to participate in receiving an introduction to IPM and any planning for IPM training, or related activities, in the host village.

Day 3 – Plans for each group/village attending are critiqued and improved by the forum participants. These plans often deal with experiments, new IPM field schools to be organized, monitoring field school graduates' fields, etc.

The enthusiasm generated by quarterly programme forums helps to propel IPM programmes forward. Farmers learn about technologies, as well as leadership, organizational and programme management issues. During the course of this project, quarterly programme forums and farmers' cross-visits have provided:

o   opportunities for systematic training on insect ecology and other IPM technical topics
o   opportunities for seed material exchange and scheduling future seed exchanges, for example, the routine exchanges between regions needed for soybeans
o   opportunities for training in specific learning methods and exchanging experiences and ideas about programme management

101

- o political legitimization of farmers' activities and IPM programmes (if the local government in village A approves and supports an activity or programme, they can be approved in village B)
- o increased enthusiasm and camaraderie and the development of role models for farmer-trainers/leaders
- o opportunities to see IPM in practice, which help newcomers visualize a better farming system for their area and begin forming more ambitious goals for their own involvement in the programme.

Dilts and Hate also stress the importance given to building farmer organizations in the government/FAO programme in Indonesia.

Building farmer organizations (Dilts and Hate)
The goal of the farmer field school is not just to impart skills to a set of individual farmers. The goal of the programme is to develop an organized group of farmer 'experts', which can serve other farmers and the village as a whole. Numerous activities are undertaken to build this support group, including exercises in communication, leadership and collaboration skills. The initial field school programme is seen as a 'primary school' and after this the group is ready to move on to follow-up programmes in farmer-to-farmer training, farmer field studies or horizontal communication programmes.

Links with research

In the World Education IPM farmer field school programme in Indonesia, much emphasis has been placed on instituting collaboration with professional researchers. Kingsley and Musante describe how such a relationship between farmers and researchers has been sought.

Establishing collaborative linkages with researchers (Kingsley and Musante)
The development of biological controls and resistant varieties for local crops and conditions benefits from significant collaboration between farmers and research agencies. These relationships are especially important in the development of IPM for vegetable crops. Farmers participating in the programmes make good colleagues for researchers, because they are making systematic observations of pest and disease problems in their fields and their knowledge is easy to access through routine farmer field schools and organized quarterly programme forums. Farmers immediately benefit from the basic ecological knowledge that some researchers bring to the field, which helps to focus farmers' own studies of insect ecology. For example, farmers from two NGOs in North Sumatra are working with local researchers to test the feasibility of improving the quality of potato seed through tissue culture and rapid *in-vitro* propagation. This linkage began through the farmers' initiative to organize a visit to a local research station. Other farmers participating in IPM programmes in the highlands have adapted researchers' inputs on snap-pea pests as a basis for their own development of IPM practices for this crop.

Through IPM field programmes, farmers are also able to make specific and informed demands on outside agencies. In many lowland IPM field school sites, for example, participating farmers have requested that field schools expand their topical coverage to include IPM on hot peppers. However, IPM practices for hot peppers are not yet well developed. In response, a three-day hot pepper workshop was organized with farmers, NGO field staff, seed company representatives and researchers to plan on-farm trials, develop guides on field studies and pest, plant and disease ecology, and suggest observation and analytical skills for farmers and field staff. This 'integrated college' seems to be an effective strategy for quickly developing technically sound responses to farmers' requests for technical assistance. Farmers in Central Java and in North Sumatra have begun on-farm trials on hot peppers. Their results and findings will become inputs for the further development of IPM knowledge and practices for this crop, as well as for learning materials.

IPM field programmes have established informal, ongoing, collaborative linkages with the International Potato Centre (CIP), Clemson University agricultural scientists, FAO Regional IPM project staff, and researchers from the Horticultural Research Centre. Usually, it is the role of local NGOs or World Education to organize and co-ordinate the visits on which the linkages are based. These relationships not only increase the technical sophistication of NGO and farmers' organization field programmes; they also help researchers gain a better understanding of local farming conditions, practices and problems.

Training of farmers and professionals

All involved in farmer-to-farmer extension and in supporting farmers' research perceive an important role for professional extensionists and researchers. However, these roles are usually radically different from those played by professionals working in conventional extension and research systems. Thus, training of both farmer-trainers and professional extension and research staff, whether from the pubic sector or NGO sector, is crucial to the success of the farmer field school IPM programmes and other farmer-led efforts. In the World Education IPM programme in Indonesia, the emphasis shifted from professional staff to using farmers for training purposes, and to training of these farmer-trainers.

Training farmer-trainers (Kingsley and Musante)
NGOs working in rural areas in Indonesia are often run by agricultural university graduates who are very interested in environmental problems. Excited by IPM concepts, many of these graduates originally requested training from the World Education project so that they could lead farmer field schools. In general, they fared badly in these training roles, lacking the practical know-how and years of experience farmers have in planting a crop and bringing it to harvest. Since the first year of the project, there has been a rapid move towards an all-farmer IPM training staff within NGO IPM programmes. Conversely, NGO university graduates have taken greater responsibility for programme co-ordination, administration and the quantitative aspects of programme evaluation.

Candidates for field school trainers/leaders are now selected from among interested farmers who are already IPM field school alumni or practitioners and, if possible, they are chosen by farmers in their community to be developed as IPM leaders. Training organized by local NGO IPM programmes involves a season-long training of trainers. This takes place in villages where there are active IPM farmers field schools. The two main training components are as follows:

103

o For three to four days per week, participants study the technical aspects of IPM and training and facilitation skills, and learn how to organize activities within a community.
o During on-the-job learning trainees must deal with real-life problems in organizing the start-up and operation of field schools with officials and farmers in neighbouring villages. These field schools are usually started in response to a very damaging pest problem in the area, such as rat infestations or stemborer outbreaks, and focus on collective or individual action directed at that particular problem. Often these field schools continue for a second season where the new field school leaders continue to be supported and mentored by a more experienced IPM trainer/leader.

The main strategy is to help the participants to learn by doing, while keeping the 'lessons' as close to real field conditions as possible. Local farmers in the training site village benefit from hosting a group of trainees, through their facilitation of field schools and assistance they give to individuals in IPM outside of field school activities.

Testing of trainees is first done by experienced IPM farmers during quarterly programme forums. Farmers' questions to trainees primarily focus on how a trainee would address what the farmers consider to be the important social and technical issues in a village. Trainees are also tested by NGO staff and farmers on their ability to develop a strategy for entering a new village, the initial approaches they use, and the way they would develop a plan together with villagers, prepare a curriculum for the field school, outline the process desired, and conduct evaluation and follow-up planning. Trainees are then asked to develop specific follow-up plans for becoming field school facilitators in their own villages.

The project has found that when farmer-trainers are leading IPM field schools, rather than non-farmers, the learning process is clearly more grounded and practical, and IPM spreads much more quickly in farming communities. All IPM field school farmer-trainers trained by the project (about 40 people) are presently leading field schools for NGOs, farmers' organizations or government agencies.

Maningding draws out several lessons about the training of professionals and farmers from his involvement in the IPM farmer field school project in Benguet province in the Philippines. He also notes the important role graduates from farmer field schools play in training other farmers, as well as professional extension staff.

Lessons learned about training (Maningding)
o Prospective clientele or participants must be consulted and involved in planning and designing the training programme. There should be a comprehensive training needs assessment before training is designed.
o A balanced training programme must be designed which takes into consideration sufficient coverage of cognitive skills; generous provision of manipulative skills and systematic discovery.
o A training methodology should be adopted which takes into account the following considerations: the farmers' specific training needs, level of education, technology and farming experience; the size of the farmers' groups; the technologies to be introduced; the budgetary support available; the venue; the abilities and skills of the trainers and resource persons available; the training support facilities and equipment available.
o Trainers should possess the following skills and values if the season-long courses are to be effective: technical skills; managerial competence; resourcefulness and initiative; problem-solving and decision-making abilities; and knowledge of the participants and their personality, behaviour and attitude differences. They should also be considerate, understanding and patient.

104

In the process of organizing and conducting farmer field schools, existing networks of farmers' groups are revitalized as farmer graduates train other farmers in farmer field school methods. They also conduct problem-focused field experiments and develop horizontal communication and support methodologies and materials. Farmer graduates also train government officials or field staff and, consequently, the results of farmer research feed into the field staff's development programmes. Both government field staff and farmers become skilled and highly motivated facilitators of IPM training and implementation.

Selection of participants

How should participants in farmer field schools be chosen? Maningding describes how participants in the farmer field school are selected in the IPM project in the Philippines. Public-sector extension agents and local government officials all play a significant role.

Selecting participants in a farmer field school (Maningding)

Each extension worker works with five to ten farmers' groups. The extension worker selects two farmer groups from the extension area, and the participants for the field schools are selected from these groups. The farmer groups are generally selected on the basis of the extension worker's knowledge of the group — how active it is — and on the advice of local government officials. The participation of local government officials in the selection of farmers' groups is important. Such officials are briefed about the goals of IPM and the farmer field school. Their support of field schools helps to eliminate any misunderstanding at the local level. The training team then meets with leaders of selected farmers' groups and briefs them on the purposes of IPM and the goals of the field schools. The final selection of participants in the farmer field school is made with their help.

Participants are selected on the basis of the following criteria:

o Participants must be active farmers. This means that they must have access to land and must actively farm that land. Whether they actually own the land is not important, nor is the size of the land-holdings.

o The participants must be able to attend the field school sessions. They must have the time to attend every session, because each session builds on earlier ones and each is on a different stage of plant growth.

o The participants must be willing and able to act as informants about IPM for the rest of the members of their farmer group. They must be able to communicate to the members of their group and be willing and able to accept responsibility for helping their neighbours.

o The participants must be interested in learning and interacting with their fellow farmers, especially in the process of agro-ecosystem analysis and in resolving problems and issues of pesticide use.

Gender issues

One of the problems experienced by the farmer field school projects has been the lesser degree to which women seem able to participate. Kingsley and Musante expand on why this may be and what measures can be taken to further enable women's participation.

Involving women in farmer field schools (Kingsley and Musante)

One immediate problem of the project is the need for greater involvement of women farmers in field school activities. Overall, women's participation has been low. A recent project review suggested that, while the farmer field school model is well suited to women's involvement, project and local NGO staff need to give greater deliberate attention to means of increasing women's participation (van de Fliert and Velasco 1994). Project and NGO staff have responded by recruiting and training women farmer-trainers and beginning all-women's farmer field schools, which will be integrated with other farmer groups in evening meetings and quarterly forums. In some areas it has been possible for some women to participate fully with men in farmer field schools; but in general, women farmers have indicated they would prefer their own group. Participatory approaches, such as participatory rural appraisal methods, will be used to analyse women's social roles and economic activities in the community and examine ways to make programme activities more accessible and relevant to women farmers. It is also expected that more women farmer-trainers will be developed from women farmers' groups.

9 Problem census/problem solving

THIS CHAPTER FOCUSES on a methodology known as 'problem census/problem solving' (PC/PS). This is a way for field extension staff and farmers together to identify farming problems and possible solutions. It can be seen as one of the basket of methods within participatory rural appraisal.

In both the cases highlighted here, the PC/PS approach is being used on a pilot basis by government extension services in South Asia. In both Nepal and Bangladesh, the extension services have identified the lack of farmers' participation as a key weakness in the prevailing training and visit system. They are testing the PC/PS approach to see whether it can be used to improve the responsiveness of the extension, research and support services to rural people's needs and priorities.

Nepal

Bimoli and Manandhar describe one such attempt from the Terai (southern plains) region in Nepal. They describe a pilot project in Rangeli Village Development Committee (VDC, the lowest administrative unit of government), Morang district, where the PC/PS approach was introduced.

Problem census/problem solving in Nepal (Bimoli and Manandhar)

The Rangeli VDC, located 25 km east of the Morang district headquarters, has 2 461 households with a total population of 12 190. Its cultivated area is 1069 hectares. In 1992–93, following the implementation of the problem census/problem solving approach, previously formed farmer reference groups were restructured. Out of the nine reference groups, five are now made up of small farmers, three of medium-scale farmers and one of large-scale farmers. The farmers' groups range in size from 9 to 17 members and the total number of member farmers is 120 (about 5 per cent of the total household population).

A meeting of the Rangeli pilot VDC. The PC/PS technique was applied in the Rangeli pilot VDC during the winter to help farmers identify needs and problems specific to production during this season, and to find solutions to them. The meeting described below was held in January 1994, was attended by 17 farmers and lasted about four hours. Farmers were provided with large sheets of paper and pens so they could record the outcomes of their discussions. The discussion and recording were facilitated by extension workers. The whole process was conducted informally and in the local language... The extension workers assisting the farmers were from the same locality and spoke the same dialect as the farmers.

The group leader began by describing the purpose of the meeting. Farmers were requested to discuss their problems in cultivating winter vegetable crops, solutions to the problems, and other important issues affecting their crop production and productivity. Once the group was clear as to what was requested, they were divided into small sub-groups of four to six members based on individuals' specific interests. Each sub-group was asked to select a discussion co-ordinator and a recorder to list the final set of problems identified.

After each sub-group identified its members' needs, priorities and problems, the extension worker helped the recorders present the findings. These were then discussed by the group as a whole. Once problems from all the sub-groups had been presented and discussed, the problems common to all were identified. The same sub-groups were than requested to discuss all the problems recorded, to identify the major ones and prioritize them. Prioritized problems were recorded on a sheet of paper and solutions to them were discussed. After a long discussion, a consensus was built on an action plan.

During the meeting, the farmers identified more than 15 problems. From that initial set of problems and after further discussions, they prioritized the problems as follows:

o lack of quality improved seeds
o lack of fertilizers
o agricultural loans amounting to NRs10 000 (about US$200) should be provided in cash
o lack of irrigation facilities
o inadequate subsidy on sprayers.

The farmers and extension staff agreed on several actions to address these problems.

Lack of quality improved seeds. The farmers' reliance on government (the Agricultural Input Corporation) and private seed suppliers led to problems of untimeliness, unavailability and poor quality of seed, so the members of the group decided to start multiplying seeds in their own locality.

Lack of fertilizers. In Nepal, fertilizers are procured and distributed throughout the country by the Agricultural Input Corporation. Since this was a nationwide problem which the farmers were unable to solve locally, they relayed their concerns to the relevant agency through the extension officer. In the meantime, they decided to establish demonstrations of compost-making and green manuring.

Agricultural loans amounting to NRs10 000 (about US$200) should be provided in cash. Farmers have to fill in lengthy paperwork to get a loan from the Agricultural Development Bank, particularly to receive a loan in cash. It is more common for farmers to receive coupons with which to purchase fertilizer and other related inputs from nearby co-operatives. They decided to raise this matter in the District Agricultural Coordination Committee meeting, in which the Agricultural Development Bank is also represented.

Lack of irrigation facilities. Farmers decided to maintain their old canals through their own efforts and also to approach the funding agency for money with which to construct deep and shallow tube wells.

Inadequate subsidy on sprayers. Spraying equipment is costly because it has to be imported from other countries. A 25 per cent subsidy is provided by the government at present. Despite this subsidy, for many farmers it remains a costly purchase. In addition, equipment owned by a single individual is under-utilized. The farmers' groups therefore decided to procure spraying equipment through the group welfare fund and rent it out to group members, as well as other farmers.

This particular farmers' group is picking up things gradually and showing great interest in and enthusiasm for incorporating their felt needs into the planning process and coming up with their own ways for meeting those needs. The extension agents working with the group are also gradually getting acquainted with the approach through engaging in the PC/PS process.

Strengths of the PC/PS process

o Group meetings have become regular and communication gaps between farmers, extension staff and researchers have lessened.
o The presence of extension staff in the community has become regular.
o Strong linkages among involved institutions have developed. Information and advice from extension have diffused quickly, and farmers' feedback is equally rapidly obtained.
o The approach has become a means of creating an appropriate technology diffusion environment, where individuals share ideas and exchange skills and knowledge. A platform has been created on which farmers discuss common problems and issues.
o An environment has been created in which joint efforts are applied to solving individual as well as common problems.
o The approach has built up farmers' confidence and trust in extension staff and other agencies related to their activities.
o The approach has encouraged poor and small farmers to participate meaningfully in agricultural development activities.
o Regular meetings with the farmers' group have facilitated the assessment of training needs for farmers and extension staff.
o The approach has created awareness among the rural communities of the benefits of organizing themselves in a group to serve their mutual interests.
o Group and participatory needs assessments have helped in developing realistic plans and programmes.
o Co-ordination amongst agriculturally related line agencies has improved. Pressure exerted by farmers' groups is also bringing these agencies on joint visits and is encouraging them jointly to cater to the needs of the groups.
o Substantial amounts of funds have been raised from among the members of the Rangeli group and put into the group welfare fund, which has been earmarked for common needs and interests.

Problems and recommendations

o Extension agents, farmer group leaders and members, as well as the other top facilitators, have little understanding of the objectives and procedures of the PC/PS process and need to be regularly oriented and trained in the process.
o Some of the problems identified by farmers require multi-agency co-operation in order for solutions to be found, and extension staff lack the knowledge and skills to foster the necessary co-operation. Regular meetings and interaction among agriculture-related agencies is necessary to foster the group problems and needs and to avoid confusion and duplication of implementation.
o During the prioritization processes, problems which are not within the mandate of extension agents are identified. Either the group can solve these themselves or the extension agent can suggest immediate solutions, such as a large irrigation scheme, motorable roads connecting the village, electric lines to run water pumps, etc. Action plans should be prioritized using three categories: short-, medium- or long-term. It is also useful to identify which agents are needed for each activity. Farmers can start with short-term action plans which they can carry out themselves, and simultaneously approach the relevant agencies for other activities while further planning medium- and long-term action plans.
o The establishment and maintenance of inter-agency co-ordination at the district and operational levels have always been a critical issue in Nepal. Poor linkages among research, extension and farmers is another serious problem. Another concerns the functioning of national and international NGOs, some of which work in isolation from other parties and provide free or highly subsidized agricultural inputs to farmer groups.

This has created confusion and presented obstacles to the successful implementation of PC/PS. An inter-agency memorandum of understanding is needed to ensure all assistance to farmers, from whatever source, is provided through a single channel and co-ordinated by the district agricultural development officer.

o Monitoring and evaluation of group activities are either weak or non-existent. A system should be developed to monitor group activities regularly so that all project participants can know whether it is moving along the right track and get feedback on their on-going and planned activities.

It is very early to give definite conclusions about the PC/PS approach. There are many areas which still need improvement. It is always difficult to give up one system and abruptly adopt another, and it requires great determination and mental preparation to discard ideas of longstanding or an acquired working culture and to switch to another, quite new approach. Despite these difficulties the approach appears to be appropriate, less costly than traditional extension methods, and more useful and effective in serving large numbers of farmers.

Bangladesh

Bhuiyan and Walker present a similar experience with the problem census methodology in a pilot project run by the Department of Agricultural Extension in Jessore district in southwest Bangladesh. The procedure to elicit problems and suggest solutions used here is slightly different from that used in Nepal and described by Bimoli and Manandhar above.

The problem census approach in Bangladesh (Bhuiyan and Walker)

The problem census is a participatory, group-based extension method which enables farmers to identify their needs and problems, and recommend appropriate solutions and action. The problem census method has been described in detail by Bruce Crouch of the University of Queensland in Australia (Crouch 1991). It builds on the knowledge and experience of the farmers involved. The problem census method could be considered one of the techniques in the participatory rural appraisal menu, towards which the Department of Agricultural Extension in Bangladesh is hoping to move in the long run. The procedure that the department has adopted consists of the a number of iterative activities as follows:

1. Defining a topic for investigation and arranging a meeting with a group of 20 to 30 male or female farmers from the same socio-economic category to discuss these. Examples of such topics include soil fertility, access to information and rice cultivation.
2. Splitting the farmers into small working groups of five or six, seated in a circle with paper and pens.
3. Each working group discussing problems in relation to the same topic, and recording the outcome of their discussions.
4. Bringing the working groups together to share and collate their problem lists and compile them.
5. Enabling farmers to select the ten most important problems from the compiled list.
6. Re-forming the working groups with each group ranking the ten key problems.
7. Bringing the working groups together to share their rankings. The rankings of each smaller group are added up to give an indication of importance to the group as a whole.
8. Enabling farmers to propose and discuss solutions.
9. Explaining the kinds of assistance the department may be able to provide the debating this is carried out before ending the census.

Table 9.1: Problem census results in Jessore district, Bangladesh

Problem	Group				Total
	1	2	3	4	
Poverty	9	9	9	5	32
No women's organizations	5	7	6	8	26
High prices of grain but low labour rates	2	8	7	9	26
High interest rates on NGO loans	6	6	8	3	23
Shortage of seeds	7	4	3	7	21
No capital to invest in income generation	8	5	5	2	20
High birth rates due to illiteracy	4	2	2	9	17
No treatment facilities for poultry	3	3	4	4	14
Shortage of land	1	1	1	6	9

Jessore District Pilot Programme. In October 1994, all 263 block supervisors in Jessore District and their senior staff were trained in the problem census technique. Within one month, they facilitated 450 problem census exercises, meeting with over 15 000 farmers. Some 25 per cent of these were women, and 42 per cent were landless, marginal or small-scale farmers. The proportion of the total population of the district involved was relatively low, but with more time more people will gain the opportunity to participate.

Table 9.1 shows the results from one of the problem census meetings. The participants were small-scale female farmers from one village. The topic discussed was problems faced in the pre-monsoon cropping season. The figures below each working group indicate their rankings of these problems, 10 being most important. The total is simply the sum of small working groups' rankings. The main areas of concern in this case are pure poverty and the lack of social organization, followed by high loan interest rates and a shortage of seeds.

It should be noted that problems identified here were general in nature, and there was little scope for the Department of Agriculture to assist in addressing them, because they fell outside of its remit. There remains a need for increased facilitation skills at the field level and enhanced co-operation between agencies involved in agricultural development, as the problems farmers face are not confined to the particular function of any one agency.

Participatory approaches to needs assessments and opportunity analyses must feed directly into viable action plans and implementation. In Jessore District, for the first time in the department's history, all the staff came together as a team to consider the results of the problem censuses and to develop an action plan in the form of a logical framework. Within two months, an extension programme had been prepared, in consultation with other organizations (such as NGOs, research and other government departments) and is now being implemented.

Lessons. In order to assess the suitability of this bottom-up system, a process evaluation was conducted (ASSP, 1995; Nasiruddin, 1995). The evaluation was primarily concerned with determining the successful and unsuccessful aspects of bottom-up planning and the training required to put it into place. As such, it concentrated on process, rather than the products or impact. The elements of the process evaluation were:

o discussions with farmers who participated in problem census exercises
o discussions with staff of the department involved
o comparisons of the bottom-up extension plan with those implemented in the past.

The process evaluation was therefore dominated by those who were most involved — farmers and field staff. On the positive side, the evaluation showed that the problem census has:

o proven a practical and simple tool for needs assessment by encouraging farmer participation in problem identification and problem solving
o enabled block-, *thana-* and district-level staff of the department to gain a better understanding of farmers' problems and needs
o improved relationships between block supervisors and farmers
o shown potential for improving access to agricultural information
o increased the spirit of co-operation between farmers, between the department and farmers, and between the department and other organizations
o started to develop farmers' awareness about the process of self-development
o enabled the department to prepare a bottom-up extension plan which reflects local farmers' needs.

Too often, when discussing participatory approaches to extension, there is a tendency to concentrate on strengths. However, it is also important to recognize weaknesses and learn from mistakes in order to develop these approaches fully. Table 9.2 shows the weaknesses in the process identified by the evaluation, along with suggestions for future improvements. Again, these comments on the process came mainly from farmers and block supervisors.

The pilot programme is on the verge of completion, the process has been evaluated and lessons have been learnt. Now, the approach is to be adopted, gradually and in phases, across Bangladesh. Additional participatory techniques will also be piloted, and those which appear successful will be expanded. A set of modular training programmes is being developed, drawing from the pilot and the lessons learnt from it. The Department of Agricultural Extension is gradually becoming a learning organization, developing its own future, rather than waiting for a new donor blueprint.

Table 9.2: Weaknesses and possible improvements in the problem census process, Jessore district, Bangladesh

Weakness	Possible improvement
There was no survey of agroecological conditions.	A participatory survey of local resources should be completed as part of the input to extension programme planning. Additional participatory methodologies, such as resource mapping, could be applied. The department is currently conducting field visits to NGOs using these techniques with a view to piloting them in the future.
It proved difficult for block supervisors to gather homogenous groups of farmers together.	A system of wealth ranking may be introduced.

Table 9.2 *(continued)*

Weakness	*Possible improvement*
The problem census identified general problems which did not serve well as an input to extension planning. Generally formulated problems are open to outside interpretation which may not reflect real farm-level constraints.	Field-staff skills in probing and facilitation need to be improved. The facilitators must attain the skills to clearly define the nature of the problems. Questions should be refined and more specific.
The problems identified by female farmers were similar to those of males, even though the nature of women's problems is different.	Improve the probing and facilitation skills of block supervisors and then train them in working with female farmers.
As it depends to a certain extent on the ability to read and write, the problem census in its present form hinders the participation of illiterate farmers.	The active participation of illiterate individuals can be encouraged by using diagrams and pictures. Staff will need to enhance their facilitation skills to achieve this.
The staff of the department have poor skills in determining, or helping farmers to determine the best solutions to identified problems.	Improve the problem-solving skills of the staff of the department. Facilitators must enable farmers to express root causes of problems in order to find appropriate solutions.
Due to the department's history of input supply, farmers still expect field staff to supply free inputs and find it hard to see their new role as facilitators.	
Block supervisors, as facilitators, will not be able to cover all farmers, even with a group approach.	Farmers themselves have the capacity to facilitate self-development. Farmers could be identified and trained as 'farmer facilitators'.
Farmers were not fully involved in the planning process.	Involve farmers in planning by inviting them to planning workshops. Train field staff in participatory planning, to enable them to facilitate farmers' own planning.
The extension plan could not cover all the problems identified.	Links with other organizations, made during the process, need to be continually strengthened.
The extension plan is directed at all farmers, even though only a small proportion participated in the problem census.	The plan should target the farmers who were involved in the problem census. As each cycle of needs assessment and planning passes, more and more farmers will receive a better service.

10 NGO–government collaboration

DURING THE 1990s several factors have led (some would say 'pushed') government agencies and NGOs towards more collaborative efforts in agricultural research and extension. Although traditionally dominated by the public sector, in many parts of the world these services have been effectively provided to thousands of communities through innovative, resource-intensive NGO programmes. At the same time, public-sector capabilities have been clipped due to shrinking budgets, the declining relative contribution of agriculture to the economy, and poor returns on investments. Therefore, perceived institutional comparative advantages have moved NGOs and governments to work together in order to provide better research and extension support to agricultural production.

Many types of collaborative arrangements have evolved, and much study in recent years has focused on this increasingly common strategy (Farrington *et al.* 1993). While a detailed typology of the diversity of collaborative arrangements is not warranted here, three main types of NGO–government collaboration are presented in this book:

o Government agencies seek collaboration with NGOs in order to see their programme efforts and activities spread more widely.
o NGOs initiate collaboration with government agencies for help in 'scaling up' their programme successes to reach a larger number of communities.
o Government agencies seek NGOs' help to become more responsive, especially to poor farmers' needs.

Strategic alliances between NGOs and government agencies are gaining popularity in many countries, especially in Asia. This chapter will highlight some which focused exclusively on NGO–government collaboration. However, the rationale and practice of NGO–government collaboration is also an underlying theme in several of the papers presented in Chapters 8 and 9.

Why are NGOs and government agencies willing to work together?

In explaining the underlying beliefs of a collaborative programme in Udaipur district of Rajasthan, India, Sharda and Ballabh provide an interesting background to the rationale for NGO–government collaborative efforts. The collaborative work focused on a government farm science centre, *Krishi Vigyan Kendra* (KVK), found in most districts of India. The KVK had earlier been the focal point of a government-NGO forum which met regularly to discuss and appreciate each side's work objectives, working styles and constraints. Sharda and Ballabh, both government representatives, ask how NGOs can contribute to the more effective provision of research and extension services to poor farmers.

Reasons for collaboration in India (Sharda and Ballabh)

At the start of the 1990s it was widely felt that government research and extension was failing adequately to address the needs of farmers — their clients. Also, the governments were finding the costs of these systems to be very high. The idea of government-NGO collaboration was mooted at this time to cut costs and make the system more need-based.

A large number of NGOs have tried to address problems faced by farmers. In most cases, however, the solution has been to create a parallel infrastructure by the NGO; examples include credit schemes, irrigation systems and, recently, NGO-managed block extension services. However, as the scale and area of operation of these parallel services expand, they often acquire the same inefficient characteristics of the systems that they aim to replace. Therefore, collaboration between government agencies and NGOs has been proposed as a way to make the state services more client-driven and to reduce costs. The basic assumption was that the three sets of actors — farmers, NGOs and government agencies — involved have unique strengths, and that collaboration would exploit these strengths.

It was thought that the NGOs would be able to play an effective intermediary role — by organizing farmer groups, developing farmers' skills and abilities to articulate needs, and assisting government workers in responding to these needs. The NGOs have regular two-way dialogues with farmers and hence have first-hand information about their needs and demands. The government research and extension agencies have financial and human resources, and have a large geographical spread which would enable them to address the problems raised through the NGOs.

Collaborative linkages between government agencies and NGOs focus primarily on concrete, time-bound activities (e.g., training, projects) but can include a multitude of activities. A few examples are presented below. Peacock describes a FarmAfrica project in the highlands of Ethiopia, designed to assist women in small-scale goat production. Women were chosen as the focus of the programme, because they, with their children, look after goats and traditionally milk livestock.

Background to the Dairy Goat Project in Ethiopia (Peacock)

The Dairy Goat Project began under the Dergue communist regime. It found that it was having to break new ground in several areas. First, goats had a very bad reputation among government officers, who appeared to blame them for environmental destruction. Ignorance, misconceptions and cultural prejudices abounded at the start of the project, necessitating a public awareness campaign. Efforts were therefore made to inform government staff of the value of goats to some of the poorest members of their society, and the potential role goats could play in improving their lives.

The second new area was involving women in a serious agricultural extension programme. Most activities previously directed at women's activities, whether under government or NGOs, had involved stove-making, sewing or possibly vegetable growing and were carried out under the auspices of a home economics programme, which is not part of mainstream agricultural extension. There was little understanding of the particular problems of women, so it was difficult to design appropriate extension strategies for them.

Finally there was little experience of operating an extension programme through farmers' voluntarily forming themselves into groups. The Dergue regime operated in a dictatorial manner. Participation was more often coerced than invited, and genuine participation in development activities was rare. New attitudes had to be instilled in the minds of extension staff, not only to work with women, but to work with them in an open and voluntary way. In addition, the legal framework within which groups were allowed to operate was not clear and is only now evolving after the change in government in 1991.

FarmAfrica decided that it was most cost-effective and more sustainable to implement a national project, such as the Dairy Goat Project, through collaboration with existing organizations. The collaborators are the Ministry of Agriculture, Alemaya University of Agriculture, Awassa College of Agriculture and NGOs with field programmes such as CARE, SOS Sahel, ActionAid and Redd Barna. The project now works with 1400 families in Eastern Hararge, Oromia Region and Konso, Welayta, and Gurage zones of the Southern Region.

Nguyen Kim Hai describes a very different institutional context for NGO–government collaboration in Vietnam since 1991. While there are still very few local NGOs in Vietnam, international NGOs have been working on innovative rural development programmes for several years, following on from initial humanitarian assistance and emergency aid efforts. One such NGO, Coopération International pour le Dévéloppement et la Solidarité (CIDSE), was asked to help develop the extension system of Bac Thai province (comprising seven districts with 158 communes, and approximately 90 000 households) in northern Vietnam. Working with a staff of about 166 provincial extension personnel, CIDSE–VIETNAM-Vietnam has attempted to modify the ways government extension personnel interact with local communities.

Extension in Bac Thai province, Vietnam (Nguyen Kim Hai)

Economic reforms in Vietnam in recent years have created substantial changes in the relationship between the state organizations and farmers, as well as within the local co-operatives. The framework for the provision of agricultural support services has changed drastically, but public service institutions have been slow to adjust to the requirements of the new situation. Following the economic reforms, the average size of production units dropped from several hundred hectares in an average co-operative production unit, to much smaller family production units of only a few hectares. Therefore, the number of extension 'clients' increased tremendously. However, the number of staff employed by state agricultural services has been reduced due to re-organization and budgetary constraints. Many thousands of agricultural technicians have lost their jobs, particularly at district and commune levels, thus considerably reducing the capacity of the extension system. Moreover, farmers now have to make their own decisions about what farming practices to use, and they face many difficulties in managing their own farms. Previously they were accustomed to work according to the decisions of the co-operatives.

Co-operatives and other agricultural service systems in Bac Thai were having difficulty reaching individual farmers due to a lack of appropriate extension methods and technology to meet the farmers' new situation. CIDSE agreed to provide support to the province to fill some of these gaps. Seven mountainous districts in the northern part of Bac Thai, the poorest part of the province, were chosen to participate in the extension programme.

117

Changing the working methodology of extensionists. In 1991 CIDSE began supporting the development of the government's extension programme in Bac Thai province. It began with an initial one-year pilot project, focusing on working methodologies and entitled 'training and demonstration plots'. More than 100 district and provincial staff from the agriculture, forestry and irrigation sectors, involved in the implementation of the project, were given guidance in:

o identifying farmers' technical needs through working with villagers
o planning with farmers, based on their needs and setting up farmer interest-groups
o setting up demonstration plots to illustrate technological solutions to farmers' problems
o providing technical assistance by working with farmers on demonstration plots and group meetings
o evaluating project results with farmers
o evaluating the project's achievements and constraints and implications for the orientation of the Bac Thai agricultural service system.

The most important effects of the pilot project were to shift the working methodology of the technical and extension staff towards a farmer-based approach, and to strengthen the commitment of the provincial people's committee to build an extension service that was responsive to the needs of farmers.

Early in 1992, based on the results of the pilot project and an exposure trip to Thailand, a new extension programme for Bac Thai province was initiated and designed through collaboration between CIDSE and representatives of the Bac Thai agricultural and forestry departments. The programme was called the Bac Thai Extension Programme for Mountainous Region Development and was implemented between 1992 and 1994. The programme objectives were to:

o improve the capacity of district and provincial extension agents to introduce innovations to farmers and to monitor the implementation of such technical measures
o increase and broaden the technical knowledge of provincial and district officers and farmers in relation to new cropping practices and improved chicken and pig production
o promote the production of seedlings for valuable tree crops and improve the design, usage and maintenance of small-scale irrigation schemes
o create a network of village and farmer groups engaged in managing village funds, land use agreements and demonstrations
o improve district and provincial extension agents' understanding of family farming practices.

Ishii-Eitemann and Kaophong describe the Regional Initiative in Sustainable Agriculture (RISA) which was created as a result of discussions between Save the Children–USA and the Rockefeller Brothers Fund. The RISA programme aims to explore how an international NGO can respond to the persistent institutional barriers encountered in rural development efforts. The multi-year programme has a geographical focus in Thailand and Laos, and facilitates linkages to other countries within the region, namely Vietnam, Indonesia and the Philippines. Field work within Thailand has focused on farmer training for integrated pest control using the farmer-field school approach (see Chapter 8). Programme efforts have centred around building a three-way partnership between farmers, NGOs and government agencies.

118

Regional Initiative in Sustainable Agriculture, Southeast Asia (Ishii-Eitemann and Kaophong)

Background. Throughout Asia the conflicting demands to increase agricultural production for food security while conserving a dwindling natural resource base have placed poor farmers in seemingly no-win situations. Local people's organizations and grassroots NGOs have responded by working at the family, community and village level to find ecologically and economically sustainable solutions. The extent to which these organizations can defuse the agro-environmental crisis at the national level, however, is severely limited due to minimal extension of their own experiences to other communities and a chronic lack of resources to influence policy (e.g., funding, technical knowledge, management capabilities, advocacy skills). Meanwhile, larger development institutions with financial, technical and extension resources (such as government) and those with skills in research, analysis and documentation (such as academic and research institutes), conduct their own projects in rural and agricultural development. Frequently, however, the outcome of these large-scale research and extension projects do not effectively meet the daily needs of the rural poor.

Development analysts increasingly point to the gaping chasm separating these diverse development institutions and argue that collaboration between these groups is the only way forward. Yet models of successful partnerships between rural associations, NGOs, research institutes and the state are few, while those that do exist are rarely known to the individuals leading development initiatives in their respective organizations.

An institutional response. The underlying premiss of the RISA project is that while local and international NGOs have accumulated vast experiences in family and community organizing at the grassroots level, government-affiliated development institutions and academic and research-based groups have often overlooked their unique skills. Moreover, local NGOs and people's organizations are frequently unable or unwilling to seek and utilize the technical expertise and resources of universities, research and government institutes.

While the value of inter-agency partnerships is increasingly recognized in some quarters, the number of successful collaborations which have been studied, documented and shared amongst implementing agencies remains few. In practice, most development initiatives are still based upon a single or specific type of implementing organization and fall short of reaching their goals precisely because they work in isolation from each other or distrust the motives of dissimilar development institutions. The potential is therefore not fully realized for creating viable rural development strategies, grounded in the reality of farmers' lives, adaptable to diverse local conditions, enriched by ongoing research, and extended throughout the country or region.

Focusing inter-agency working groups. RISA aims to test that a project promoting collaboration between diverse institutions and agencies can evoke a synergy among partnering members, establishing the grounds for a sustainable sharing of knowledge and resources. Broadly, the goal of RISA is to identify and promote effective means for developing the institutional capacity of local and national organizations within Southeast Asia in promoting farmer-centred sustainable agriculture. However, initial efforts in forging inter-agency collaboration towards this end revealed that broad, abstract goals such as 'sustainability' are less effective than concrete ones in attracting participation. While enthusiastic about general principles of partnership and sustainable development, in practice many partner NGOs find it difficult to commit staff time and effort to additional collaborative activities unless project outputs are specific, unique and not readily obtainable through other, simpler means. Highly structured and compartmentalized government agencies also respond more positively to proposals for collaboration with NGOs when the project clearly identifies the technical division whose participation is sought (e.g., disease management, weed control and soil improvement). At this point, a realistic assessment of work plans and timetables became possible, and inter-agency collaboration could proceed from general discussion to the planning of activities and commitment of staff time.

How do NGOs and government agencies work together?

NGO–government collaboration can take on various forms. Common collaborative activities include problem identification, planning, technology development, and the provision of critical production inputs such as information, credit, seeds and animals. Workshop participants did not report collaboration in more difficult areas such as conflict resolution, land tenure and institutional development. This would seem appropriate: since there are already enough uncertainties in NGO–government collaboration, it would seem sensible to focus on less threatening or difficult tasks. In fact, Sanghi, Kanda and Dayal (quoted later in this chapter) point out that certain skills such as conflict resolution may not be found among either government or NGO extension staff, and so gaps in these areas will not be addressed simply through collaboration.

Peacock describes a set of activities within the FarmAfrica dairy goat project in Ethiopia, which involves both government and NGO extension agents. The project made deliberate efforts to access government resources, especially where the government had facilities the NGO lacked, such as for credit provision and technical training of women paravets.

Modes of collaboration in the Dairy Goat Project in Ethiopia (Peacock)

Credit. The poorest women, often widows, are identified by the community and receive two goats on credit. The credit may be repaid in cash or in kind, the latter by passing on a weaned kid to a new family. The women form a group of 15–30 members who elect a committee and draw up by-laws. The group itself manages the credit repayment and selects new families who they think need to receive goats. Women involved with the project have shown themselves to be responsible in disbursing credit to appropriate families and accurate in maintaining records and receiving repayments.

Based on the success of its own women's credit programme, the project has played a major role in lobbying the Agricultural and Industrial Development Bank to supply credit funds to women, who were not previously allowed to obtain loans. It is now possible for a women's group to receive funds directly from the bank, with the approval of the local Ministry of Agriculture extension staff.

Training. The women involved in the project follow a basic training course in improved goat husbandry which covers forage development, health care and general management. Extension staff are trained to use a simple extension package consisting of a set of flip charts and guidelines in their use. The package is designed to be used in a very interactive, participatory way, encouraging dialogue and discussion of issues while learning new ideas. The package can be divided up into meetings of different lengths according to the wishes of the group. The package itself is continually revised in the light of the experience of the groups.

Women paravets. Ethiopia, like most African countries, suffers from a chronic shortage of trained, mobile and equipped veterinary staff. Most farmers have limited or no

120

access to veterinary services. However perhaps as much as 80–90 per cent of livestock diseases could be controlled through the simple vaccinations, and the use of anthelmintics and acaricides. These drugs do not have to be administered by highly trained professionals, but can be properly administered by trained farmers, including women farmers.

It was considered vital to the success of the programme to have a more effective goat health programme than the existing veterinary service allowed. It took time to persuade the authorities that illiterate women could correctly use basic veterinary drugs and could learn simple veterinary techniques, but eventually the project was allowed to train women as paravets.

Each goat group selects two women to be trained as paravets. They attend a five- to seven-day initial training course which is organized in their own or a nearby village, and are invited to bring local goats to the course so that trainees see a variety of cases. The training is very practical and participatory in nature, allowing practical skills to be taught and practised in a familiar environment. The paravets are trained to examine a sick goat, use anthelmintics and acaricides, dress wounds, trim feet and castrate. The women are also trained to keep simple pictorial records, allowing the project to monitor their activities.

At the end of the course there is a small graduation ceremony where the trainees receive a basic veterinary kit and a certificate of attendance, and where they publicly commit themselves to serving the members of the goat group. The paravets charge a small mark-up on the price of drugs and a small fee for their work.

The paravet programme is supervised jointly by the local Ministry of Agriculture veterinary officer and the goat group committee. Follow-up training is organized to allow feedback and the discussion and solving problems. So far the paravets have performed very well. A few have dropped out due to family problems or pregnancy, but most return after some time.

Recent changes in legislation have allowed private veterinary drug shops to be established in rural areas. The project will help five paravets or animal health assistants to open drug shops in project areas, to ensure continuity in the supply of drugs after the project ends in 1997.

Breeding programme. The project aims gradually to intensify the production from local goats through improving their management, but there comes a point beyond which local goats cannot be further improved and should be upgraded. Once a woman has achieved a reasonable level of management and has repaid her debt she receives a crossbred goat on credit. At the start of the project, crossbreeds were bred on an experimental basis at a local agricultural university and at a college. However as the groups became more established and the demand for crossbreeds outstripped the supply, local-level crossbreeding was encouraged through community buck stations. One buck is allocated to a group, which selects a family to look after it and to which members take their local goats for crossbreeding. Group members agree to take feed to the buck or help the buck keeper in other ways. In order to ensure the sustainability of the breed improvement, local farmers with superior management skills and larger farms have been selected to be breeders of pure stock and supply them to local groups. The Ethiopian Goat Improvement Association has been registered as a national organization to promote improved goat farming throughout the country.

The Bac Thai project in Vietnam took a very formal approach to establishing a collaborative structure in which project activities would be carried out. However, CIDSE did not deploy their own field extension workers, but rather worked to strengthen the methodological skills of the public-sector provincial extension staff.

Organizing the extension system in Bac Thai (Nguyen Kim Hai)

The organization of the extension system was established, with a programme steering committee made up of representatives of different government sectors and mass organizations, such as the Bac Thai Agricultural Department, Forestry Department, Irrigation Department, Farmers' Association and Women's Union. The vice-chairman of Bac Thai People's Committee is chairman of the steering committee.

The programme is directly implemented by the Bac Thai Extension Centre, under the supervision and guidance of the programme steering committee. This provincial extension centre employs six full-time members of staff who are in charge of training, planning, information development, monitoring, evaluation and financing.

The extension system has an extension board at district level with four part-time staff, representatives of the programme steering committee and different sectors of the district, and one full-time extension co-ordinator. The next level of the extension system is occupied by the Inter-Communal Centres, of which there are between four and six per district (38 in total), each staffed by three to four extension workers with complementary technical backgrounds.

Nguyen Kim Hai goes on to describe the range of activities undertaken within the project, many of which focused on transforming government extension personnel 'to become facilitators, rather than providers of immediate solutions.' Several other activities were important, including the deliberate strategy of directly involving farmers or groups of farmers in planning extension activities, and providing study visits to government extension workers to learn about other successful extension approaches.

Extension activities in Bac Thai, Vietnam (Nguyen Kim Hai)

Farmer interest groups. Through intensified discussions about the role and function of farmer interest groups more emphasis was laid on the selection of group members, group size and group activities. Moreover, the extension worker's role as group facilitator was more precisely defined and realized. Group size in general was raised from 3–5 members to 8–15 in late spring 1993. In 1993, 559 groups were established, compared to 828 in 1992, as a result of a more careful approach, but by the end of 1993 around 5300 households in total were participating in farmer interest groups.

Through monitoring and internal surveys it was found that the performance of 30 per cent of the groups was still weak. This was mainly due to lack of a clear agenda when meeting, or too much discussion about the rotating loan fund system, instead of new technologies.

Setting up demonstration plots. Demonstration plots were defined through discussion as involving a simple farming practice which is new to the group members, requires limited external inputs, and fits in with the present farming system as a solution to a specified problem farmers have identified.

Rotating loan funds were set up in each group for the establishment of demonstration plots. The repayment and rotation of the loan funds among group members caused no major difficulties. However, it was often the case that the groups were not very flexible in using the loan fund and in recruiting new group members to participate in the loan system. Between 1992 and 1993, a total of 2052 demonstration plots were established. During 1994, only experimental plots and very few demonstration plots were funded from central project funds, the rest being funded by the interest groups themselves. The revolving fund principle has enabled the continuation of the learning process from demonstration plots for about 1400 farmers' groups. In later cases more than one loan was provided to the larger groups in order to satisfy the need for more visual extension activities.

The loans (always less than US$10 per demonstration plot) should be regarded only as an incentive, rather than capital support. In cases of failure of the demonstration plot, a project fund is available to compensate for any losses. However, up to now, no claims for such compensation have been made, indicating that the demonstration plots have had satisfactory results for the farmers.

Increasing farmer participation in extension work. During 1993 and 1994 around 190 'field workshops' among farmers were organized with support from the project, reaching an estimated 5800 households. These topical discussion meetings were often centred on certain demonstration plots or group activities. During the field meetings the farmers explained the new techniques they were trying; this is an important achievement compared to the past, when only extension technicians gave demonstrations of new techniques. Field workshops, if they are well-prepared, offer opportunities for discussion on the specific problems identified by farmer groups, and on possible solutions. Farmers at the field workshops typically discuss the various social implications of these solutions, as well as the technical aspects...

The major follow-up activity resulting from the new farmer-based extension methodology was the planning process for the farmer support activities. Especially in the beginning, extension workers tended to fall back into the habit of offering the technologies they were already familiar with to farmers, either by taking over the planning of activities from the farmers, or by waiting for top-down package programmes from the district level. The five technical framework programmes initially offered under the extension programme were 'abused' in this way. They were misinterpreted as package programmes, for example, 'peanut on sloping land' or 'maize as a second-season crop', or 'special-breed chicken raising'. Some extension workers who had specialist knowledge of particular technologies or 'packages' anticipated the farmers' needs with their solutions. However, this phenomenon was easily traced through monitoring, and tackled in discussions with the extension workers.

The first step in avoiding these problems was to require all plans for demonstration plots and other activities to come directly from the farmer interest-group members. Once this rule had been established, a new problem appeared: the lack of flexibility and ability of the extension workers, district and province levels in responding to the farmers' requests. This problem has recently led to the formulation of criteria for procedures on planning and the acceptance of farmers' plans to be supported by the extension service. This coincided with a wider discussion on what the extension policy for the province should be and which groups of farmers should be targeted. It must therefore be regarded as an on-going debate in an on-going process of consolidating and strengthening the extension system.

Developing low-external input technology. In order to establish clear and direct flows of new technologies from researchers to farmer groups, researchers were invited to support farmers in testing their low-cost, low external input technologies through on-farm experimental trials. Extension workers facilitated discussion among the farmer interest groups and ensured farmers properly compared new technologies with their existing practices.

One technology tested in this way was the introduction of nitrogen-fixing bacteria in rice fields, reducing considerably the need for expensive chemical fertilizers. Another example was the technique of quick rice seedling production, helpful to farmers living at higher altitudes, where there is a critically short period for growing two crops a year. These trials provided greater feedback to research than the demonstration plots. At the same time the capacity of farmers to do experiments by themselves was highlighted, as well as the high level of interest they showed in participating in trials.

123

Study tours. Study tours to see agroforestry extension models in other provinces were arranged, in order to get new ideas and inspiration. Visits to potential learning sites were carefully prepared, planned and implemented. The types of places visited were model forest farms and an agroforestry project supported by the Swedish International Development Authority in Yen Bai province. In Thanh Hoa province agroforestry models in Dong Son district were visited, all with the participation of extension workers and staff from provincial and district departments. At the end of 1993 a study tour was prepared to examine the results and effectiveness of various extension attempts in northeast Thailand. After a preparatory visit by programme staff in December, 11 provincial and district extension staff took part in the study tour, with staff from Khon Kaen University and CIDSE facilitating the visit.

On all study tours farmers, and then local extension agents, were interviewed and questioned on the approach, methodology, effectiveness and results of the extension approach. Both government and non-government extension services were closely studied. Critical questions for the study tour participants to consider were indicated, such as: whether a particular project was serving the real needs of farmers, the extent of farmers' participation in the process, funding, the planning process, and report flows.

The major lessons learned from the study tour, as expressed by the extension worker participants, were:

o do not do the work farmers can do themselves (such as planning)
o do not just bring money to farmers
o do not put pressure on them to follow a particular course of action.

The visits helped to underline that the purpose of extension work is to support farmers, to help them to organize activities among themselves, to utilize their own capital as much as possible, and whenever necessary provide loans in order to increase production both for their home consumption and for the sale of any surplus. In general, the study tours provided the participants with a clear insight into the development path, as well as showing them the results which extension could provide to farmers in the long term.

Garg describes the Rajasthan state government's efforts to bring about change to the formal extension service through testing innovative extension approaches in which government and NGOs collaborate. He describes a deliberate decision by the state government to replace government extension workers with NGO staff in specific geographic areas. Unfortunately, this idea was combined with the strategy of transferring some of the costs of these services to the NGO and ultimately to the farmers themselves, and so encountered some resistance.

Extension service delivery by NGOs in Rajasthan (Garg)

NGOs were seen primarily as facilitators which can mobilize rural communities to analyse and prioritize their local needs, help them conceive, design and plan remedial interventions, and assist in creating local stakeholders through contributory funding, implementation, management and ultimately taking up ownership of the project. The government is keen on funding these projects identified and evolved by farmers in close association with NGOs.

The concept of an alternative extension delivery system was debated in the agriculture department and discussed with several NGOs as well. It was thereafter decided to operationalize collaboration by handing over a geographical unit of the extension system to an NGO by withdrawal of government staff from that unit. The NGO was to function as part and parcel of the extension system. Besides providing the extension services, the NGO was to implement all agricultural development programmes of the department. The NGO was also to share not less than 20 per cent of the costs in the first year, with the amount to be progressively increased to 50 per cent over the next two to three years. The NGO was supposed to charge the remaining part of their costs to the farmers for the services rendered. It was presumed that the farmers would be willing to pay for those costs if they were getting good quality economic services.

The concept was initially found to be quite impractical both by NGOs and government implementing agencies. The NGOs found themselves unwilling to take over wholesale responsibility for extension and charge farmers even a small percentage of the costs. However, the government persisted with the proposal and eventually found an NGO willing to work with the approach. More NGOs have since joined.

Benefits from collaboration

One of the most notable potential impacts of NGO–government collaboration is that it allows extension institutions to avoid duplicated efforts in the field. But do the potential savings justify the cost, time and effort invested in establishing effective collaborative linkages and trying to make them work? Does (or can) collaboration lead to greater impact than separate government and NGO initiatives? And is eliminating such duplication in fact desirable? (see Garforth's comments on creating a market for extension services in Chapter 3).

This section focuses on the institutional benefits of collaboration. The field-level benefits are covered in Chapter 12.

In the Bac Thai extension programme in Vietnam, Nguyen Kim Hai explains that a significant impact has been reached: a provincial extension policy, the first of its kind in Vietnam. Additionally, it is interesting to note that the continuation of the collaborative effort was guaranteed when the government partner requested further assistance from CIDSE.

Provincial extension policy in Bac Thai, Vietnam (Nguyen Kim Hai)
After two years of the programme of co-operation between CIDSE and Bac Thai province in extension work, the extension staff at all levels raised the need for further support. However, it was felt that some issues needed to be clarified prior to continued programme planning. Based on its experience in Thailand, CIDSE staff generated a discussion of these issues by raising several questions at a two-day internal evaluation workshop:

o What direction should the extension system in Bac Thai take? This question relates to the fact that the recently established national extension service, together with more and more incoming commercial firms, would like to use the extension system for their top-down package programmes. Is this desirable?

o Who are or should be the beneficiaries/clients of the extension system. If the poor, how to make time, funds and staff available? And if the poor, what extension methodology should be followed?

o How will the extension programme function if forestry and agricultural extension workers work separately with the farmers? How can 40 forestry extension workers work efficiently when they have to cover 158 communes?

o If participatory rural appraisal forms the basis of the farmer-based approach and the appraisals are carried out in teams, should the inter-communal centres be the smallest unit from which teams of extension workers operate?

o What are the roles and duties of the different levels in the extension system, from individual extension workers to the provincial extension programme steering committee?

Regular discussions with provincial policy makers, who consulted with district extension staff and extension workers, resulted in a consensus: to establish a provincial extension policy to which those major questions could be referred, at the same time providing options for a clearer direction.

Provincial extension policy. As a result of the internal evaluation workshop and the following rounds of discussion, various issues were prepared to be included in a provincial extension policy, to be formulated by the provincial People's Committee. In August 1994, when these policy preparations were completed, a further two-day workshop was organized for all staff concerned, to refine and discuss the newly formulated direction of the extension system.

With this extension policy formulation — unique for a province in Vietnam — the farmer-based methodology is much better anchored and better focused on poor farmers and ethnic minorities. At the same time as the policy was decreed, the provincial extension working group formally became the acting body for extension, and recently the Extension Centre has become a more independent sub-department under the Agricultural Department. This implies that the daily decision making, planning and implementation in the extension system will now be done by more staff involved at district and provincial level.

Although they do not mention concrete gains, Shinde and Rangnekar of the BAIF Development Research Foundation, among the oldest and largest Indian NGOs, discuss some of the activities which have prompted improved collaboration between NGOs and government agencies working in Rajasthan. Although BAIF has a historical technical focus on livestock development, the collaborative work in Rajasthan embraced a number of wider issues, including water resources development, crop improvement and pest control. The 'change in attitude and approach of officials of various organizations' mentioned, while sometimes difficult to measure, is the foundation on which further collaboration can be based.

Benefits of collaboration in Rajasthan (Shinde and Rangnekar)

Promoting interaction between various agencies has been one of the endeavours of BAIF wherever it is involved. Success in promoting interaction in Udaipur has been outstanding in view of the pro-active role of the Ford Foundation and the positive response from government departments, NGOs, the University of Agriculture, and others. NGOs and government agencies involved in agriculture, education, environment, and awareness-related activities in and around the project areas were identified and contacts were established. Joint meetings were arranged between NGOs, government agencies and farmers as a way to develop understanding and collaboration. Most of the NGOs and some of the government agencies responded favourably; for example, the extension units of the state agriculture department actively participated in discussions, and development and training activities; and the state agriculture university arranged field trials, as well as promoted interaction between various agencies. The Rajasthan state government has also taken the initiative in promoting NGO involvement, and has developed mechanisms to promote NGO participation.

126

The zonal agricultural research committee at Udaipur is one of the few in the country in which NGOs are invited to participate and make suggestions.

Orientation and training programmes for the staff of BAIF and other organizations were arranged to promote interaction among various agencies and adoption of participatory and systems approaches for development planning and field research. These learning opportunities involved representatives from various NGOs, government agencies, and the agricultural university. The impact of these workshops has been very positive, as can be seen in the form of a change in the attitude and approach of officials of various organizations.

Problems encountered in collaboration

Although benefits have resulted from NGO–government collaboration, problems persist. It is an uneasy partnership which in many cases is still built around a lack of trust and deep suspicion on both sides. Difficulties over ownership and control of individual (or joint) resources often remain an obstacle. Differing institutional agendas may prevent collaboration from being based upon a shared vision and common objectives. Government agencies may wish to implement change more rapidly than NGOs feel is sustainable.

We begin this section with a brief, but important, comment from Nguyen Kim Hai that emphasizes a basic tenet of NGO–government collaborative efforts and the opposing perspectives and priorities of the two different types of institutions.

Taking a long-term view in Vietnam (Nguyen Kim Hai)
It should be stressed that for the sake of sustainability the extension programme had to be slowed down several times and made less ambitious, because of its aim to build involvement in extension at the grassroots level, rather than to work by directly relieving the sufferings of the target poor. This also means that the results should not only be measured during the life of the project itself, but from the longer-term results as well.

Sharda and Ballabh raise a number of key issues from their collaborative experiences with NGOs in Rajasthan. A very unsettling distinction arises between 'process' — which is an important tenet of the approaches used by NGOs — and the 'impact' or 'outcome' — which usually drives government extension efforts.

Problems in collaboration in Rajasthan (Sharda and Ballabh)
Recent discussion about the collaborative work undertaken has raised several issues. The first relates to the 'contracting' arrangement inherent in all collaborative activities. The collaborating NGOs fear that increased collaboration would actually mean their having to manage field-level government activities. While collaboration would prevent parallel services by phasing out government services in collaborative areas, it would also prevent the NGOs from carrying out their core task: that of contacting and motivating groups.

There is also a feeling that a large number of ills in the government system are political in nature and would hence take sustained efforts to resolve. Because they are large, the participating NGOs find it easier to undertake these activities themselves, rather than trying to improve the government system. This 'do-it-yourself' attitude might also be due to the fact that Udaipur district has a very large number of NGOs which are competing for the attention of a limited number of communities.

127

The attempts at collaboration have also been confined to the top levels of the government agencies and the NGOs. Instead of making government facilities more accessible to the communities directly, these attempts have introduced another level in their interactions with the formal extension system. The collaborative efforts are also extremely person-dependent, and no systematic solutions have been found to date.

The second issue relates to the balance that has to be achieved between the expressed needs of the farmers and the technical advice given by the research and extension departments. Improved varieties of maize, which promise good results under erratic rainfall, have been rejected by farmers, apparently on the basis of taste. The NGOs demand need-based efforts from the government agencies, whereas the government agencies ask the NGOs to promote new technologies which are technically more appropriate for the region. The government agencies feel that this increased emphasis on *expressed* needs of the farmers by the NGOs, at times, obscures the farmers' *real* needs...

The participation of small NGOs in these collaborative efforts has been negligible. The participants in the KVK forum and the collaborative work are the large NGOs who have resources and the staff to implement programmes alone. The small, resource-poor NGOs have not participated at all — even though they stand to gain the most from these initiatives. There are also very few examples of NGO–NGO collaboration, despite, or because of, the common roots of most NGOs in the district.

Outlining the government perspective of the collaborative work in Rajasthan, Garg highlights the critical dimension of how collaboration is perceived from within the 'formal' extension service providers — those who have traditionally been at the forefront of government extension efforts. He emphasizes the key issue of control over the extension process and its accompanying systems: will it continue to be in the hands of state and national governments, or will it increasingly come under the decision-making domain of local communities, farmers groups and farmers themselves?

Extension workers' perceptions of collaboration in Rajasthan (Garg)

The further extension of the concept shall depend upon the ability of these few pioneering NGOs to deliver much better information than the stock governmental functionaries and create public demand for them. That is not going to be easy. The (extension) establishment has already started getting 'worked up'. The agriculture supervisors' (i.e., village extension workers') association has filed a protest, and the public representatives (i.e., certain politicians) have also commented against the arrangement. However, the government is taking necessary steps to allay their fears and remove apprehensions. The supervisors' association was invited for discussions and the concept was explained to them in detail. These fears are perhaps rooted in the possibility of the concept gaining momentum and affecting their interests (which they are currently enjoying from a monopolistic position). The government has also decided to watch the results of experiments and allow the extension workers to see the alternative approach working.

In their description of two government-initiated research/extension projects in Andhra Pradesh in India — an alternative pest control programme for red hairy caterpillar, and a tank-conversion programme — Sanghi, Kanda and Dayal point out the costs associated with NGO–government collaboration. Many of the successful process-oriented methodologies require resources that are scarce, or which compete for other uses (e.g., because they require more extension staff).

Costs of collaboration in Andhra Pradesh (Sanghi, Kanda and Dayal)

The extension of group-based technologies (such as the conversion of irrigation tanks to function as storage reservoirs to raise the water table and permit more efficient pumped irrigation) requires social skills to ensure that the necessary group actions associated with the technological intervention are accomplished. The availability of such skills is relatively better with NGOs. Hence, there is a need to explore new institutional arrangements in which government agencies and NGOs can work as equal partners, and to ensure that the necessary financial resources will be provided for meeting the administrative expenses of the participating NGO.

Farmer-led extension approaches require financial resources: for example for the organization of exposure visits, honoraria for resource farmers, village animators, cultural groups, facilitation of group discussions, etc. Presently, under government-sector programmes these items are not generally approved for expenditure, with the result that field staff hesitate to implement them even though they are convinced of their effectiveness. Hence, proper provision should be made to meet these requirements.

In describing the FarmAfrica goat project in Ethiopia, Peacock (see above) presents a similar perspective, but wonders if, given current realities, governments will in fact be able to provide resources for such intensive extension approaches. She argues that other forces, such as regionalization or decentralization, may provide support to farmer-farmer extension initiatives.

While collaboration led to field-level impact in the IPM work in Thailand, Ishii-Eitemann and Kaophong rightly point out a more difficult task: getting NGOs and government agencies to undertake collaboration as a programme strategy. NGO–government collaboration can be realized for definite, short-term activities, but larger barriers and suspicions between the two types of institutions may prohibit true collaboration on a sustained basis.

Different styles in Thailand (Ishii-Eitemann and Kaophong)

While the participating farmers demonstrated a clear ability to weigh the diverse and complex agro-ecological ideas exchanged throughout the training, facilitating the collaboration between local and international NGOs, government trainers and researchers proved, ironically, to be the most challenging aspect of the entire exercise. Among the participating NGOs, none had worked this intensively over an extended period of time together and, naturally, differences in working styles, personal and organizational values, commitment and approaches to inter-agency collaboration emerged, often pulling the training in multiple directions. Communication between the more ideologically oriented non-governmental groups, the more practical-minded of the development workers and extensionists, and specialists from the more conventional research and development institutions was not always successful either. Some NGOs indicated that they had joined the IPM Working Group in order to acquire specific technical skills, but were far less interested in building long-term relationships with the participating government agencies. Responsibilities in facilitating the progress of the training over five months and in holding the disparate group of strong-minded individuals together were not equally shared, with the result that some organizers felt overly tired at the training's end, while others explained that in their initial commitment to organizing an IPM training they had not realized that the process of partnering would itself need so much patience and conscious nurturing.

At the institutional level, the participating NGOs expressed satisfaction with their increased technical knowledge, but did not initially appear interested in continuing the inter-agency collaboration beyond the duration of the IPM training itself. While the participating NGOs, researchers and government extensionists had significantly deepened their understanding of and respect for each other as individuals, the longer-term goal of establishing self-sustaining NGO–government partnerships appeared far from realization.

Lessons learned from collaboration

While the collaborative strategies used and the activities undertaken vary, several common lessons seem to emerge from the cases cited in this chapter.

o Farmers can be very active partners in extension and can set an agenda and direct a process in which government agencies and NGOs can participate to meet the needs of the farmers and their communities.
o Whatever extension approach is used, it should ensure that farmers are encouraged to share their experiences with others.
o Collaboration between government agencies and NGOs is usually more difficult than originally thought.
o Despite this, benefits (sometimes quite significant) can be achieved.
o During the process of collaboration, stereotypical views held by one group of the other partner can be broken down, even if quite slowly.
o It is important to get the agenda and parameters of collaboration right at the outset.

Nguyen Kim Hai focuses on some human and institutional requirements necessary to facilitate NGO–government collaboration within the context of farmer-led extension.

Guidelines and lessons on collaboration in Vietnam (Nguyen Kim Hai)

o For any intervention to be successfully institutionalized, there must be a certain level of commitment to the programme from local extension authorities and in particular from the province. This commitment must result in the provision of sufficient and skilled staff for the programme to be realistic.
o Co-operation must be based on mutual understanding of the problems and mutual social commitment, i.e., support for resource-poor farm families.
o Extension staff and outsiders can only assist, but the local people need to do the work. CIDSE considers that there are no CIDSE extension programmes or projects in Vietnam; there are only programmes and projects supported by CIDSE.
o The involvement of existing (suitable) institutions in extension work should be maximized, rather than creating a new system from scratch.
o Investment in human resources and institution building is important. It takes time and requires high investment, but it is an important and decisive factor for the sustainability of a programme or project.
o Bottom-up methods and approaches used in extension work should be developed to provide better tools for targeting farmers, monitoring the effectiveness of such target-

ing, and assessing the impact of the extension programme on the livelihoods of the target group.

o An extension system should encourage farmers to communicate among themselves in order to identify and analyse their problems, prioritize them and find solutions. The project activities should be mainly implemented by farmers' interest groups.

o The role of the extension worker is very important. Time is needed to develop this role and change old ways of thinking. It is important to pay continued attention to their incentives. If these are too low they cannot be expected to work effectively. However, types of incentives should be many, varying from 'feeling welcome at farmers houses,' to the size of their salary.

o Start on a small scale; then if successful, expand later.

Although the larger goal of constant NGO–government collaboration has not yet been achieved, Ishii-Eitemann and Kaophong explain that significant gains and lessons have already been realized from the collaboration between Save the Children and the public sector in Thailand.

Lessons learned in Thailand (Ishii-Eitemann and Kaophong)

The five-month exercise in 1994 in inter-agency collaboration yielded a rich set of experiences regarding both the enormous benefits of working together and the challenges and difficulties in communicating creatively across traditional institutional barriers.

The field-orientation and 'organized flexibility' of the working group proved successful approaches to fulfilling the educational goals of the training. Farmers themselves shaped the evolution of the training's structure and direction, and were central decision-makers regarding the content of the curriculum and the ecological questions posed in field studies they designed, with the technical assistance of training support staff. While the initial outline was based upon the successful farmer field school IPM programme developed by FAO in the Philippines and Indonesia, and partially tested in some parts of Thailand, the actual curriculum continually evolved to meet the needs, interests and field problems encountered by farmers in their own villages. While ecological pest management provided the framework for posing ecological questions, subsequent discussions and field exercises embraced wider agricultural issues of soil fertility, organic nutrient inputs, rice growth and development, natural farming, weed management, mulching and intercropping. In group evaluations, farmers emphasized that the enquiry-based learning approach enabled them to better understand the ecological interactions taking place in their fields, and therefore increased their confidence in experimenting and resolving problems on their own.

The Department of Agricultural Extension provided a dedicated and enthusiastic trainer, who was invaluable to the success of the training. The trainer easily established a close rapport with both farmers and NGO staff alike, disproving the common assumption among NGOs that governments are necessarily part of the problem. NGOs learned that government officers can be strong allies in promoting ecological agriculture, and may be very willing to share their technical expertise in a meaningful way. At the same time, the extensionist learned that the 'NGO community' is not a homogeneous one, always in conflict with government, but is rich in diversity and contains potential supporters and partners. Much work remains, however, for those individuals who took part in the exercise to convince their own institutions of the merits of such collaborative efforts.

One lesson learned was the need for greater clarity in the initial stages of organizing intensive inter-agency collaborations. This should include frank group discussion by participating organizations about the degree of commitment and explicit roles and responsibilities which they expect of themselves, of their partners, and of the collaborative process itself. While loose interactions such as those commonly found in information networks do not always require closely shared vision and goals for the network to function, the more intensive, even intimate, nature of long-term collaboration often does.

11 Other approaches to farmer-led extension

VARIOUS OTHER APPROACHES to farmer-led extension have been experimented with. This chapter describes five:

o supporting farmers' research (a fish cage-culture project in Bangladesh)
o limiting external inputs to facilitation only (a food-security project in Zimbabwe)
o helping farmers access information from various sources (a horticultural project in Egypt)
o a combination of institution-based training and farmer-based approaches (hybrid rice production in India)
o providing training in specific techniques to farmers, who then provide these services to other farmers for a fee (community agricultural workers in Nepal).

Some of these are adaptations of, or borrow from, the approaches described in earlier chapters. The fish cage-culture project in Bangladesh, for example, has much in common with the farmer field schools described in Chapter 8. The projects in Zimbabwe and Egypt share features of the problem census/problem solving methodology described in Chapter 9. The rice production project in India, though based in a government institute, is inspired in part by farmer-led approaches. Nevertheless, there are sufficient differences to warrant a separate chapter for this group.

Supporting farmers' research

Similar principles, strategies and methods to those used in the IPM farmer field schools described in Chapter 8 have been adopted by a public-sector aquaculture project in Bangladesh. This project is implemented by the Northwest Fisheries Extension Project (NFEP), supported by the British Department for International Development (DFID) and CARE. It is particularly interesting because it was initiated by a female Bangladeshi farmer, and CARE has studied the learning processes involved very closely. It also encapsulates another strategy adopted by some public-sector agencies in a bid to increase the responsiveness of their services to their clients' needs — namely collaboration with NGOs. The strategy of public-sector collaboration with NGOs is discussed in more detail in Chapter 10.

The project, described below by Kamp, involved 50 women — all poor, illiterate, and without income-generating opportunities. Neither they nor their families had any experience in aquaculture. While they lived next to water bodies, none owned them, so CARE negotiated access on their behalf so they could place fish cages in the water.

Teaching the teacher to fish in Bangladesh (Kamp)

Background and context. Cage culture of fish is practised in many countries in Asia and other parts of the world, but not currently in Bangladesh. The initiative for the trials in this study came from a woman whose husband was involved in CARE's IPM programme for rice, which incorporated the culturing of fish in rice fields. One day her son brought some live fish from their rice fields for her to cook. Feeling sorry for the fish, she refused to kill them and instead placed them in a clay pot and fed them each day. After some time she noticed that the fish were growing. She became interested in the potential for cultivating fish in confined areas and approached the CARE staff working with her husband to provide her with support and guidance. After discussions with her and a few of her interested neighbours, it was decided that a small group of women would experiment with cage culture with the support of CARE and NFEP. Subsequently, three other groups in different villages were also formed to experiment with cage culture of fish.

Cages were built using nylon fish netting purchased in a market in Dhaka and were attached to a bamboo framework which could be placed in the water. The cages were approximately four feet (1.3m) wide, six feet (2m) long, and six feet (2m) high, and were placed in the water so that the bamboo structure was firmly in the mud with the cage material suspended in the water...

Origins of the approach. At the time that the cage culture trials were being facilitated, CARE was gaining considerable experience in implementing action learning approaches through an integrated pest management programme for rice, based on FAO's Asian model. The basic approach involved facilitating an experiment or activity in a rice field with a group of 20 farmers (sub-divided into smaller groups), and providing them with the opportunity to discuss and validate what they observed, reflect on how what they learned fitted in with their existing knowledge, and finally to plan to use this new knowledge in a practical way on their farms. CARE's strategy was to provide opportunities for farmers to gain an understanding of basic concepts from which, together, they could develop appropriate practices, which would vary considerably from farmer to farmer.

In contrast, NFEP had considerable experience in aquaculture extension using fairly traditional approaches. Their strategy was to teach farmers the most appropriate practices for cultivating fish, ensuring that the farmers remembered the practice — the same practice — correctly. There were obvious significant differences between the two approaches, both philosophically and operationally. Sometimes these differences between CARE's and NFEP's approaches led to considerable friendly 'dialogue'.

From the start, the training for the women involved in cage culture would best be termed the 'NFEP approach'. Women followed the instructions they were given regarding stocking rates, species composition and feeding. In fact, NFEP provided what they considered to be the 'right' fish in the 'right' quantities. CARE worked with the women to develop monitoring systems they could use and understand to record feed inputs and growth rates. After they sold the fish from the first cycle, the women began to make changes.

First, the women changed the species mix. Next they changed the stocking density. They further changed the feed composition and timing, and finally their harvesting strategy. Almost every cage culture practice promoted at the start of the programme was subsequently changed by the participants with remarkable speed.

Once the basics of feeding were understood by the women, they made substantial changes to it. These incorporated seasonal fluctuations in the local availability and price of feed

134

components in relation to growth performance. The women observed which food items the fish ate first, last, and only if they were very hungry. They also had a better idea than the extension staff which food types were easily available and when, their relative costs, and how to access them. They also experimented with simple, short-term preparation techniques, such as silaging, to make foods more palatable.

The women began to sell the larger fish and restock new fingerlings in small increments to replace those fish sold. This, it turns out, conformed to their household needs for a continuous flow of money to meet on-going expenses. This was very different practice from the original advice given to them to sell all their fish at one time once they had got to a certain age. In addition, they harvested fish for home consumption, considerably increasing the frequency and amount of fish eaten by their own families.

Although a polyculture of fish was initially introduced to the participants, in a relatively short period of time the women changed to a monoculture based on the two species of fish most commonly used in cage culture in Southeast Asia: common carp and tilapia. The women also noted differences in growth response of the two species of tilapia available, one being selected and preferred by the women as the faster growing of the two species.

One lesson from the trials was the importance of access to water bodies. In the locations where the pilot activities took place, not one cage is currently active. From discussions with the women, this was found to be as a result of loss of access rather than due to technical reasons. After the pilot project ended the women began to lose access to the water bodies, since they no longer had the support of the project. Within six months from the end of the pilot, they no longer had access to the original areas in which they had placed their cages.

What it was that had enabled the women to learn so fast, attain such high levels of self-confidence that they could ignore the advice of the 'experts' and develop their own effective management strategies for a technology of which they had no previous experience, was of particular interest to all concerned. CARE had experienced this speed of learning and adaptation in its IPM project, but was not expecting it from the cage culture trials. Similarly, NFEP had not experienced such dramatic results in aquaculture extension before.

Impact and evaluation. When it became apparent that the women were developing their own management strategies and that CARE could learn much from their experiences, a new monitoring system was developed. This provided reliable data from participants' experiences on the types and quantities of feed supplied to the fish, fish species, stocking rates, costs, and harvest quantities over a period of one year. Feed preparation, feeding methods and other qualitative data not recorded during the first period of trials were now collected.

To document how the women learned and what affected their management decisions, a focus group session in each area was facilitated with as many cage culture participants as possible. A total of 33 women participated in these sessions... The women unanimously felt that there was no difference between the source of learning and the source of their subsequent management decisions. Ninety-one per cent of participants rated *themselves* the *most important* source of learning and subsequent influence on management decisions. Seventy-six per cent of the participants rated the experiences of *other women* the *second most important* source of learning and management decisions. And finally, 79 per cent of them rated the *extensionist* as the *least important* source of learning and management decisions. Not one of the 33 participants rated the extensionist as the most important source of learning or management influence, in spite of their technical competence.

After a period of reflection on what had happened, discussions with the participants and the ranking exercises, the key elements responsible for the rate of learning and adaptation were identified. Not surprisingly, these mirror the elements which were found to be responsible for rapid learning in the IPM project:

135

o To begin the action-learning process in IPM, an experiment or activity in which the farmers are active participants is facilitated. The expected outcome of the experiment is known to the facilitator, but not the farmers. This process was mirrored with the cage culture participants, except that neither the facilitator nor the women involved knew what the outcome of the experiment would be. The women were fully involved in the experiments, however, including the monitoring of food inputs, timing of feeding, and fish growth. The women learned as much as the staff did and, as it turned out, even more. They were following our experiments and began designing and implementing their own.

o The women were experimenting with cage culture as individuals, but did so in physical clusters of cages where they could not conceal what they were doing from other participants. This meant that not only was each woman able to monitor the experiment she was personally involved in, but she could also monitor the same experiment being done by her neighbours. This provided them with a number of replications from which they could analyse the results and arrive at a more accurate and reliable conclusion. This provided them with a greater sense of self-confidence in their own results.

o The proximity of the cages also allowed women to monitor and evaluate the impact of experiments designed and carried out by their neighbours, even those that they did not try themselves. They could easily adopt practices which seemed to have a positive impact on fish growth and profitability, or verify the practice in their own cages.

o Initially women were brought together as a group to teach them about cage culture. When it was realized that little was being learned from the staff after the initial period, the meetings were continued but their purpose changed. Now the women were brought together to discuss what they had done and what the impact had been on fish growth. This served to reinforce and disperse the learning which had taken place, something considered to be of critical importance since Bangladeshi farmers do not generally give up their cultivation secrets to others, often not even to family members. But they do love to talk and, in the artificial environment created in a group setting, the most tight-lipped farmer soon begins to provide the details of his or her secrets of success. During these sessions the women discussed what happened and why they thought it happened.

o Group settings also provided an opportunity for the extensionist to validate individual and group observations with scientific knowledge. If the group came to mistaken conclusions, the extensionist could attempt to get them to reconsider the results, try the experiment in a different way, or plan new experiments. In the group setting, self-confidence was boosted and the women gained respect from their peers.

o Finally, these meetings provided the participants with opportunities to plan their subsequent activities based on what they themselves and their neighbours had learned, given the limitations and goals of their specific households. The meetings also provided an opportunity for the extensionist to 'endorse' their plans. This again resulted in greater self-confidence.

Guidelines and lessons. CARE's experiences with the women involved in this project provided insights into extension approaches which have broad implications:

o A focus should be placed on the role of the extensionist as a *catalyst* for learning, rather than a source of technical expertise. This is not to say that such expertise is not important, but the dynamics involved in learning appear to be a more limiting factor to technology transfer than the technical competence of staff. The experiences suggest a very different role for extensionists than those on which traditional extension systems are based.

o In countries where a culture of sharing knowledge does not exist, as in Bangladesh, extension systems should be planned in such a way that 'technology secrets' are more difficult to conceal. In the case of cage culture, this entailed facilitating experiments in cages in close proximity to each other.

o A greater emphasis on learning the concepts underlying specific practices should be considered in contrast to teaching specific practices. The more specific the practice, the less likely it is to be applicable to a significant number of farmers.

o The value of personal experience as a catalyst and conduit for learning cannot be over-stated. The more this is structured like an experiment, with farmers involved in all the steps, including collection and analysis of data and the development of appropriate management practices, the greater the comprehension, retention, and empowerment effects.

o The concept of 'critical mass' is important to ensure that farmers have a significant number of experiences to monitor and evaluate. Not only does this provide a greater number of experiences on which to base decisions, but also a larger number of opportunities for other farmers to observe similar results, resulting in an enhanced spread effect. An insufficient 'mass' could result in inaccurate conclusions or low adoption rates.

o Working in groups, rather than as individuals, results in the application of a broader range of local knowledge and experiences, better synthesis, and the development of practices applicable to a wider range of household and farm situations.

o An extension organization and its staff can play a critical role beyond the provision of technical expertise or extension. The cage culture project, for example, was made possible by CARE's intervention with owners and leaseholders of water bodies to gain and ensure access for the women involved in the project. An emphasis on providing technical expertise or extension advice alone will not necessarily result in success.

Limiting inputs to facilitation only

The primary role of professional extension and research staff as *facilitators* is seen by many as critical. This principle has been put clearly into practice in a project in Zimbabwe supported by the Intermediate Technology Development Group (ITDG) in collaboration with two government organizations: the agricultural extension service and the Department of Research and Specialist Services.

Unusually for development projects, this project offers farmers nothing, except a member of staff whose only job is to help farmers solve their own problems. This project provides important insights into the possibilities and potentials posed by facilitation and is a particularly good example of what can be done once farmers' needs and priorities have been agreed upon. It raises the question of whether all extension officers, whether public or NGO, should focus solely on facilitating farmers' efforts to resolve their own problems. The project is described below by Murwira, Vela, Bungu and Mapepa.

The Chivi Food Security Project in Zimbabwe (Murwira et al.)

In 1991 a project officer was hired to initiate the food security project in Chivi District. The ambition of the project has always remained that of realizing the potential of the community to identify and manage their own development. This includes making better use of the public services available to them and influencing inappropriate inputs so that they better complement what the community is already doing. This means more than enabling farmers to better survive periods of hardship such as the drought of 1991–92. It means catalysing the invisible talents of individuals and community institutions to build strong structures which will raise the communities' productivity and enable them to withstand adversity. The project would be characterized by the following:

o a low input, participatory approach
o building on local knowledge
o community leadership
o an absence of material support, including food-for-work programmes
o an absence of free inputs.

The project would only facilitate development through a process of unlocking the potential of the community to help itself and through linking the community with sources of training and technical expertise. The project had the following objectives:

o to help farmers' institutions in identifying their priority needs and strengthening their capacity
o to work with local institutions to identify and develop technological options to solving problems, by building on existing traditional knowledge
o to influence government agricultural policies to take into account the production needs of small-scale farmers, such as the communal farmers in Chivi.

As an initial step the project was introduced to the district authorities. It was, however, very difficult for anybody to explain what the project was all about. The tendency with most NGOs is to define clearly the goal, purpose and nature of activities which they are going to be undertaking before interacting with the community. Sometimes they even go to the extent of defining the period of stay and expected output. Such is the tendency of most projects which develop a paternalistic attitude and prescriptive solutions to people's problems and would normally treat people as objects of poverty. The project, in line with its objectives, felt that it was up to the community to identify its priority needs and develop appropriate solutions for the same. ITDG would act only as a facilitator.

The project conducted a survey of local institutions, which identified such players as traditional leaders, farmers' clubs and garden groups. A wealth-ranking study of all households in the project area (Ward 21 of Chivi District) was then done by village residents, and two of the poorest villages were selected for further activities. Murwira *et al.* describe the method used for wealth ranking, and then how this information was used to develop a list of needs and design extension approaches.

Chivi project implementation (Murwira et al.)
Wealth ranking. The purpose of the wealth-ranking study was to provide the organization with information about the poverty or wealth status of every household in the community. Such information would assist in the selection of a sample for the household needs survey, as it would be easier to pick samples from various wealth ranks within the community.

To conduct the wealth-ranking study, four or five members in a village who had knowledge about every household in their village, were selected to rank each household in their village according to its level of poverty or wealth. Each of the selected rankers was asked to do the ranking privately to avoid influencing each other. Selected rankers preferably included both

Table 11.1: Wealth ranks of households identified by villagers in the Chivi Food Security Project, Zimbabwe

Rank	All households		Female-headed households (12% of total)	
	No.	%	No.	%
1	282	24	1	1
2	334	28	22	16
3	339	29	57	42
4	229	19	56	41
Total	1184	100	136	100

men and women. At the end of each ranking, the ranker was asked to share the characteristics of households in each wealth rank category.

The results of the wealth-ranking study are shown in Tables 11.1 and 11.2. They show that 41 per cent of the households headed by women were among the poorest group.

Samples for the needs-assessment survey are usually taken from the bottom wealth ranks to ensure that the identified needs do not become biased in favour of those in the top wealth ranks. The wealth-ranking information can also be used as a monitoring tool during the implementation of the project. For example, project staff can use the information to check whether the poor members of the community are being elected to leadership positions, involved in decision-making processes, and are actively involved in project activities; and to ensure that the activities of the project are having a positive impact on the lives of the poor.

Needs-assessment survey. Using the wealth-ranking information, a needs-assessment survey was carried out in two of the poorest villages in the ward. The results of both the institutional survey and needs-assessment survey were shared with the community at an open meeting. The community leadership confirmed the findings. During the feedback meeting, the community selected two villages to initiate the work, and farmers' clubs and garden groups were selected to become institutional bases for the work.

Planning meeting. Farmers' clubs and garden groups in Ward 21 had a three-day planning workshop. They prioritized their needs as shown in Table 11.3.

Responding to prioritized needs. In early 1992 the project undertook the process of responding to prioritized needs. Two issues took a major priority after thorough analysis, that is the water problem and the need to strengthen the capacity of the groups. 'Training for transformation' was identified as one of the tools for strengthening local groups and empowering them to tackle their problems on a self-reliant basis.

With regard to the problem of water for both field cropping and garden activities, the project began by investigating traditional or local practices of soil and water conservation. The advantages and disadvantages of each technique were examined by ITDG staff and the farmers together. Both farmer and gardener representatives were exposed to techniques being used in similar geographical areas. The representatives were selected by the farmers themselves. The following areas were visited:

Table 11.2: Wealth characteristics of households in the Chivi Food Security Project, Zimbabwe

Wealth rank 1 households

- have a reliable monthly income (i.e., salary or pension)
- have savings in form of either cash or food
- have adequate draught power — cattle or donkeys and implements (scotch cart, wheelbarrow and plough)
- have well-built homes (asbestos roofing or metal sheets and brick walls plastered with cement mortar) with enough rooms to provide decent accommodation for at least two visitors
- are self-reliant and self-sufficient in terms of food production, and usually have surplus food to sell at the end of each cropping season
- can afford to send their children to secondary schools with boarding facilities
- have almost everything at their disposal to create wealth
- may cultivate with tractors at times.

Wealth rank 2 households

- have reasonable draught power
- have some assistance provided by children at work
- are usually self-sufficient, but may not have surplus food for sale
- have adequate shelter or good homesteads, which may not necessarily be roofed with iron or asbestos sheets
- can afford sending children to secondary school.

Wealth rank 3 households

- are capable of producing only enough food for themselves
- donkeys usually dominate in the provision of draught power
- homes or houses are generally poor and sometimes inadequate to accommodate all residents decently
- in terms of education, their children may only go as far as the seventh grade
- many members in this group are widows who struggle to survive
- frequently offer their services as casual hired labour to earn income
- family sizes are usually large.

Wealth rank 4 households

- lack of draught power
- mostly school leavers, widows and aged, also disabled people
- can hardly make ends meet
- usually have one hut
- usually survive on handouts
- rely also on wild fruits such as *marula* nuts
- sometimes can be described as assetless or destitute.

Table 11.3: Farmers' and gardeners' priority needs, Chivi Food Security Project, Zimbabwe

Farmers	Gardeners
1. Insufficient water	Insufficient water
2. Insufficient draught power	Pest management
3. Lack of suitable seed varieties	Fencing for the gardens
4. Lack of co-operation	Poor crop diversity
5. Lack of farming knowledge and skills	Lack of farming knowledge and skills
6. Increasing landlessness	Lack of co-operation
7.	Poor access to inputs

o Two local research stations (Chiredzi and Makoholi). Farmers were exposed to the work on no-till tied ridges, sub-surface irrigation using home-made clay pipes and pots, *fanya juus*, mulch ripping and half-moon ridges.
o Individual innovative farmers. Farmers were exposed to the work on infiltration pits and rainwater harvesting using reservoirs, guttering and rock catchment methods.
o Fambidzanai Training Centre. Farmers were exposed to the use of plastics, inverted bottles and mulching.

Feedback. At the end of the exposure visits the representatives gave feedback to the rest of the community on the techniques they had seen. The community from the two villages selected the techniques which they wanted to test in their own area. They also discussed who was going to do the testing.

Monitoring and evaluation. During the testing period farmers continued to monitor progress with each technique. At the end of each cropping season the techniques being tested were reviewed. Those which did not perform well were either rejected or modified to improve their performance and suitability for solving the water crisis.

Extension approaches. A similar process was followed in response to all other prioritized needs, and the same approach has been used in the remaining four villages of Ward 21. It has also been replicated in Ward 4 by the extension worker in that area. Training for transformation, participatory rural appraisal, etc., have continued to be used as tools for strengthening local farmer communities in:

o identifying and developing appropriate solutions to their own problems
o actively participating in decision-making processes
o owning and controlling their productive resources
o putting in place structures for dealing with any issues which may arise from time to time
o developing capacity to plan, implement and evaluate their activities
o building confidence to be able to:

• articulate their needs, especially with service providers (i.e., creating a demand structure)
• experiment with innovations and new technologies, even though they may not yet have been scientifically proven
• spread knowledge on a farmer-to-farmer basis
• influence policy in their favour.

141

Helping farmers to access information

Farouk and Worsley write about a project in Egypt supported by CARE, in which the objective is also to support farmers' own research, but the type of intervention could be described as minimalist. This is not to understate the enormous effort put into the project by the development agency, but to highlight the range of interventions that are being tried in pursuit of supporting farmers' own research. In some sense, this project can be seen as holding a position at the opposite end of a spectrum from farmer field schools, where staff inputs are highly intensive. The CARE–Egypt project is interesting not only because it represents an innovative means of supporting farmer research, but also because it offers a possible means of reducing the intensity of external agency input and thereby enabling greater breadth of support. However, the authors do note that there are limits on the degree to which farmers can be relied on alone as the agents of methodological spread.

The CARE–Egypt FarmLink project (Farouk and Worsley)

Project overview. FarmLink is a farmer-participatory agricultural extension project that works to increase the economic output of 8000 small farmers' horticultural production. Through a participatory analysis process held in each project village, small farmers can articulate their needs. Based on these, FarmLink searches for sources of information that can provide answers, and connects farmers to these sources. Community-selected innovative farmers are invited to visit these sources at the expense of the project. Through discussion and demonstration, sources of information and farmers can share experiences, information and materials. The project refers to these visits as 'links'. After a series of links, innovative farmers can select technologies and ideas that best meet the conditions of their village, resource base, experience and needs. On returning home, the farmers actively try out new ideas on a small scale. Successful innovations at the experimental stage are rapidly adopted to become normal practice. Since technologies adopted in this way are selected on the basis of village needs, they are germane to the needs of neighbouring farmers. Once established in the fields of the innovative farmers, other farmers rapidly follow suit.

In April 1993, the CARE Egypt FarmLink Project started to work in Abou Taha hamlet of Menshat Demmo village, in the Fayoum Governorate of Upper Egypt. Having established permission from the village authorities and the agricultural co-operative, the CARE agricultural extension officer, Muhammad Farid, held a farmer's meeting. Hishem Muhammad Ali, a farmer with only 1.6 hectares of land, was one of those who attended. It was made clear at this first meeting that FarmLink was not going to give away any inputs. Many farmers consequently lost interest at this stage. The extension officer explained how FarmLink could help farmers to see up-to-date horticultural crop technologies and marketing strategies.

The following week, a workshop for all interested farmers was held in the village. Everyone had their own agenda. The village leader wanted to know about specific issues that related only to him, but the rest had more basic needs. The extension officer invited the assembled farmers to draw different diagrams to explain their farming systems. Hishem and his colleagues drew a map of the agricultural land and time diagrams to show how various things changed with time. This was the first time that anyone outside the village had asked farmers about their needs. After everyone was satisfied that they all had a common understanding of the community farming system, the extension officer introduced some new methodologies. Using different ranking tools, the assembled farmers ranked their

142

horticultural needs by crop. Some farmers were particularly interested in cantaloupe cultivation and others in cowpea. Farmers were then divided into groups according to their selected crop. Hishem opted to join the cowpea group, since this was a crop that he grew, but from which he could not get good yields.

The cowpea group met again with the FarmLink extension officer and used a series of flow diagrams to identify where problems were occurring and where opportunities were available. The group identified poor seed quality, lack of knowledge of correct irrigation and fertilizer regimes, and little understanding of different planting methods. In addition, the cowpea group was asked to select some delegates to participate in the project on behalf of the group. Using a modified wealth-ranking methodology, the farmers identified criteria that described an innovative farmer and a traditional, conservative farmer. Key village members were asked to rank the names of the farmers in the cowpea group according to the defined criteria. Hishem's name was placed close to the 'innovative' end of the scale. He and several other farmers were therefore selected to be part of the linking programme.

During the next two weeks, the extension officer worked with the FarmLink technical resource specialist to identify sources of information that could provide the needed information about cowpeas. Through communication with the Ministry of Agriculture and other agricultural organizations in Egypt, three sources were found. These were the Kanater Research Institute in the southern tip of the Egyptian delta, an experimental farm associated with this institute, and the Vegetable Research Institute in Cairo. Transportation was arranged and towards the end of June, a group of 16 farmers was taken to visit these sources of information. During their visit, they were exposed to a range of new varieties, fertilizer systems, irrigation methods and planting regimes.

On returning to his village, Hishem Muhammad Ali decided to purchase enough seed of a variety of cowpea called Karim #7 to plant an area of 525m^2. He had seen this in the fields of the Kanater experimental farm, and had learnt from researchers how to grow it. The yield he obtained from this improved seed was twice that he normally obtained, and twice the yield of his neighbours' cowpeas. When it was time to sell the crop, Hishem tried to send his cowpeas to the market. His neighbours insisted that they be allowed to buy his crop to use as seed for the next season. As a result, the entire crop was retained in the village for this purpose. Given his success with new cowpea technologies (variety, fertilizer, irrigation and plant spacing) the FarmLink project used Hishem as a source of information for a link visit by seven innovative farmers from another village. These farmers, equally impressed by his results, pressed Hishem for seed. Unable to supply any more, he directed them back to the research station at Giza. These farmers proceeded to purchase seed from this source, and to test Karim #7 in their own fields.

In addition to these knock-on effects, Hishem passed on information to another three farmers in his village who also adopted the new variety and associated husbandry technologies. Through one farmer therefore, many others in the Abou Taha hamlet have increased their yields and income. When asked how the FarmLink project had benefited him, one innovative farmer from Sohag said: 'Before the project came to my village, I was blind to the opportunities available in other parts of the country. Now, the scales have dropped from my eyes. If I need more information, I am now able to seek it myself.'

Project methodology. The paradigm used by the FarmLink project is popularly known as the 'farmer first' approach. Figure 11.1 represents how this has been incorporated into the project. When farm households address problems in their farming systems, there is a naturally occurring cycle of events. Individual farm households identify their own needs through a growing awareness of a problem or opportunity that faces a household. If this problem/ opportunity is perceived as important enough to warrant attention, the farmer begins to show interest in one or more possibilities that might answer the need. Once these possibilities have been identified, the individual makes a mental evaluation of them and, if there are potential solutions, provisionally selects one or more to test. Through the testing of an innovation, farmers tend to adapt it to meet their individual needs and resources and if successful, finally adopt it into the farming system.

FarmLink recognizes the inherent knowledge and skills of small farmers, and works to enhance their decision-making ability. Through a process of participatory analysis, FarmLink elicits a series of community-identified needs in the horticultural sector. Information sources that can provide answers to these needs are then sought. Community-selected innovative farmers are taken to visit these sources of information. This interaction leads to an exchange of ideas, and farmers are able to see new and improved technologies for themselves. Having gone through this experience, farmers are observed to test one or more innovations before finally adopting them into their farming systems. FarmLink staff conduct periodic follow-up visits to assess the way in which new ideas are being incorporated into the systems of linked farmers and their neighbours.

In a changing economic environment where the farming community has to adapt to survive, there are individuals who have independently sought and found new ways to manage their farming activities. Most of these farmers are located in the Northern Delta region of Egypt. It is in this region that the government has its major research and development centres, where many new technologies have been tested and introduced into the surrounding farming communities.

Within Egypt there are many sources of agricultural knowledge. Ranging from government and private research stations, through traders and skilled farmers, these resources remain relatively untapped. In the north of the country, farmers who have exploited the opportunity created by liberalization in the horticultural sector to establish large farms on new, reclaimed

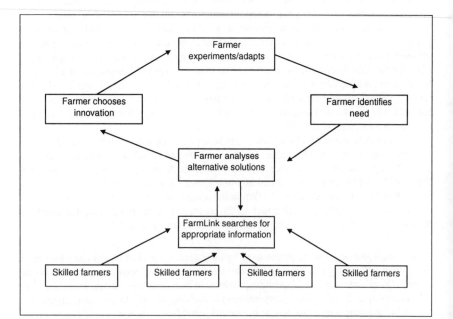

Figure 11.1: Schematic diagram of the FarmLink approach

144

desert lands, have imported technologies from around the world and use them to produce high quality fruit and vegetables. New and improved technologies have been adapted to Egyptian climatic conditions and are potentially useful to all farmers. However, few smallholder farmers in Upper Egypt have heard of, let alone seen these technologies.

FarmLink was initiated to help bridge the gap between 'those who want to know' and 'those who know'. Farmers take all the decisions regarding the direction in which they wish to move. The use of farmers as central decision-makers creates a dynamic project. Its life and the changes in its approach over time are now very much governed by the needs of its participants.

Relations with external agents. FarmLink maintains formal relations with the departments of agriculture in each of the two governorates where it works. These relationships work at the level of information sharing and joint action. Information sharing is managed through regular meetings and field trips with department of agriculture members, including participation in field trips. Joint action is managed at the level of access to new villages, establishment of protocol and use of government sources of information. FarmLink maintains no formal relationships with sources of information, but pays many of them according to use. For the future, CARE–Egypt is planning to expand its activities to work more closely with departments of agriculture by introducing an institution-building component.

Impact and evaluation. By the end of March 1995, FarmLink had facilitated access by 1570 innovative farmers to new and improved technologies. The project has involved work with over 24 farmer-selected crops, ranging from annuals to perennial tree crops, and farmers have been linked to 554 sources of information.

Of the 1570 linked innovative farmers, 975 have tested new technologies, 766 have adopted these technologies, and 662 have indicated benefit. The inevitable delay between linking, testing, adoption and benefit means that these figures will rise to approach the total number of innovative farmers linked. The project has targeted 1920 farmers for linking, 20 per cent over and above the number originally intended. This is in recognition of the fact that not all linked innovative farmers will be successful.

Project impact is not only defined by the success of technology transfer to innovative farmers. The diffusion of information and corresponding impact on other farmers is critical. Indications of diffusion are therefore measured regularly. Over the life of the project, 562 innovative farmers have indicated the names of 1762 other farmers who are applying new technologies as a result of the innovative farmers' communication with them. This is a ratio of 1 to 3.14. In other words, on average seven innovative farmers are disseminating innovations to 22 other farmers. If this ratio was applied to the total number of innovative farmers so far linked, the project could claim to have reached about 6500 small farm households. More realistically however, this ratio applied to innovative farmers that have at least tested new technologies, suggests that about 4000 farm households have been reached.

Combining institution-based training and farmer-led extension

It can be very difficult for government extension systems to adopt farmer-led approaches. This section provides an example of how this has been done in a hybrid rice extension project in India implemented by the National Institute of Agricultural Extension Management (MANAGE) in Hyderabad. The editors feel that Arora's description, below, offers a note of optimism in a country (India) whose public-sector agencies have not so far been distinguished by interactive and farmer-participatory approaches to extension. MANAGE's highly innovative approach demonstrates several features from which others could learn:

o a capacity to work productively with other types of organization (a university; an NGO) in ways which few others in India have achieved (see also Chapter 10)
o the involvement of farmers in research, testing and adaptation of a highly specialized technology (hybrid rice seed production)
o an attempt to combine face-to-face, distance learning and mass-media approaches, thus avoiding some of the expense of using face-to-face approaches where not necessary
o a combination of practical, hands-on experience with the latest available communication technologies
o a concern to ensure that all partners in the process find it financially sustainable.

Distance learning for farmers: The MANAGE way (Arora)

The National Institute of Agricultural Extension Management (MANAGE) in Hyderabad is a management training institute set up by the government of India with a mandate to develop new extension management systems and techniques with a view to make them more farmer-responsive and farmer-friendly. In 1994, it was given the responsibility of promoting the concept of distance learning so that a large number of farmers could benefit from it.

In recent years, MANAGE has experimented with an extension approach built around farmers' practical skill upgrading to absorb new technologies. The trained farmers then become resource persons to train other farmers in the new skills as well as act as vehicles for farmer-to-farmer extension.

Background. MANAGE conducted seven experimental training programmes for farmers' skill upgrading with a view to understand the real training needs of farmers, identifying gaps in existing training infrastructure and work out objectives, methodologies, content and duration of farmers' training programmes using distance learning techniques in future. These ranged from IPM for red-hairy caterpillar on castor, to seed production and processing and IPM for root-grub and *Spodoptera* on groundnut.

These programmes revealed

o Mere information about new technology or training in traditional skills does not satisfy farmers. They want new skills related to new technologies.
o Farmers desire practical field training with hands-on experience.
o Farmers are busy and cannot afford to devote more than a day or two at a time for training.
o Once farmers become aware of and motivated to use new technology, they are quite willing to invest their time and resources to acquire the necessary skills and inputs.
o Themes like integrated pest management, integrated nutrient management, integrated watershed management, vermiculture, organic farming, sericulture, etc., which are relatively new and need new skills, are likely to be more acceptable to farmers than are traditional production technologies.

Distance learning approach. Conventional distance learning methods like correspondence courses and electronic media were inappropriate on account of the tremendous diversity in agro-climatic conditions and languages, as well as the low level of literacy.

146

Based on its experiments, MANAGE developed its own concept of distance learning for farmers' skill upgrading. It comprises three phases of development, from simple face-to-face training to more complex and sophisticated mass communication methods. It also envisages collaboration with a grassroots-level institution involved with farmers' training such as a farmers' training centre or an NGO or a *Krishi Vigyan Kendra* (farm science centre, KVK).

Phase one begins with motivation of farmers through exposure visits to successful examples, followed by face-to-face training in skills involved in the new technologies at the collaborating institution. In the second phase, the trained farmers are used as resource persons to train other farmers in the new skills as well as act as extension agents for other farmers. The farmer-trainers are backstopped with technical support and training materials such as self-study work books, audio-visuals, etc. In the last phase, MANAGE will produce audio-visuals, short films and television programmes on common, general management principles and practices relevant to diverse farming audiences but with common management problems.

The discussion below describes how this approach was implemented for hybrid rice seed production.

Phase 1

MANAGE decided to put into practice the first phase of its concept of distance learning for farmers in the winter (*rabi*) season of 1994–95. MANAGE collaborated with Shri Aurobindo Institute of Rural Development (an NGO in Nalgonda district of Andhra Pradesh) during the preparation period, and developed a skill-development training programme design for hybrid rice seed production technology. Several concepts were refined and many features were added to the training programme to make it well rounded and sustainable. The salient features are described below :

Programme design. In view of the lessons learnt from the experimental farmers' training programmes, it was decided that the farmers would be invited to come for training on 8–10 days during the whole winter cropping season. Starting with an initial two-day introductory visit to the KVK, the farmers would come before different stages of the crop such as land preparation, nursery raising, transplanting, panicle initiation, synchronization, harvesting, etc. Each visit would be limited to one day. Each visit would be used for imparting new skills relating to the relevant stage through hands-on field practicals, method demonstration, sharing of experiences, doubt clarification, etc. The face-to-face training was to be supplemented with a simple self-study work book to be used by farmers as reference material regarding new skills acquired for improving productivity. This institutional training at the KVK was to be followed by practice back on the field, for which each farmer was asked to set apart one-quarter to one-half hectare of his own land. The farmers would share their experiences on the subsequent visit not only about skill application but, more importantly, on the innovations and refinements they had made in the management practices to make the technology more relevant to their specific locations.

Technological package. MANAGE commissioned scientists of the Directorate of Rice Research, Hyderabad, and Andhra Pradesh Agricultural University, who had developed the new hybrids in Andhra Pradesh, to give the technical material for the total technology package. MANAGE and KVK scientists then identified the elements of new knowledge and skills required by the farmers at different stages of the crop in terms of various management and cultural practices. The KVK scientists then carried out a feedback survey with the farmers to identify gaps in the farmers' knowledge and skills to enable greater focus on their real training needs.

147

MANAGE developed a simple matrix as a tool around which training should be organized. This matrix had crop growth stages on the vertical axis, and management practices (such as the management of water, weeds, pests and diseases) on the horizontal axis. It allowed both the skills needed at any stage of the crop, and the skills for any practice across all crop stages, to be identified.

The matrix was then used to develop self-study material around all the relevant skills under different management practices for each growth stage. After obtaining the new skills, farmers were invited to share their experience back at the farm so their improvements and innovations could be incorporated to make the technology package more location-specific. This then became the final 'product' for dissemination.

Production of training and self-study materials. Based on the skill gap grid, small booklets of 8–10 pages each were brought out covering the new skills required for each stage of the hybrid seed production cycle. MANAGE also developed a standard format for the self-study material, with each skill being dealt with on one page. Each page indicated the 'what', 'how to' and 'why' for each skill in a few short sentences in simple and easy language from the farmers' perspective. Each page also had the key skill shown pictorially. There was also space provided for the farmers to make notes about their difficulties, innovations and improvements to enable them to share these with the other farmers at the next visit for training.

These booklets were made bilingual in English and the local language, for quick adaptation elsewhere. The development and publication of the self-study workbooks were taken up as a joint effort between MANAGE and Wiley Eastern Co., (now New Age International Ltd.,) and are being marketed commercially.

Critical production inputs. While trainee-farmers were expected to make arrangement for fertilizers, pesticides and the like on their own, production inputs, (thirum for seed treatment and giberallic acid for growth regulation) were procured in bulk by the KVK. The KVK also made arrangements with the Directorate of Rice Research and the Andhra Pradesh Agricultural University to supply the breeder seed for producing the parent-lines at the KVK farm. MANAGE gave a loan of Rs1 000 000 (about US$30 000) to Nalgonda KVK to develop its farm infrastructure for parent-line production. The parent lines were then supplied to the trainee-farmers on a cash-and-carry basis, or on credit (to be repaid from the proceeds of the sale of the hybrid rice seed to the KVK).

Financial sustainability. Right from the start, it was felt that skill upgrading training should be taken up only for technologies likely to bring direct and early financial gain to the selected farmers. Once convinced and motivated, the farmers were expected to register themselves voluntarily for the training programme by paying the cost of different items: registration fees, transport, board and lodging, follow-up visit by KVK staff, self-study material, critical production inputs, etc. In the hybrid rice seed production programme, these costs amounted to Rs1300 (about $40) per farmer for the whole of the cropping season. However, since the incremental income for the farmers from the hybrid seeds produced on half a hectare of land exceeded Rs10 000 (about $300), the trainee-farmers were quite willing to pay the costs. This enabled the programme to be replicated on a larger scale in the ensuing seasons.

Even from the point of view of the KVK, the programme was commercially viable. MANAGE trained the KVK scientists and field staff free of charge. The farmers paid for all the materials, services and logistical arrangements. MANAGE provided loans to the KVK for operational costs of training. However, the income derived by the KVK from the marketing of the hybrid seed was enough to enable them to repay the MANAGE loan within one year and still leave them with some profit.

148

MANAGE picked up the bill for capacity enhancement of the KVK scientists and field staff, focused exposure visits of farmers, development of self-study materials (only the actual cost of printing the self-study booklets was recovered from the farmers). However, MANAGE expects to recover its investments through the commercial sale of its information products (self-study booklets in Phase 1, audio-visuals in Phase 2, and distance learning programmes in Phase 3).

Farmers' training in rabi 1994–95. Based on the above concepts, the first training programme for hybrid rice seed production was implemented at Nalgonda KVK in November, 1994. Sixty farmers were selected from villages near the KVK on the basis of their exposure visit to the KVK farm, their willingness to set apart half a hectare of land for seed production, assured source of irrigation, agreement to pay the operational costs of the training programme, and undertaking to supply the hybrid seeds to the KVK at a mutually agreed price.

All the 60 farmers, including one woman farmer, successfully completed their training. The average productivity was around 1.1 tonnes per hectare of F1 seed, with some farmers achieving 1.5 tonnes per hectare. Each farmer earned a net profit of roughly Rs10 000 (about $300), and the cost of critical production inputs supplied by the KVK was fully recovered from the sale proceeds. The KVK also made some profit through the commercial marketing of the hybrid seeds.

Phase 2

The success of the hybrid rice seed production training programme in *rabi* 1994–95 led to a much larger demand in *kharif* (rainy season) 1995. Realizing the logistical and other technical supervision difficulties in scaling up the training programme, MANAGE and Nalgonda KVK introduced the following changes in the programme to move into Phase 2 of the distance learning concept.

Selection of farmers. There were over 500 applications. Since the availability of parent-lines was limited, only 210 new farmers were accepted after the exposure visits. Also since *kharif* is the rainy season and more prone to pest and disease attacks and low yields, each farmer was asked to set apart only 1/10th of a hectare as his practice field for which critical production inputs were agreed to be supplied by the KVK. The 60 farmers trained in *rabi* 1994–95 were also supplied the critical inputs at the revised rate to enable them to carry forward their production programme. Besides, these farmers were used to comparing and contrasting the management practices in *rabi* and *kharif* seasons to further refine and fine-tune the technological package for the two seasons.

Critical inputs production infrastructure. As the MANAGE-KVK training programme had shown great promise of being commercially viable with the production of 25 tonnes of hybrid seeds in *rabi,* it was decided to upscale the operation from *rabi* 1995–96 in order to have a larger impact on the overall rice production scenario in the district. Accordingly, Nalgonda KVK placed a much higher request with the agricultural university for breeder seeds for the production of parent lines. At the same time, MANAGE provided a loan of Rs0.9 million (about $25 000) to the KVK to develop its own infrastructure for systematic large-scale production of parent-lines. This enabled the KVK to take up a training-cum-production programme on 72 hectares in *rabi* 1995–96 and produce over 100 tonnes of hybrid seeds.

Farmer-to-farmer training. With the increase in the number of trainee farmers, MANAGE and the KVK decided to decentralize the institutional face-to-face training. For

149

this, the KVK invited the trained farmers to take up training for other farmers in their village or neighbouring areas. Seven farmers came forward to act as resource persons. Accordingly, arrangements were made to attach 10 to 12 farmers to each of these seven farmers; these will visit the trained farmer's field to get practical demonstration and hands-on experience of the new skills required. The selected farmer-trainers were given some exposure to training methods to improve their effectiveness. Besides, on the agreed dates, these farmer-trainers were backstopped with a technical field worker of the KVK. Thus, out of 210 new farmers, 70 were attached to the training fields of the farmers-trainers, and the remaining 140 were trained at the KVK farm. The new farmer-trainers were given the designation of *mitra kisan* ('farmer friend'). The KVK scientists, field staff and the *mitra kisans* also supervised the field practice for the new farmers on their own farms. While the training was structured around the self-study booklets produced by MANAGE, the KVK scientists interacted with the *mitra kisans* and the new farmers to identify further innovations and refinements of the technology package.

In *rabi* 1995–96, 12 farmers came forward to be the *mitra kisans* and act as resource persons to train other farmers. Enough new farmers were selected to enable 10 farmers to be attached to each of the 12 *mitra kisans*. Another 16 farmers were attached directly to the KVK.

Training of extension officers. Looking at the success of the *rabi* 1994–95 programme, the State Department of Agriculture deputed a group of 20 subject-matter specialists and extension officers to the KVK to undergo training in hybrid rice seed production technology, as well as the commercial production of hybrid rice. The KVK also supplied quantities of hybrid rice seeds to the department for extending the hybrid rice production technology among farmers in other areas.

Farmer-to-farmer extension. Most of the farmers who produced hybrid seeds under the programme retained a part of their seed production for commercial production of hybrid rice on their own fields. They also supplied seeds to some of their neighbouring farmers and friends. Because of their rigorous practical training in all aspects the new technology, they became willing instruments in transferring the hybrid rice technology to other farmers. This was an unintended but promising spin off. However, the exact nature and extent of this is not known.

Audio-visual material production. To enable the rapid spread of hybrid rice technology in other areas, in *rabi* 1996–97 MANAGE plans to produce audio-visual materials on the production of hybrid rice and hybrid rice seed. Similarly, audio-visuals will also be prepared in MANAGE's other extension programmes as the first round of training and technology refinement is completed and the technology package is finalized.

Audio-visual materials will also be used in the institute's programme on sodic land reclamation, since this takes longer than a single season. In summer, land reclamation and development have to be undertaken, followed by rice cultivation during the *kharif* season and wheat cultivation in the *rabi*. While skills training, as envisaged above, may be used for selected farmers, its extension to a large number of farmers should be attempted through electronic media. Accordingly since *kharif* 1996, in addition to self-study booklets, MANAGE has prepared audio-visual materials to capture the new skills required by the farmers. It is hoped to introduce the audio-visual cassettes for training farmers on a large scale in *kharif* 1997 in Sultanpur district of Uttar Pradesh.

Phase 3

MANAGE proposes to use advances in information technology for the third phase of its distance learning programme for farmers. It proposes to produce multi-media training packages based on computer, video and satellite technologies. These are essentially knowledge-based programmes in English and are meant to be used as information and training products for self-study by extension officers and scientists. These can also be used by the farmers with a working knowledge of English. The package includes:

o a CD-ROM-based expert system on pest and disease management for rice
o multi-media interactive training packages on watershed development, rainfed rice and other technologies and approaches, using video laser disk and video CD-ROM
o electronic communication networks, including Internet connections to access information and make the MANAGE library available to users elsewhere, television broadcasting of training packages and live programmes, and video conferencing. MANAGE is encouraging institutions such as the state agricultural universities and KVKs to provide similar facilities to complete the network.

Conclusion

There are three rising trends of complexity. Farmers' needs are changing from simple cultural practices to complex commercialized farming. Scientists are developing newer and more advanced technologies requiring a variety of skills. And communication has become extremely sophisticated with advances in information technology. MANAGE has attempted to employ extension methods ranging from face-to-face interaction to the mass media to design an appropriate 'fit' between the nature of technology and the range of skills required by the farmers. MANAGE has taken the first few steps. Much more needs to be done.

Another important factor for long-term impact is the financial viability and sustainability of the skill upgrading programme. The institutional arrangements and operational modalities have been designed with a view to creating abiding financial interests of the stakeholders in the extension approach developed by MANAGE. It is hoped that, with more experience and further refinement, it could be evolved into a sustainable extension management system.

Provision of fee-based service paid by farmers

The final case in this chapter describes how ActionAid–Nepal has trained farmers as community agricultural workers, who then earn their living by providing advice and other services to other farmers for a fee. The project is one example of attempts being made in several countries, in both the public and NGO sectors, to ensure farmers have control over services through their monetary votes. In some instances farmers are being given some or all of the money with which to purchase services. However in the case below, the emphasis is on the supply side of service delivery. The approach is based on the assumption that farmers will pay for services or information that will make their farming more productive, and that these services or information can be provided by local sources, rather than by the public sector.

Thapa argues that this approach brings various benefits to those served. The data he cites come from interviews with 30 community agricultural workers in 11 village development committees (the smallest unit of local government) in Sindhupalchowk district in Nepal.

Community-based agricultural extension workers in Nepal (Thapa)

Community agricultural workers (CAWs) are unpaid local agricultural community extension agents and have been operating since 1988. They provide assistance to farmers through
training, the production and dissemination of improved seeds and other technologies and
veterinary and crop protection services. Assistance is offered in agriculture, forest development and livestock production.

How farmer-led agricultural extension started. In 1988 local farmers (both male and female) from each village development committee were selected for training to become CAWs.
The following criteria — formulated by ActionAid–Nepal agricultural staff in consultation
with community members, community development committees and local ActionAid staff
— were used as the basis for selecting these farmers:

o Age: Between 25 and 45 years.
o Marital status: Married.
o Social class: Poor to middle class, having 6–12 months' food sufficiency from their
  own land.
o Leadership: Co-operative, honest, interested in social work and committed.
o Ethnic group: Priority was given to Tamang.
o Education: Preferably literate.

Training in agriculture and livestock development was organized for CAWs in order to
provide them with the necessary technical knowledge and skills. The training was conducted by ActionAid, in collaboration with leading agricultural research stations and training and extension agencies of Nepal. In addition, a series of follow-up training courses and
observation tours were organized to maintain and upgrade their knowledge and skills and to
establish links with government and non-governmental agencies. Necessary basic equipment and veterinary drugs worth NRs3000 ($60) were provided to CAWs to enable them to
establish their extension services and, initially, a monthly sum of NRs150 ($3) was paid by
ActionAid to each CAW as an incentive. However, this payment was discontinued in 1992.
Some 94 percent of the local farmers who were trained and equipped to become CAWs
have established their own agro-vet extension service in their locality.

Why this approach? The conventional extension approach adopted by ActionAid initially,
which used outside extension agents (ActionAid employees), was costly, top-down, unsustainable, and locally unmanageable. It was only later recognized that outsiders can merely
facilitate, and that local people have to do the job if it is to be done effectively. Having
realized the pitfalls of the earlier approach, however, ActionAid developed the concept of
CAWs who would replace external extension agents in disseminating agricultural innovations amongst subsistence farmers. It was thought that local agents would be able to provide more timely and appropriate services to their neighbours in the remote hills of Nepal,
which suffer from a serious lack of transportation and communication facilities. By developing a cadre of unpaid, local CAWs, ActionAid hoped to make the extension system more
efficient, cost-effective and sustainable. The approach also aimed to develop local human
resources as a means of empowering local people.

Distribution of CAWs by age and sex. The average age of the 30 CAWs who were surveyed
was 33. The majority were between 21 and 40 years old, while about 17 per cent were
between 41 and 55. Age did not have any effect on the quality of extension services provided by the CAW, but female CAWs (less than 7 per cent of the sample) were less effective
due to their lack of education and lack of time.

152

Educational status. The CAWs' standard of education varied greatly. The majority of those surveyed (53 per cent) were literate, but had only a basic level of education. The more educated CAWs were more effective than their lesser educated counterparts, because the former could better understand the extension posters, pamphlets and booklets and manufacturers' instructions on the use of fertilizers and pesticides.

Distribution of CAWs by agro-climatic zone. A look at the geographical distribution of CAWs showed that 20 per cent of them came from the high hills (above 1800m), 57 per cent from the mid-hills (1250–1800m), and 23 per cent from the foothills (760–1250m). The CAWs were more active in the mid-hills and foothills where there was greater potential for higher cropping intensities and increased productivity compared with the high hill areas. The mid- and foothills also had better access to markets, and farmers were more informed about improved agricultural technologies. These factors may have been responsible for a greater demand for the CAWs' services in the mid- and foothills.

Training received by CAWs. The training provided to the CAWs included:

o veterinary skills
o agro-forestry
o agronomy
o horticulture
o entrepreneurship and leadership skills.

In practice, the CAWs concentrated on the provision of veterinary services, seed multiplication and distribution, plant protection measures and pruning fruit trees, because these were the services most in demand from farmers. These services were also the most financially rewarding for both farmers and CAWs. The training in entrepreneurship and leadership skills were intended to increase CAWs' managerial capacity and it was expected these would be important in the running of their businesses.

The CAWs' use and distribution of basic equipment. Nearly all (97 per cent) of the CAWs surveyed had been using the veterinary kit box supplied to them by ActionAid. This indicated that the CAWs had strong incentives to use the kit, which largely arose from the sale of veterinary drugs to farmers. The sprayers, castrators and secateurs provided by ActionAid were also widely used by the CAWs. As was the case with veterinary services, CAWs were able to charge the farmers for the services relating to the use of this equipment.

Activities preference ranking. The different extension activities were scored for preference on a ranking of 0–10. The majority of the CAWs ranked veterinary services first. They charged NRs100–300 ($2–6) for treating a case of dystocia or retained placenta in buffalo and goats. They charged NRs10–15 ($0.20–0.30) for castrating bucks, and NRs20–40 ($0.40–0.80) for castrating bulls. They also sold veterinary drugs and seeds, charging 20–25 per cent more than the wholesalers' prices. The CAWs regularly conducted training for farmers in their constituencies on subjects like animal diseases, kitchen gardening, compost-making, pruning fruit trees and cultivating cereal crops. The motivating factor for them in conducting training sessions was a fee of NRs75 ($1.50) per day which they were paid by ActionAid. CAWs also used the training sessions as an opportunity to promote their businesses.

Some CAWs (33 per cent of those surveyed) have developed nurseries for fodder trees and horticultural crops on their farms and earn additional income by selling saplings to farmers. A large majority (80 per cent) also earned money from selling vegetable seeds. The income that the CAWs earned from selling their services and commodities was seen as one of the major motivating factors for engaging in their work.

153

Of the different extension activities in which they were engaged, the CAWs gave least preference to the sale of insecticides and pesticides, because of the risks in handling them. Apparently these activities are also not very profitable.

Area covered by CAWs. Most of the CAWs surveyed (63 per cent) limited their activities to their local vicinity (a cluster of three wards within the village development committee), but the most active ones (10 per cent) served the entire VDC and some (27 per cent) even went to other VDCs. The area they covered was determined by money-making opportunities, demand from farmers and also by the size, population and accessibility of the wards and VDCs.

Links with government offices and NGOs. Many of the CAWs had established links with government agriculture service centres in order to obtain mini-kits (small packets of improved seeds, with or without fertilizer), technical advice, and supply of vaccines and pesticides during outbreak of epidemic crop or livestock diseases. In addition, they frequently visited the government agricultural research station in Kathmandu to obtain foundation seed, vaccines and diagnoses of plant and animal diseases. They also maintained links with private agro-vet dealers in Kathmandu, from whom they purchased seeds, chemicals and veterinary drugs. They regularly utilize the facilities (loans, equipment) provided by the agricultural development bank and input corporation. However, 13 per cent of the CAWs surveyed did not have any links with outside agencies.

Income earned from extension activities by the CAWs. The number of clients and type of services provided by the CAWs decided the amount of cash they earned: those serving more clients also earned more money. As mentioned above, the provision of veterinary services and drugs, and the sale of seeds and seedlings were more remunerative than other activities. The majority of CAWs earned NRs1000 ($20) or more per year (see Table 11.4). Only very few (less than 7 per cent of those surveyed) earned no income from their services. The CAWs spent some of their income on the promotion of their agro-vet enterprises. They also used it for buying goods for daily consumption and those who had debts used it to pay these off.

Job satisfaction. The overwhelming majority of the CAWs surveyed (90 per cent) were 'very satisfied' or 'satisfied' with their job. Reasons given for this satisfaction were that they were self-employed, their own farm productivity had increased, and they felt that their social prestige had increased. However, some of them were dissatisfied with the lack of a credit scheme and their lack of knowledge, skills and professional confidence.

Institutional development. About 77 per cent of the CAWs had become members of the Community Agriculture and Livestock Resource Centre (CALRC), an association set up and registered by CAWs themselves in 1993 to help strengthen their positions through institutional support. The objectives of the association were to:

o   supply agricultural inputs to farmers at a reasonable price
o   disseminate agricultural innovations among subsistence farmers
o   institutionalize the CAW agriculture extension system to make it more sustainable.

Most of the CAWs surveyed (67 per cent) were found to understand the objectives of their association and were confident that they could run the association themselves. However, it had been inactive during the six months prior to the survey owing to a lack of leadership, effective communication, management skills and co-ordination among the CAWs and the donor agency (ActionAid–Nepal). In addition, there was no budget for running

Table 11.4: Community agricultural workers' annual cash income from extension services, Nepal

Annual income (NRs)		No. of CAWs	% of CAWs
No income		2	7
1000 or less	(<$20)	14	47
1000–3000	($20–60)	4	13
3000–5000	($60–100)	3	10
5000–10 000	($100–200)	4	13
10 000–20 000	($200–400)	3	10
Total		30	100

the association. In May 1995 the CAWs decided to revitalize the CALRC by reforming the existing executive committee, conducting regular meetings, making monthly savings (NRs10 ($0.20) per month per CAW), establishing an office, preparing working rules for themselves, and forming geographically based subcommittees. The CAWs hope to benefit from the CALRC's revitalization in terms of organizational linkages which could sustain the future growth of their activities. In addition, the CARLC has the potential to act as a means through which the farmer-run, CAW-based agricultural extension system could become institutionalized.

Future plans. The majority of the CAWs surveyed had a clear plan for their businesses in the future. Most of them planned to promote the agro-vet side of their business and establish horticultural or agro-forestry nurseries, because they received more income from these aspects of the business than from others. Some CAWs also had plans for increasing the productivity of their own farms to allow for commercial production so that their socio-economic standing would be improved.

Distribution of CAWs by landholding. The average size of surveyed CAWs' landholding (irrigated and upland) was 0.87 hectares (the quality of the land being better in the mid- and low hills than in the high hills). Only 17 per cent of the CAWs had a surplus of food and income, while 83 per cent of them came from poor families. They had no savings, but their agricultural extension services provided an important contribution to their livelihoods.

Impact on agricultural productivity. Since the initiation of the ActionAid–Nepal agricultural extension programme in 1983, the overall agricultural productivity of the area has increased, partly due to the introduction of new crop seeds (potato, maize, barley, finger millet, radish and cauliflower) and improved breeds of livestock (goat, buffalo).

A study on the impact of the programme (Adhikari and Baniya, 1991) was conducted in 1991 with the objective of assessing changes in food self-sufficiency and farm productivity in different agroecological zones. The findings were as follows.

o The households participating in ActionAid's programme in the high hills had an average of 1.68 months more food self-sufficiency than their non-ActionAid counterparts; in the mid-hills about 4.5 months. These differences were due to improvements in the production of crops and livestock.

- o Crop yields of new varieties compared to existing varieties had increased by an average of 28 per cent as a result of the introduction of summer varieties of maize, paddy and millet (ActionAid–Nepal, 1992). For example, the average productivity of millet increased by 49 per cent, rice by 19 per cent, wheat by 42 per cent, and maize by 22 per cent.
- o Sixty-two percent of households in the high hills parts of the programme area and 73 per cent of the mid-hills households had participated in the ActionAid programme. (The survey concentrated on the mid- and high hills areas).

Problems faced by CAWs. Despite many successes, CAWs also faced some problems. The following were reported.

- o A lack of knowledge and skills. Two months' training in general agriculture was not enough. Many CAWs lacked the technical knowledge and skills to handle veterinary cases, like retained placenta and dystocia, or to assess proper drug dosages. They also . said they needed more training on fruit tree propagation, vegetable seed production and record keeping.
- o Lack of credit. Some of the poorer CAWs could not run their business smoothly, due to cash-flow problems.
- o Delayed payment by clients. In the villages, farmers tended to take the agricultural inputs (seeds, veterinary medicines) on credit from CAWs. They did not make payments on time and this hindered the CAWs' business. In addition, CAWs' close relatives did not pay for inputs.
- o Lack of follow-up. A systematic follow-up mechanism by ActionAid staff was lacking, and as a result, technical support became weak.
- o Lack of equipment. There was a lack of necessary equipment (e.g., castrators, secateurs, sprayers, veterinary kit-boxes and measuring glasses), and the CAWs felt it was difficult to provide effective services because of this.

Lessons learned

- o The CAWs with good literacy and Nepalese and English languages were more effective as agricultural agents than others, because they could more easily understand manufacturer's instructions, for example on the use of fertilizers and pesticides, as well as extension literature such as posters, pamphlets and booklets.
- o The CAWs were found to provide a sustainable agricultural extension service in comparison with that provided by outsider extensionists, because they could more easily reach remote areas and the management costs were low.
- o CAWs were more approachable than outsiders and they were reliable in providing services as and when required by farmers.
- o Agricultural training could not be really effective without a proper assessment of the CAWs' and farmers' agroclimatic zones, the accessibility of markets in their areas, and the common problems related to crops, livestock and agroforestry.
- o The working efficiency, quality and excellence of the CAWs tended to decline if regular follow-up in the form of meetings and workshops was lacking.
- o The CAWs local institution, the CALRC, did not function well in the absence of good leadership, a budget, common understanding and managerial skills among its members.
- o Benefits in terms of fees, social prestige and power were the factors which motivated the CAWs to undertake and continue their non-salaried agricultural extension work.

Recommendations

- o A quarterly, one-day workshop of CAWs should be organized in order to enable them to share ideas and experiences with each other.
- o Needs-based training should be given to the CAWs. The agroclimatic zones, markets and common problems relating to crops, livestock, vegetable seed production and agro-forestry should be properly assessed and taken into consideration in designing the training for each CAW. Necessary equipment should be provided to CAWs along with the training.
- o Regular follow-up and coaching in the field needs to be improved to increase the CAWs' capacities in terms of technical and managerial skills and knowledge.
- o CAWs, especially those who are not very literate or numerate, should be encouraged to attend non-formal education classes to increase their capacity to run their business.
- o A revolving fund should be created to ensure the smooth and sustainable running of the CALRC.
- o Co-ordination and linkages with different government and non-governmental organizations, such as the agriculture development offices, service centres, the agricultural inputs corporation, seed companies and private dealers should be strengthened.
- o The CAWs' professional ethics should be strengthened to overcome some of the problems related to the services they provide to the community.

12 Impact assessment and evaluation

A KEY WEAKNESS in farmer-led extension is the dearth of critical evaluation and assessment of both processes and impact. As is the case with other participatory methodologies, supporters of farmer-led extension and research are convinced it is effective in empowering small farmers and increasing productivity, but they have very little hard evidence to offer sceptics. The lack of well-documented quantitative or qualitative analyses may undermine the credibility of the approach.

Anecdotal information about benefits abounds. The excerpt below is an example: it provides some data on milk yields as well as a qualitative description of the project's performance during a drought and some other benefits.

Impact of the Dairy Goat Project in Ethiopia (Peacock)
Most families have managed to increase their flock of goats to a size which they are able to manage with the labour and feed available. As the flock increases, excess males are sold for cash.

The crossbred goats have so far performed very well and yield one to two litres of milk per day while rearing a kid, compared to an average yield of 300–500 ml per day from local breeds. Several women have started to sell milk and earn the equivalent of the daily wage rate by doing so. In addition male crossbreeds command a premium price. Taken together, the crossbred goats are making a considerable impact on child nutrition and family incomes.

The project was sorely tested during the drought in 1994 in southern Ethiopia. There was widespread famine in the Welayta area of the southern region, but there has been clear evidence that families owning goats were able to sell them and earn sufficient funds from doing so to feed their families until the next harvest. As the families selected were considered to be the poorest in their community, the project has obviously had a major impact on some of the most vulnerable groups.

The increase in self-esteem and personal confidence among women involved in the project is not something that can be easily measured, yet is plain to see. One group in Konso, the poorest of all the project sites, have constructed a tiny meeting hut for themselves, which is turning into a small social centre for the community. Individual women tell countless stories of how their goats, or membership of their group, has helped them. A widowed grandmother in Hararge, struggling to bring up her orphaned grandson, now has milk for the child and enough left over to sell and enable her to buy grain. Other women have managed to start petty trading activities through borrowing money from their group.

This description gives some indication of the (very positive) impact the programme has had on a few families. But it does not show the number of families who have gained in this way relative to the number of people given assistance, nor the possible long-term impact of the programme. This type of information frequently leads

159

to more questions than it answers. How many families in total are involved in the programme? How many women have sold what quantity of milk, at what price? What is the overall impact on women's incomes, families' nutritional status and food security?

The challenges in trying to monitor and evaluate programmes are clearly articulated by Sinaga and Wodicka in describing the experiences of the Tananua Foundation in Indonesia.

Weaknesses in evaluation in Indonesia (Sinaga and Wodicka)
Although this programme has been on-going for 15 years now, there has never been a concerted attempt to have its impact assessed by an independent team. This is a major weakness, but it should not detract from the fact that monitoring and evaluation have been on-going activities since the beginning of the programme. Evaluations have been informal and have been carried out at every opportunity — during quarterly meetings, cross-visits, training, regular staff meetings, farmer field days, etc.

Documentation of the progress of the programme and the achievements of farmers has also been weak. Quarterly reports, annual reports, and periodic visitor reports are available, but do not necessarily provide the type of critical analysis that is needed to assess overall programme impact. In other words, many of the outputs of the programme have been recorded, such as number of adopters of different technologies, metres of terraced contour lines built, number of trees planted, etc. However, the more significant indicators for assessing impact, such as the contribution of various practices to crop production, food security, and incomes, have been more difficult to measure. The lack of baseline data, appropriate technical backup and time have often been cited as reasons for the paucity of impact assessment efforts.

Such problems are common to many development activities, but farmer-led extension and research also create some of their own. Perhaps the two most important differences in evaluating farmer-led extension and research lie in the need to examine:

o the increase in farmers' capacity to generate, analyse and disseminate information about improved agricultural technologies and innovations
o the changes in the policy environment that open up opportunities for farmer involvement in extension and research.

One should beware of quantitative proxy indicators of a qualitative process. Evaluation and impact assessment cannot be expressed in quantitative measures alone. It is often the qualitative context which gives the numbers meaning or significance. In addition, qualitative measures often better reflect the processes involved, which many exponents of farmer-led extension view as at least as important as the physical 'products' that result.

This is not to say that there is no place for quantitative data analysis. The impact of farmer-led extension cannot be measured merely by the number of people adopting specific innovations. It is also necessary to assess the increased capacity of farmers to participate in setting and implementing the research and extension agendas and, in turn, the contribution which specific innovations make to farmers' wider

160

ability to adapt and spread technologies. As in other evaluation exercises, there should be a balance of qualitative and quantitative indicators, and cross-validation or 'triangulation' of the results from different methods. And because the farmer-led extension process is so unpredictable and flexible, the evaluation framework should also be flexible enough to accommodate the unexpected.

Individual or household-level assessment

At the individual or household level, many projects use crop yields and projected financial gains to demonstrate impact. Some of the papers cited here used more creative indicators to measure impact, such as the length of time food stores lasted, or behavioural changes on the part of project participants.

De Freitas expresses the impact of a project on farmers and households through the increase in yield, area under cultivation using the new technology, and possible cash gains from the sale of the crops.

Measures of project impact in Brazil (de Freitas)
A survey carried out at the state level has shown that the area under minimum tillage and no-tillage amounts to 120 000 ha. Since 1991, more than 1000 agricultural machines and pieces of equipment adapted to water and soil conservation have been acquired by farmers living in watershed areas for collective use.

Yields have multiplied practically 2.5 times where cover crop techniques have been used. Assuming that the produced corn was all marketed, this would represent an annual circulation of US$165 000 among farmers engaged in the project.

Kingsley and Musante describe the success of the integrated pest management (IPM) farmer field school (see also Chapter 8). In the first season, pesticide purchases fell to US$0.56 per hectare in 1993, from $29 per hectare in the previous year. At the same time, unhulled rice yields rose from 6.2 to 7.2 t/ha for the same farmers applying IPM. This quantitative impact is important because it demonstrates that there were not only behaviour changes, but also a decline in risks to people's health. As Kingsley and Musante describe below, in the second season the yields were slightly lower in the IPM fields, but farmers were still satisfied because of the lower costs and the health benefits.

Impact of farmer field schools in North Sumatra (Kingsley and Musante)
The IPM field schools continued in the second season of rice with the same participants, because farmers wanted to prove the effectiveness of IPM in this season when pest problems are more severe. In fact, in the second season there was a serious stemborer outbreak which affected all farmers in Karang Anyar, with estimates of moderate damage affecting 20–50 per cent of farmers' fields... Despite this, the 34 participating farmers produced an average 3.2t/ha, again with practically no applications of pesticide. This yield was 186kg (5 per cent) less than 26 non-participants sampled, who produced 3.4t/ha. However, the amount that the non-participants spent on pesticides (average Rp46 000/ha (about $20/ha)) was the equivalent of the price of 155kg of rice. With the small difference in yield, farmers in the programme remained enthusiastic about IPM practices, because they knew that the stemborer

attack had affected all farmers' fields and they thought that they had benefited in other ways, such as decreased labour costs, better health and fields free from pesticides, allowing for further development of other cultivation practices such as rice-fish culture (Sabirin 1994).

The experience of IPM field schools for rice in other NGO or farmers' organization programmes in Lampung and Central Java has shown that farmers' greater understanding of insect and plant ecology is indicated by radical reductions in pesticide use and active management of indigenous natural enemy insect populations and field conditions. In all cases, rice yields have remained stable or have increased due to improved fertilization regimens developed as part of the field school trials. Savings of about Rp300 000–500 000 ($140–230) per season per group, after rice IPM training, are recorded in most lowland sites. The cost of providing season-long training through NGOs or farmers' organizations is approximately Rp500 000–800 000 ($230–370) per group. Thus the costs of training are recovered after only one or two seasons. In locations where activities continue after the first field school, as in Karang Anyar, farmers have applied IPM principles to other crops and production problems such as IPM for soybeans and hot peppers, rat control and rice-fish cultivation or duck raising, as well as organizing saving groups and bulk purchases of fertilizer.

Murwira *et al.* assess the impact of the ITDG-supported project in Chivi district, Zimbabwe (Chapter 11), in terms of organizational capacity (using indicators such as the number of groups formed and their total membership) and the technologies now being used to address problems identified by farmers and gardeners.

Impact and sustainability in Zimbabwe (Murwira et al.)

Since 1991, in terms of organizational capacity, the garden groups have increased in number from 10 to 40. A group gardens area committee, with 12 members drawn from all the six ward villages, now exists to enhance co-ordination between all group gardens in the ward. Membership of the garden groups has expanded from 300 to over 1200.

Likewise, the number of farmers' clubs increased from nine to 34, and now stands at 33. The original area committee, which used to comprise six persons from three villages, has been expanded to 12 to ensure adequate representation of all six villages in the ward. Club membership has increased from 161 to over 865.

Garden groups' activities

The following activities are now being undertaken by the garden groups to alleviate some of their problems.

Water. The following techniques are now being practised on a wider scale:
o sub-surface irrigation using clay pipes
o mulching using grass and leaf mould
o use of ferro-cement rings to source water easily from dry riverbed wells
o use of plastics laid about 60cm beneath the surface of vegetable beds.

Pest management. A wider range of local plant materials has replaced the use of expensive and unavailable chemicals as a means of pest management. Some of these plants are *murunjurunju, majacha, mutovhoti, mutsviri, sooty*, chilli, garlic and onion. Intercropping is also being practised.

162

Fencing. Gardeners have acquired skills in fence-making and are now producing their own fences. A total of 35 x 50 kg rolls of plain wire have been procured at a total cost of Z$9145 (about US$1000). So far one garden has been completely fenced, and three gardens are near completion. Other garden groups are at various stages in producing their own fences and fencing their own gardens. Four gardens have been live-fenced.

Crop diversity. All garden groups are growing at least the following vegetables: rape (leaf), lettuce, chou moellier, carrots, potatoes, tomatoes, chilli, beans, pumpkins, cabbage, spinach, peas, maize and cucumber. In the past gardeners were growing an average of only four types of vegetable.

Skills and knowledge. Information sharing has been intensified through farmer-to-farmer mechanisms and garden competitions at ward level. The latter are held annually and followed by a field day hosted by the garden judged to be the best of them all. Gardeners decide on the criteria for selecting the best garden. Gardeners are now also able to facilitate their own meetings and discipline their own members.

Farmers' clubs activities

The following activities are also being undertaken by farmers' clubs to help solve their problems.

Water. This problem is being tackled through the construction of infiltration pits, tied ridges, mulch ripping, *fanya juus*, rainwater harvesting, rock-catchment water harvesting, winter ploughing and spreading ant-hill soil in the crop fields.

Draught power. The need is being minimized by labour parties, improvement of tools, establishing no-till tied ridges and *humwes* (sharing resources).

Seed varieties. Farmers are holding seed fairs on an annual basis and share knowledge with each other on various seed varieties, including about their performance. Farmers also exchange seeds and organize field days. A number of new seed varieties, or some of those which had disappeared due to monocultural practices, are now resurfacing, for example, castor, cassava, millet and sorghum varieties. Knowledge and skills continue to be shared in the same ways as in garden groups.

Sustainability

The key to the sustainability of the Chivi food security project activities is that the project acts merely as a facilitator, stimulating a process of community development. Although there may not be any guarantees that the process will remain irreversible, the fact that there is no heavy investment in project specific institutions, personnel or activities, which run the risk of collapse at the end of the project, provides positive indicators. The involvement of agricultural extension service staff in the whole process also suggests that project activities will be sustained even after the withdrawal of project staff.

Pandit (see also Chapter 5) describes an impact study carried out in the area where the Nepal Agroforestry Foundation operates, showing that group extension efforts have been very effective in bringing success to the programme. He also mentions in passing the presence of a 'control' village (one which the project activities have not affected, that can be used for comparison purposes). Using a control is an important technique, yet is strangely rare in evaluations of farmer-led extension.

Project impacts in Nepal (Pandit)

Since the extension strategy of the Nepal Agroforestry Foundation (NAF) was developed and designed by grassroots NGOs there have not been serious problems in using the extension and training approaches used. Nevertheless, small changes have been brought into the system, including administrative changes. Farmers' representation on the NAF board of directors has been increased. The approach seems to be agreeable to all involved to date, provided that the programmes are farmer-based. It has been observed by many that the farmer-to-farmer, bottom-up extension approach is quite successful and easy to implement.

Below are presented some of the findings of a study (Pandit 1994) conducted in two villages namely Kunwari (project village) and Gaikhura (control village) of Ramechhap district of Nepal to assess the impact of the NAF support programme with TSS, a local NGO supported by it. The regression model used in this study suggests that 84 per cent of the variation in total farm income between the project and the control village is due to fodder-tree adoption by farmers.

The study showed that group extension efforts were very effective. Fifty-seven per cent of the 60 farmers interviewed confirmed that the farmers' group helped to control grazing. Almost all agreed that livestock income increased as a result of farmer group formation. Twenty-three per cent of the farmers expressed the confidence to run their programme themselves. More than 50 per cent were in favour of the statement 'farmer groups are self-supporting and sustainable'. The study showed that only 23 per cent of farming households in the project village were living below subsistence levels. This is quite a satisfactory result when compared to the national average of 49 per cent.

A few farmers were asked how effective the extension methods being used by the NGO staff farmers were. The extension method most preferred by farmers was cross-visits, followed by participatory discussions. More than 50 per cent of the farmers interviewed responded that a one-way lecture was not effective. Flipcharts and flannel graphs were the most efficient tools to motivate farmers to plant trees on their farms. Demonstrations of the results of green manuring cover crops (velvet bean, jack bean, sun-hemp) motivated some farmers in the project sites to adopt this technology. The effect of using green manure cover crops on soils was compared with control situations. Samples were taken to Kathmandu for laboratory tests. The findings showed that cover crop plots contained significantly higher amounts of organic matter and nitrogen than did non-cover crop plots. Farmers reported that growing velvet beans in upland terraces provided fodder to livestock, increased maize production and consequently improved soil fertility in a sustainable manner. However, this technology is not yet adopted extensively by the farmers. Why? The problem appears to be that the small size of landholdings means that the farmer wants to use all the land available to them for growing edible crops such as millet, potato and other local legumes (kidney beans, soybeans).

Despite the examples above, much of what is lacking in evaluations is the actual impact on families and communities in terms of the changes in quality of life, as perceived both by community members and outsiders.

Project-level assessment

Project-level assessment enables both project staff and participants to scrutinize the process and methods used by the project. Some of the indicators used to describe the benefits of the project have been: cost-effectiveness, rates and degrees of diffusion of information, and number of beneficiaries reached. Measuring the outcome of the project by looking at the project's cost-effectiveness can be done relatively simply by dividing the project budget by the number of beneficiaries.

Sinaga and Wodicka give details of the Tananua Foundation's annual costs below. In 1984 the programme cost US$17 per farmer served; this rose to more than $50 in 1989 because of a technical problem, and has since fallen again to $11 as the number of farmers involved has increased.

Programme costs in Indonesia (Sinaga and Wodicka)

Table 12.1 provides basic data on the cost of the programme between 1984/85 and 1993/94, along with the total number of farmers reported to be active in it. The calculation of dollar investment per farmer over the years provides a crude idea of programme costs. Analysis of such an indicator is complicated by the fact that there is no comparative data to measure relative cost-effectiveness. Nevertheless, this is an initial attempt to show how inexpensive a farmer-based extension programme, combining the use of extension workers and trained farmer extensionists, can be.

It should be noted that the dollar figures are not exact, but are an approximation of the total costs incurred by the programme each year. It should also be noted that these dollar figures cover salaries, transportation (including investment in motorbikes), inputs such as seeds, cross-visits and meetings, and training costs.

Table 12.1 shows that the highest average cost per farmer occurred in 1988/89 at $52 and that the cost per farmer has been decreasing ever since to a low of $11. The increase in costs starting in 1985/86 can be attributed to the widespread devastation of *Leucaena* (the 'miracle tree' of agro-forestry, used by almost every farmer as hedgerow material) by the psyllid or 'jumping louse', and the resulting decline in farmer interest in adopting it or continuing to maintain soil and water conservation practices. The psyllid arrived in Sumba in mid-1985, and by early 1986, the *Leucaena* was virtually destroyed. This event led to a broad reassessment of technical approaches and programme strategies in Sumba and the rest of Southeast Asia. The recovery path was a slow one as new species were tested to replace the miracle tree. It was only towards the late 1980s that farmers started gaining confidence in the new species.

Table 12.1: Costs of the Tananua programme, Sumba, Indonesia, 1984–94

Year	84/85	85/86	86/87	87/88	88/89	89/90	90/91	91/92	92/93	93/94
Inputs (US$)	10 749	15 237	17 236	18 608	20 404	21 767	22 200	22 467	25 027	28 100
Farmers	650	750	537	N/A	393	449	828	861	1 593	2 614
Villages	8	8	10	N/A	15	13	15	13	18	29
$/farmer	17	20	32	N/A	52	48	27	26	16	11
$/village	1 344	1 905	1 724	N/A	1 360	1 674	1 480	1 728	1 390	969

Aside from illustrating the low cost of an effective farmer-led approach to extension in the context of marginal and resource-poor upland farmers, this rudimentary analysis also shows that long-term programmes are needed to respond to the calamities faced by such farmers. Without a long-term commitment to working with farmers, this programme could have ended in total failure had it been terminated after a period of five years. There is no question though, that more comparative analyses are needed to refine our understanding of the effectiveness of such approaches to extension.

Regional or national-level assessment

One of the ways of measuring the impact of a programme on a regional or national level is to look at other organizations that are using some of the farmer-led extension or research approaches promoted by the organization. For example, Bunch (see below) discusses how 'people-centred agricultural development' principles and methods are being picked up by other local and international NGOs and government agencies. Influencing other organizations (both government and NGO) to use similar methods or technologies, or to open the opportunity for farmers to take more of a lead in the research and extension agenda, represents an expanded programme impact, without increasing the actual programme itself.

Many programmes which attempt this level of assessment use the number of people involved or the number of hectares of land under a certain technology as indicators of national or regional impact. Measuring the impact a project has had through influencing other organizations is very difficult because the indicators are not clearly defined. For example, van Veldhuizen and Waters-Bayer (1995) describe how the Information Centre for Low-External Input Sustainable Agriculture (ILEIA) can quantify the number of organizations using a term promoted by it ('participatory technology development') but cannot ensure quality control over the use of the methodology. Nevertheless, some authors mention such regional or national indicators of success.

Holt-Gimenez (see Chapters 4 and 5) states that since 1989, the *campesino-a-campesino* extension methodology has spread to an estimated 300 farmer-promoters and 3000 beneficiaries in Nicaragua. The movement has succeeded in regenerating thousands of hectares of degenerated soils.

Dilts and Hate (Chapter 8) describe how the 'upstream' intensive training of extension officers in the integrated pest management field school approach in Indonesia has paid off. Over 2000 field workers have graduated from the IPM programme and the drop-out rate has been next to zero. At the present rate of spread, where field workers manage one field school per season, the Indonesian national IPM programme will reach one million farmer graduates by 1998.

Another way to look at cost-effectiveness is described below by Bunch.

Cost-effectiveness of people-centred agricultural development principles (Bunch)

The people-centred agricultural development (PCAD) approach has not only proven itself capable of achieving high rates of farmer adoption and increased productivity, but, even more important, has done so at much less cost than other extension systems. Inasmuch as the farmers become a major factor in the spread of both agricultural technologies and the development process, costs are considerably reduced. Instead of having to work with each individual group of farmers, the more expensive professional personnel become managers of farmer-extensionists, who do most of the teaching. Therefore, each professional extension worker trains, supports, and backstops a group of six to 10 farmer-extensionists. In this manner, each extensionist can reach, intensively but indirectly, some 150 to 200 farmers. Even though the farmer-extensionists are also paid a small stipend (after the first year) the reduction in costs per farmer reached is dramatic.

World Neighbors and Cosecha in Central America have a standard of being able to sustainably triple the productivity of farmers' basic grain production (from levels of between 400 and 800kg/ha) for a total programme cost of less than US$400 (in 1995 dollars) per farm family, including administration, salaries, transportation, etc. That is, if a programme costs a total of $50 000 each year for eight years, for a total of $400 000, then about 1000 farmers should have sustainably tripled their productivity of basic grains.

Some of World Neighbors' programmes have not attained this goal. Their first programmes in Mexico (in Oaxaca and Tlaxcala states) were more costly. However, the San Martin programme in Guatemala was a good deal more efficient than this, and the Guinope programme in Honduras cost almost exactly what the goal would indicate. The World Neighbors Cantarranas programme cost about $450 per family that tripled its productivity, while a programme in Honduras run by students from a college in Oregon, USA, spent less than $300 per family.

In any case, these figures are a good deal lower than those of virtually any other methodology. Many programme proposals describe efforts that cost a total of several thousand dollars per family benefited, while some cost well over $10 000 per family. And most of the programmes resulting from these proposals never reach all the people they hoped to, nor did many of those people ever manage to sustainably triple their productivity. A fair number of programmes spend more than the $400 per family on artificial incentives alone.

Nature of the impact. Furthermore, included in this $400 per family cost of the PCAD programmes is leadership training, organizational strengthening, training in the basic principles of biology and agriculture, and in most cases, agricultural diversification.

But the most important question is how much of the increases in productivity are sustained after programme termination. Do yields maintain themselves after the outside intervention ends?

A recent study of three of the earlier PCAD programmes (in San Martin Jilotepeque, Guatemala, and in Guinope and Cantarranas in Honduras) showed that yields have not only maintained themselves, but have continued, in general, to increase significantly (Bunch and López, 1994). In San Martin, for instance, average maize yields before the programme (1972) in the four villages studied were 400kg/ha and at programme termination (1979) were approximately 2000kg/ha. But 15 years later (1994), with virtually no additional intervention in agricultural development by any institution, the study showed maize yields averaged close to 4500kg/ha. That is, yields had once again doubled. In the same 15 years, bean yields (beans being the second most important staple food in the area) had increased by 75 per cent. The villagers themselves had successfully carried on the process of agricultural development.

167

The picture was not, however, uniform. In Guinope and Cantarranas, where the study selected villages arranged along a scale according to perceived quality of impact (thus it included some of the villages where the impact had been least), the villages of least impact had not been able to maintain yields. Thus, more or less (although this issue needs further study), in the 25–30 per cent of villages where the response was best, yields had continued to increase after programme termination. In the 40–50 per cent of the average villages, yields had more or less maintained or increased only marginally, whereas in the 20–35 per cent of the villages where impact had been poorest, yields had decreased, though they continued to be better than the yields at programme initiation.

Other signs of innovation were roughly proportional. In the villages of poor impact, there was virtually no on-going innovation, whereas in the best villages, literally hundreds of experiments had been made, and successful innovations presently being used that originated with this farmer-initiated and farmer-managed experimentation often numbered over 10 per community.

In San Martin, whole new systems of agricultural production had appeared. One of the four villages studied had developed an intensive cattle-raising system in which they were raising some seven head per hectare. Another village had become a major producer of fruit, while two others had developed an intensive coffee-producing system. And one of the villages had even developed a small-scale (less than one hectare per family) sustainable forest management system, earning good incomes by planting out into open spaces trees that volunteered (without using a nursery), and felling each year (on the average, with some variability due to varying need) the number of trees they could harvest on a sustainable basis.

Other impacts were also studied. The number of organizations in the high-impact communities had increased, land prices had increased dramatically, incomes had increased, and out-migration had either diminished drastically (in San Martin), or had been reversed. In the Guinope programme villages, net in-migration occurred between 1990 and 1994, in spite of heavy out-migration during the 1970s — a phenomenon without precedent in Honduras, as far as we know.

One of the major conclusions of the study was that sustainability does not reside in technologies. Whereas the technologies taught in these programmes had a half-life of perhaps five years (i.e., after five years, half the technologies had been abandoned), the agricultural development process and increases in yields had continued. Thus, sustainability is not to be found in the correct choosing of technologies. Markets change, input prices increase, new technological opportunities appear, varieties degenerate, and competition becomes stiffer. Most technologies will disappear, sooner or later, in this fast-changing modern world. Our only hope for sustainability of agricultural development is not in the nature of the technology, but in the nature of the process. The study confirms that the social process, one of widespread experimentation and sharing of information, of innovation and group problem-solving, is sustainable, year after year.

Though formal studies have not yet been done, empirical evidence indicates that similar phenomena have occurred in many other programmes using the PCAD principles around the world.

Obstacles to achieving such impact. It should be frankly admitted that the PCAD principles are not capable of overcoming all obstacles. They do require well-motivated extension personnel, and they require a good understanding of how they can be applied in each particular situation. While some World Wildlife Fund-supported programmes in Mesoamerica have been highly successful, such as the Defensores de la Naturaleza programme in Guatemala and the Calakmul and Línea Biósfera programmes in southeastern Mexico, other programmes

168

using the PCAD principles, because of a lack of motivation on the part of the personnel, or extremely poor, top-down administration, have been virtually total failures.

We are often asked under what conditions the PCAD principles would not work. We doubt that they would work with mechanized, highly capitalized farmers, because they would probably not be willing to teach each other. The principles will also not work in areas for which no known group of two or three technologies will bring significant increases in yields (some of the semi-arid areas of Africa would probably be included in this category, as would the higher reaches of the Peruvian Andes).

The PCAD process is also very difficult, or even impossible, in an institutional framework that discourages decision-making at a level close to the village extensionist. Both the principles and the technologies used must be adapted according to differences in farming systems, cultures, land tenure, environmental factors, accessibility of the villages, accessibility of markets, etc. Institutions which do not provide the space for such adaptations will rarely be successful in using the PCAD approach.

The methodology is also made much more difficult where previous development programmes have been highly paternalistic, giving away all sorts of inputs, food, and other artificial incentives. Nevertheless, even in these sorts of situations, significant successes have been achieved.

How to monitor, evaluate, and measure impact?

As indicated by Sinaga and Wodicka at the beginning of this chapter, it can be difficult to establish a suitable monitoring and reporting system that provides appropriate types of information. The nature of farmer-led extension means that it is difficult (or even undesirable) to use the conventional approach of setting targets beforehand and then measuring project effectiveness by whether the target has been reached. Paper-based systems of monitoring may be inappropriate because of the diversity of activities, the low literacy levels of project implementers, and the fact that they are usually not staff members of the organization that requires the monitoring information.

Project-level monitoring

Farrington and Nelson (1997) offer an approach to using the standard 'logframe' planning tool to monitoring farmer participatory research. Perhaps this could also be adapted to farmer-led extension projects.

Below, Nguyen Kim Hai discusses how a planning, monitoring and reporting system was set up in the project supported by CIDSE in Bac Thai province in Vietnam (see also Chapter 10). This system not only provides project managers with information they can use to guide the project; it also enables project staff to learn from each other and to plan on the basis of the information acquired.

Establishing a planning, monitoring and reporting system in Vietnam (Nguyen Kim Hai)

In 1992–93, the extension centre established a provincial monitoring plan based on quarterly visits to all seven districts. Each district was visited every six months for the purpose of regular monitoring. During these visits, meetings were held with the

169

extension board including all the extension workers in the district. The inter-communal centres were also visited, and so were their activities with some farmer interest groups. To date a total of 84 monitoring visits have been made by provincial extension staff to each one of the 38 inter-communal centres in the seven districts. Discussions with the extension workers form the central activity. Their performance and the functioning of the extension system at every stage, from the initial needs assessment to the field workshops, are evaluated. Much attention is also paid to establishing the communication lines from the inter-communal centres up to the district and province. Monitoring has thus become an important opportunity for discussion and fine-tuning, as well as trouble-shooting.

This system of visits runs parallel with the 'paper line' of reporting, planning and monitoring. This direct line is often very formal, and suffers from poor reporting capacity. The monitoring visits therefore act as an important 'personalization' of the system, as individuals from all levels of the extension system sit together and observe, discuss and plan activities, with a major focus on problems. This helps to make people at every level feel that they are part of the system, and gives them a sense of ownership of it.

A round of inter-district extension exchange visits (a total of 14 in Bac Thai) was organized. Each district extension board both hosted and visited one other. The extension workers and the district extension staff visited their counterparts in another district where the extension programme was active. The purpose of these visits was to facilitate an exchange of experience between districts. In this way, the district extension staff, especially the extension workers, were encouraged to learn and to share their specific experiences and methods of working with farmers and farmer groups.

Farmer-level monitoring

Due to the nature of farmer-led extension and research, many of the methods of evaluation focus primarily on farmers' evaluation. Some of these are described below:

o Individual farmer testimony is used to demonstrate the impact of some programmes at the individual/household level (see Farouk and Worsley, Chapter 11).

o Farm planning is a tool used by the Tananua Foundation which encourages farmers to develop a plan for the future of their farm based on their current situation and those improvements they can implement on their own farms. The farm plan can be used to monitor and evaluate the progress farmers have made to improve their farms (see Sinaga and Wodicka, Chapter 5).

o Quarterly meetings are very popular as a means of evaluating the progress of program activities as well as a way for farmers to take more control of the research and extension agenda. They are used in farmer-to-farmer extension (Sinaga and Wodicka, Chapter 5) and farmer field schools (Kingsley and Musante, Chapter 8). The responsibility for hosting the meeting lies with the farmers; government agencies, NGOs and villagers are invited. Farmers thus have a large voice in setting the meeting agenda. The farmers exchange information about programmes and critically analyse the results. It is a relatively inexpensive forum for information exchange.

170

o Farmer field days in farmers' fields are another forum for exchange and evaluation (Chapter 5). Farmers from different locations can see the improvements other farmers have made, and can discuss the strengths and weaknesses of the farms they visit. Such visits may stimulate them to try these improvements for themselves.

Indicators for assessing farmer-led extension

Indicators for monitoring and evaluating the degree to which objectives of farmer-led extension and research are being met come from two sources: farmers, and project or programme managers. Farmers should be deeply involved in defining their own objectives and indicators of success. On the other hand, managers need indicators of the effectiveness and appropriateness of the approach used, to assess whether the interventions are indeed helping farmers (especially poor, marginalized farmers) improve their quality of life. Programme indicators are frequently used by external donors, policy makers and governments to determine resource allocations and the future direction of support.

Farmer-led extension practitioners agree that both programme and farmers' indicators should be developed through an interactive process between farmers and extensionists or researchers. Extensionists and researchers — and farmers themselves — need to discuss their expectations together to arrive at mutually acceptable objectives for the project, and means of monitoring whether such objectives are being met.

Table 12.2 lists some of the indicators used in current projects and programmes. They have been the subject of much discussion in the literature on farmer participatory research (Farrington and Nelson 1997). 'Other stakeholders' include internal and external agencies providing financial and other support to farmer-led extension, or those concerned with the formulation or implementation of policies affecting (or affected by) farmer-led extension. Where appropriate, the information should be disaggregated by economic and social levels and gender to ensure that inequities can be identified.

Measuring group effectiveness
Because farmer-led extension relies so much on groups of farmers, it is important to know how effective those groups are. But measuring the effectiveness of groups is difficult. Workshop participants suggested several measures.

o Count the number of volunteers who participate in the groups (but this frequently rules out poor farmers who may not have the time/ability to access the group).
o Measure the amount of time external extensionists spend with the group. This can be seen as a measure of the group's effectiveness since those with a good response are visited more often.
o Use a chart (see the example in Table 12.3) to assess participation in planning meetings.

171

Table 12.2: Some indicators for assessing farmer-led extension

Farmers' indicators

- Extent to which the extension system identifies farmers' needs.
- Farmers' access to the extension system.
- Usefulness of the technologies to improving farm production, reducing risk, enhancing output stability and sustainability, and enhancing market values.
- Extent to which farmers gain confidence and agility in decision-making — i.e., the extent to which their human resources are enhanced.
- Extent to which local membership organizations and institutions are strengthened.

Programme managers' indicators

- Involvement of marginalized groups (especially women and poor) in decision-making. This means both the actual number of marginalized people involved in decision making and the quality of their involvement.
- Participation in the extension system (recorded perhaps as the number of people who sign up and attend meetings).
- The behaviour of farmers in response to the extension system.
- Frequency and quantity of feedback from farmer participants.
- Skills and abilities of the group to make proposals to, or demands on, the extension system.
- Creation of local resource persons, such as community animal health workers.
- Ability of the group to choose the inputs and resources it would like to use.
- Inclusion of farmers' techniques in the extension agenda, such as the generation and refinement of local technologies.

Other stakeholders' indicators

- Greater relevance of ideas or technologies generated from 'outside'; reduced proportion of technologies developed by government services which remain unadopted.
- Reform of policies relevant to farmer-led extension — concerned with input/output pricing, physical and social infrastructure, etc.
- Improved quality of life for everyone.

Table 12.3: Planning meeting assessment chart

	Points
Number of people who spoke and quality of contribution	(max. 100)
• Type of people who spoke? (marginalized people)	
• What? (plans)	
• Who? (decision making)	
• When?	
Needs incorporated in plan	(max. 300)
Understanding of the plan	(max. 100)
Total	(max. 500)

Measuring how far extension is 'farmer-led'

The many approaches presented in this book are all, to some degree, 'farmer-led'. Because of the multiplicity of approaches and the difficulty of defining the concept of 'farmer-led', measuring this characteristic presents problems. Ways of looking at this include:

o Trace membership of farmer groups over time.
o Examine which extension organizations are drawn into the area over time.
o Examine the extension agenda to see whether farmers' interests are being included. The demands that come out of farmers' meetings can be seen as requests on the system. If no real changes are seen in the agenda, the system would seem to be supply-driven.
o Table 12.4 can be used to assess the extent of control farmers have in the extension system. For each of the steps in a typical programme cycle (needs assessment, planning, implementation, monitoring, and evaluation), the matrix can be used to measure the extent to which farmers control the agenda.

The last line of Table 12.4 indicates that the evaluation process itself should involve farmers, using techniques such as group meetings and participatory action research. Farmers are often not involved in creating programme objectives, nor are they encouraged to create their own objectives for the success of the programme. Many project reports focus on the lessons learned by the programme, not the farmers.

There is also limited dissemination of the documentation and results of evaluations, especially in forms that can be used by community members. Although programme staff evaluate the impact of the programme activities for donors, this evaluation information is not translated into forms that the community can use.

Table 12.4: Assessment of farmer involvement (or 'farmer-led-ness') in key extension activities

Programme steps	Input			Influence			Control		
	Govern-ment	NGO	Farm-ers	Govern-ment	NGO	Farm-ers	Govern-ment	NGO	Farm-ers
Assess needs									
Plan									
Implement									
Monitor									
Evaluate									

13 Reaching more farmers

THERE ARE MANY examples throughout the world of local-level, small-scale farmer-led extension programmes. However, there are also many programmes and agencies struggling to 'scale up' their activities. Various strategies have been tried to this end, but many challenges have been met in the process.

This chapter reviews some efforts to extend the impact of farmer-led extension efforts and looks at constraints encountered and factors which influence the success of farmer-led extension efforts.

Two terms are used here to describe different means of reaching more farmers. 'Scaling up' refers to strategies which lead to an enlargement of programme size through an increase in financial and/or human resources. 'Scaling out' refers to efforts to influence other organizations (NGOs and government) and their policies, through networking, lobbying, creating and disseminating educational materials and undertaking training, etc.

Many of the experiences described in this chapter come from NGO programmes, but there are a few examples of government attempts to incorporate farmer-led approaches into the agricultural extension and research systems. Some of the difficulties in attempting to reform large-scale organizations arise because of the enormous resources required to change an existing bureaucracy which is highly structured in its approach to extension. Nevertheless, various approaches have proved successful, including reforming the public sector from within (through problem census/problem solving), and increasing demands on the public sector (for instance through collaboration with NGOs).

Scaling up

Increasing the number of extensionists

Increasing the number of farmer extensionists and paying them for their work are two common strategies for scaling up. Both enable programmes to reach more farmers. In Indonesia, for example, the national IPM programme has scaled up the farmer-led element of its extension efforts by developing farmer-experts who facilitate learning by other farmers. The programme trains public-sector extension field officers in farmer-led extension methods. It is estimated that the programme will have produced one million farmer graduates by the end of 1998. Dilts and Hate emphasize the importance of investing in a thorough training of professional extension staff in this process. They describe the training undertaken by extension staff.

Training farmers and extensionists in Indonesia (Dilts and Hate)

If a programme is to reach hundreds of thousands of farmers and have a real impact on agricultural practice while going through normal government channels, 'upstream' training, preceding the farmer level programme is important.

In our experience, anyone can become an effective facilitator. However, thorough training of field workers cannot be over-emphasized. In the IPM model, most training resources are focused directly at the field worker and farmer levels. Before field workers can run field schools, they must become 'farmers'.

We found that few extension workers had ever actually grown a rice crop from start to finish. Hence the initial 'IPM rice training' comprised a full-time course of 3.5 months where field-worker participants handled all the work for raising a rice crop on 2 hectares of irrigated land. On these plots, trainees worked as teams to conduct a set of 'IPM classic field studies' designed to allow participants to learn the principles of IPM directly from fieldwork. Therefore, before field workers begin their activities with farmers, they themselves have done each exercise dozens of times during training. This ensures that a high quality standard in the process is maintained across all field schools. Additionally, an unwritten curriculum teaches participants respect for farmers as they learn of the difficulties of raising a rice crop, from the heat of the noonday sun to night-time rat attacks.

On top of this, the programme provides time for building the 'field management' teams that will in the future operate, manage and administer field programmes in designated areas. During the course of training, participants also receive numerous sessions on participatory planning, discussion leadership, 'people management', computer applications, evaluation techniques and training methods. Training does not end after one season. During their first season of field school implementation, monthly 'technical workshops' are held. Subsequently all participants receive a further full season's training on IPM for rotation crops. The total programme involves over a year of full-time training, including the actual implementation of a field school with farmers.

This large 'upstream' investment has paid off. Currently over 2000 field workers have graduated from the IPM programme, with a drop-out rate of next to zero. These persons, along with the farmers they have trained, and the local communities and government officials with whom they work, form a strong foundation for large-scale expansion of the programme. At the present rate of spread, where field workers manage only one field school per season along with their other duties, the Indonesian national IPM programme will have about 1 000 000 farmer graduates by 1998.

Paying farmer-extensionists

Despite the problems that have been experienced in paying farmer extensionists or researchers (see Chapter 7), this can facilitate scaling up. Sinaga and Wodicka describe one such example. When the Tananua Foundation in Indonesia started paying farmer leaders to work on a part-part time basis, its programme was able to reach more farmers and ensure wider adoption of certain agricultural practices.

Payment of farmer-advisers in Sumba, Indonesia (Sinaga and Wodicka)

The farmer-extensionists, as volunteers, represented the most delicate but yet the most important link in the extension chain. Experience showed that extensionists fared best where there was direct support from field staff. On the other hand, as the programme expanded, and fewer follow-up visits were carried out by field staff, some farmer-extensionists discontinued their activities in their own farms as well as with their neighbours. The programme tried to compensate for this by facilitating visits among farmer-extensionists, and by inviting at least three farmers from each village to attend regular meetings.

In order to respond to the growing needs of programme expansion and the difficulty of working solely through volunteer farmer extensionists, Tananua decided to form a new category of farmer-leader, known as the 'farmer-adviser'. A farmer-adviser is a farmer who has a very good farm, helps his neighbours learn improved farming techniques, and is selected by both the farmers and Tananua staff. Farmer-advisers, as opposed to farmer-extensionists, receive a small salary as compensation for the time the spend away from their farm. The obligations and rights of these farmer-advisers are explained and agreed upon together. Generally, farmer-advisers are expected to spend 10 days in a month working with their neighbours, attending meetings and maintaining records. Farmer-advisers receive a salary equal to a farm labourer's daily wage. The rationale behind this payment is to allow the farmer-adviser to hire someone to work on their farm while they are busy serving other farmers.

Scaling out

Working with and through existing national-level organizations, whether farmer associations or government or NGO sponsored programmes, can facilitate the spread of farmer-led extension. The *campesino-a-campesino* movement in Nicaragua is one example of such a strategy. As Holt-Gimenez explains, the movement expanded country-wide by working through an existing national union of farmers. The union had traditionally organized local, regional and national-level meetings or *encuentros*, and farmers took advantage of these meetings to arrange visits among themselves to share their ideas and field experiences.

Spreading the campesino-a-campesino *approach in Nicaragua* (Holt-Gimenez)
With the help of NGOs, the initial promoters spread their learning and teaching methods to other projects in the region. Still working within the NGO project framework, *campesino-a-campesino*'s overall impact remained limited at first. In scale, it was programmatically indistinguishable from hundreds of other NGO-sponsored micro-projects in sustainable agriculture which sprang up in Mesoamerica during the 'lost decade'. *Campesino-a-campesino*-type projects were small, sustainable islands in a sea of rapidly degenerating agro-ecology. It was not until 1989 that 'spontaneous innovation' and the adoption of sustainable agricultural techniques began to occur on a national scale. This was just two years after Mexican *campesinos*, working with a Mexican local development organization and the Nicaraguan Farmer's Union, initiated the first *campesino* soil and water conservation project in Nicaragua.

Within five years the conservation techniques had swept through the central dry zone and were spreading to the semi-humid mountain regions and the humid-tropics of the Nicaraguan agricultural frontier. The rapidity and ease with which these techniques travelled, without the intervention of extensionists or formal programmes, gave rise to the movement's name: *campesino-a-campesino*.

What happened in Nicaragua? First, the climate of change during the revolutionary period was particularly strong in the countryside. Traditional social and economic relation-

177

ships were profoundly altered by military conflict and the agrarian reform which re-distributed over three million acres. No social group was more affected by these changes than the *campesinos*.

Second, for the first time in history, Nicaraguan *campesinos* had easy access to each other. Indeed, open communication among *campesinos* may well turn out to be the most revolutionary aspect of the Nicaraguan revolution. Third, the first Nicaraguan *campesino-a-campesino* project was implemented by the Unión Nacionál de Agricultores y Ganaderos (UNAG), a national farmer's organization with over 100 000 members. UNAG had histori-cally organized local, national and regional *encuentros* or gatherings where *campesinos* met, ostensibly to organize the union politically and to train co-operative leaders. *Campesinos* took advantage of these *encuentros* to arrange visits among themselves to share their field experiences first-hand. This initiative was the farmers' and was absolutely unprogrammed. UNAG's soil conservation programme soon followed up on these farmer visits with project-organized field visits, sometimes between small groups of farmers and sometimes involving whole villages. All of these factors contributed to what might be called the 'scal-ing out' or spread of *campesino-a-campesino*. But a fourth factor, brought about by the collapse of the Nicaraguan economy, was the end of subsidized credit, hybrid seed and agrochemicals for *campesinos*. Practically overnight, the Nicaraguan agricultural sector went from being one characterized by state subsidies, state control, capital-intensive, high-external input production to one based on the 'free market'. This meant there was now no credit, no chemicals and no technical assistance, and for most *campesinos*, no alterna-tive.

When the Sandinista government was unseated in 1990, it marked the end of over a decade of government-run social programmes for the countryside. Foreign aid, once channelled through government ministries or mass organizations, now sought new development counterparts. In response, many local development agencies sprang up, and soon independent *campesino-a-campesino* projects began to appear all over Nica-ragua. In part this was because *campesino-a-campesino* was in vogue. Both financing NGOs and recipient local development organizations were looking for successful projects to sponsor and execute. But also as important was local demand by *campesinos* for such activities. At last count, in Nicaragua alone there were over 300 promoters and 3000 beneficiaries involved in *campesino-a-campesino* activities. Region-wide the figure is more difficult to estimate, though based on participation in regional *encuentros*, it may well be double. Is the magic in the methodology, or are revolutions and economic crises necessary for farmer-led development to emerge and spread on such a scale?

Scaling out through government extension services

There has also been successful scaling-out through working with national-scale public-sector extension networks and other public-sector bodies. Nguyen Kim Hai (Chapter 10) describes CIDSE's efforts in Vietnam to assist in the formulation of a province-wide extension policy as an important first step towards spreading its farmer-led extension approach.

Sinaga and Wodicka (see Chapter 5) describe the problems faced by World Neighbors in attempting to use an inter-agency farmer network called the Nusa Tenggara Upland Development Consortium to influence the public-sector exten-sion system.

Problems in influencing the government extension service in Indonesia (Sinaga and Wodicka)
In spite of these small successes, it has not yet been able to influence and change the extension system in a significant way. Changes are noticeable at the local level; however, policy makers have not yet been convinced of the effectiveness of these (farmer-led) approaches (to extension). In the meantime, small efforts spread throughout the country provide the best avenue for demonstrating impact. Continual exchange and sharing through the consortium activities are currently seen as one of the most effective strategies for effecting change at the local level.

Likewise, Kapoor argues that although the best means of scaling out the farmer-to-farmer extension project of the Aga Khan Rural Support Programme is through public-sector support and adoption of the strategies used by the NGO, there have been enormous difficulties in India in gaining acceptance of the approach.

Problems in institutionalizing farmer-led extension in India (Kapoor)
Despite some operational issues and difficulties, however, the effectiveness of farmer-to-farmer extension cannot be denied. It is therefore important to replicate such models by adapting them to other local situations. In India, major responsibility for carrying out developmental works lies with the state, which should, therefore, recognize the benefits of supporting the replication of AKRSP's farmer-to-farmer extension model. The knowledge and skills of the people who have already been undertaking these activities can be used in the expansion of the programmes and training of other people. The recent trend in some government departments indicates an acceptance of participatory approaches to development, with major responsibility for implementation being placed on communities. The Union Ministry of Rural Development has already accepted that the implementation of integrated watershed development should be conducted through communities. However, such recognition of the need for community involvement and confidence in their ability to provide what is needed is not yet present in all sectors of the government. Moreover, even in those departments where the necessity of community involvement in public sector development activities has been accepted, there is also a need to recognize that supporting the upgrading of local people's knowledge and skills will be essential for effective programme implementation.

Peacock describes a similar means of scaling out used by FarmAfrica, which decided to work with the public extension system and academic institutes in Ethiopia, as well as other NGOs, in order to expand its dairy goat project. However, as a result of this experience, she questions the ability and wisdom of NGOs' efforts to scale out such intensive programmes.

Problems with expanding activities in Ethiopia (Peacock)
Questions must be asked about whether the intensive group-based extension system used so successfully by the project can, realistically, be scaled up and used by government, or other NGO programmes. A group of farmers offers extension staff a valuable forum for the exchange of ideas and a channel for offering new technology. However when the level of farmers' skills is low, in relation to the technology offered, a great deal of extension staff time will be needed to help groups become firmly established. It may be hard for govern-

ments to justify allocating resources towards such endeavours. Governments must strike a balance between allocating many resources to a few farmers or a few resources to many farmers, which may be politically expedient. The FarmAfrica project's experience has shown how powerful groups of farmers, whose members share a common interest, can be in sustaining new technology once introduced.

For effective farmer-to-farmer exchange to take place, facilitating structures must be in place. Ethiopia is currently regionalizing its political and administrative structures to encourage greater regional autonomy. This offers the potential for the relatively easy exchange of ideas within a region, but may limit exchange between regions.

The decline in resources allocated to rural services by governments throughout Africa is leading many agricultural ministries to reconsider their role in extending agricultural technology to their populations. Rural communities in marginal farming areas are likely to suffer most through their inability to pay high charges for private services. New ways through which the public and private sectors can collaborate and deliver services must urgently be sought. Marginal farming communities will become increasingly marginalized unless they happen to be lucky and benefit from the attentions of an NGO.

There have been some successes in changing public-sector attitudes, though. Kingsley and Musante (Chapter 8) describe how widening the impact of World Education's IPM programme in Indonesia was undertaken through identifying and working with other NGOs and public-sector extension staff interested in using farmer field schools to promote sustainable agricultural practices in new areas and amongst new crops. Quarterly forums and cross-visits are used by World Education to introduce other NGOs and government extension officers to the concepts and practices being used.

Developing and using information materials
Strangely, there seem to have been relatively few attempts to use publications and other media (especially mass media) to support farmer-led extension activities. Sinaga and Wodicka (Chapter 5) describe how the Tananua Foundation and Studio Driya Media in Indonesia have developed and used visual materials and booklets to promote their work in Sumba.

According to Nguyen Kim Hai's description, below, of similar activities in the CIDSE-supported project in Bac Thai, Vietnam, it is not enough merely to have the right equipment. Personnel must also be skilled in developing suitable materials, operating the equipment, and using the materials appropriately as part of field activities.

Strengthening the extension information system in Vietnam (Nguyen Kim Hai)
In the first year of the project, equipment was bought for a print shop and installed in a special air-conditioned printing room to enable extension literature to be produced. Initially two information officers at the extension centre received technical training in computer use and basic printing skills. Unfortunately, up to the present the

equipment remains almost unused, for three main reasons: equipment defects; lack of technical skills and experience in working with printing; and most importantly, a lack of ideas and creativity in printed media production among the information officers.

To attempt to remedy this, a three-week media development workshop was organized, conducted by two media specialists from Indonesia. The workshop focused mainly on developing media designed to assist extension workers in their work with farmer groups. Practical technical sessions working with the above mentioned equipment were also arranged, but, as time was limited and the group of trainees too large and diverse (three information officers and nine extension workers), these efforts were not very successful. The workshop clearly revealed the need for more strengthening of media development activities in the extension programmes. Following up on this activity, in middle of 1994 three provincial information officers were sent to Studio Driya Media, a development media organization in Bandung, Indonesia, to upgrade their skills. This led to some developments.

The information officers produced a series (a total of 56 000 copies) of simple and informative technical leaflets for the technical programmes. Technical booklets on various training subjects for extension workers were also produced, as well as four issues of the new extension newsletter (8000 copies each). Five hundred copies of an extension worker handbook were produced to be used as direct field guides for extension workers in extension methodology, explaining and illustrating the 'nine-step approach'. All printing was done outside the extension centre. In the first half of 1994 a video film was made for the external promotion of the Bac Thai extension programme.

Constraints and positive influences

Possibly the two major constraints to scaling-up farmer-led extension efforts are:

o the intensity of human resource inputs required, as described by Peacock above
o successfully encouraging a change of culture among traditional development organizations towards accepting that farmers may have more to offer than learn in appropriate technological innovation.

However, there are also many other constraints on both the adoption of farmer-led modes of extension, and their impact or effectiveness once initiated. Conversely there are also many factors that stimulate and encourage such activities and their success. A wide array of these are summarized below.

In many cases the positive influences are the reverse of the constraints — for example, government support, or the lack of it. Below we focus on the positive influences on farmer-led extension and research. These positive and negative factors are rather crudely and arbitrarily divided into four categories:

o environmental factors — external to both the extension system and the community
o factors internal to the extension system but independent of the community
o factors internal to the community but independent of the extension system
o factors common to the extension system and the community.

Environmental factors

The policy environment

The importance of government policies to support farm family production and farmer-led extension cannot be over-estimated. Many of the authors highlighted this as the single most important factor in scaling up and maintaining activities. For example, Nguyen Kim Hai (Chapter 10) asserts that CIDSE's efforts in Vietnam could not have succeeded if the government policy had not shifted to support farmer-led extension.

Likewise, Bimoli and Manandhar (Chapter 9) describe how, after democracy was introduced in Nepal, government policy shifted to group extension based on the principles of self-help and volunteer leaders. This, they argue, played an important role in the adoption and spread of the problem census/problem solving approach and thus a clear articulation of farmers' demands. A similar shift in policy following the accession of a new government was described by Murwira *et al.* in Zimbabwe (Chapter 11).

In Nicaragua, Holt-Gimenez (Chapter 4) asserts that the revolution greatly assisted the development of a mass farmer-led extension movement. The end of government subsidies on credit, hybrid seeds, and agro-chemicals may also have been important in stimulating farmers to look for alternative agricultural technologies, learning methodologies and dissemination strategies.

However, such a drastic change in national government is not necessary. Maningding describes below the importance of local government support to the success of the IPM farmer field school programme in the Philippines. Such support was actively courted through dialogue and by involving local officials in the programme's activities. It should be noted, though, that the devolution of power from the national to local governments (a shift brought about by national government policy) encouraged and led to greater involvement of local officials in such programmes.

Factors influencing the effectiveness of farmer field schools in the Philippines (Maningding)

The efficiency of the implementation of the farmer field school programme was affected by the following:

o the support of local leaders and the regional, provincial and central administration management through the provision of funds or 'sourcing out' the implementation
o supervision was and is being practised at all levels of management
o responsibilities are clearly and evenly distributed and well co-ordinated
o workloads are equally divided
o organizational linkages are ensured through regular and well co-ordinated meetings and conferences
o there is a liaison with local people and authorities who have influence and rapport with the farming community, which was important during the preparation stage.

The reverse side of the coin — lack of government support — also demonstrates the importance of this factor. For example, Peacock (Chapter 10) describes how negative government attitudes towards both goats and women historically undermined the development of both, and how FarmAfrica had to address such attitudes.

The organizational environment

Collaboration between government, NGOs, private firms, and farmers' groups involved in agricultural extension and research can facilitate a farmer-led agenda by sharing resources and scaling up the approach. However, as described in Chapter 10, such collaboration may be more difficult than at first sight. It requires a significant amount of communication and commitment to exchange. Despite the difficulties, there are some examples of successful collaboration between very different organizations. For example, in Santa Catarina, Brazil, de Freitas (see Chapter 12) describes the joint implementation of a rural extension and technical assistance project by the private sector and municipal government. Similar collaborative experiences are also described by Kingsley and Musante in Indonesia (Chapter 8) and by Ishii-Eitemann and Kaophong in Thailand (Chapter 10).

Shinde and Rangnekar (below) stress the importance of inter-organizational relationships in their analysis of BAIF's activities over the last 25 years in Rajasthan.

Inter-organizational relationships in Rajasthan (Shinde and Rangnekar)

Promoting interaction between various agencies has been one of the endeavours of the BAIF wherever it is involved. Success in promoting interaction has been outstanding in Udaipur due to a pro-active role of the Ford Foundation and positive response from government departments, NGOs, the agricultural university, etc. NGOs and government departments involved in agriculture, education, environment, and awareness-related activities in and around the project areas were identified and contacts were established. Joint meetings were arranged between NGOs and with government agencies and farmers to develop understanding and collaboration. Most of the NGOs and some of the government departments responded favourably. Particular mention need be made of the training-and-visit units of the agriculture department in Udaipur district, who gave very positive responses. Their team actively participated in discussions, development activities as well as in training and extension. The state agriculture university, which has a large establishment in Udaipur, also responded well to promote interaction between various agencies and in arranging field trials. It may also be mentioned that the Rajasthan state government has also taken initiative in promoting NGO involvement. An NGO cell has been formed to promote NGO participation. The zonal agriculture research committee at Udaipur is one of the few in the country where NGOs are invited to participate and make suggestions. The Ford Foundation as well as Swiss Inter-cooperation are some of the international agencies that have taken the lead in Rajasthan to promote government–NGO interaction.

The co-ordination of approaches between various institutions may also be important. For example, farmer-led extension may be difficult to apply where previous or current development programmes have been or are highly paternalistic. Cansancio notes that 'dole-outs' from politicians in the form of free food and cigarettes undermined the self-reliance ethos his project was promoting in the uplands in the Philippines.

Problems caused by free inputs in the Philippines (Cansancio)

With the introduction of the *bayanihan/alayon* concept (group or communal labour exchanges) in the area, the notion of getting paid every time one works is slowly being lessened. In short, the materialistic orientation of the people is slowly being erased, giving way to a counterpart system.

Sometimes motivating people to be self-reliant is difficult due to dole-outs. During the campaign period, politicians give away food, money, cigarettes, and liquor. Through community-organizing strategies, communities have learned to be empowered and self-reliant. During meetings, others brought with them vegetables, corn grits, and cooked through *bayanihan*. In order to improve their quality of education, they established day-care centres and encouraged their children to pursue their studies.

Bimoli and Manandhar (Chapter 9) argue that the confusion caused in some areas of Nepal by NGOs distributing free agricultural inputs has frustrated efforts at promoting self-reliance and sustainability in some of their project areas. Co-ordination among institutions is important, as is collaboration between government agencies, since separately they do not have the mandate or resources to tackle farmers' problems.

Small-farmer mass movements can also be important in stimulating farmer-led agricultural services. This was clearly important in the development of the *campesino-a-campesino* movement described by Holt-Gimenez (Chapter 4).

Access to land and other resources

Access to land — and particularly to good-quality land — is an important determinant of the success of farmer-led extension, as it probably is with all agricultural development initiatives. The same can be said of other resources, such as labour.

Likewise, Nguyen Kim Hai describes the importance of obtaining secure tenure for farmers before CIDSE began its extension efforts in Vietnam (see Chapter 10); and Cansancio (see above) describes how activities in the Upland Development Pilot Project in the Philippines necessarily began with ensuring security of tenure for farm households through certificates of stewardship.

Family ownership of farms was also thought to be important by some participants. For example, Pham Xuan Du (Chapter 4) suggests that market-oriented reforms in Vietnam, including government policy to support the family economy, created a demand among farmers for extension services.

Access to infrastructure, markets, information and technology

The availability of infrastructure such as roads, irrigation and telecommunications is also seen as a major influence on the success of farmer-led extension and research efforts. Thapa (Chapter 11) mentions that there is more demand for community agricultural workers in the mid-hills and foothills of Nepal, where potential productivity is higher and infrastructure and access to information and markets is better than at higher elevations.

Farouk and Worsley (Chapter 11) describe how access to information impinged on CARE's efforts to initiate a farmer-led technological innovation process in Egypt. They note that although much relevant information and many technologies are available in the country, they were not always accessible to small-scale farmers. The project they describe focuses on linking small-scale farmers to such information and technology.

Existing extension and research systems

Disillusionment with previous extension or research systems can stimulate the adoption and spread of farmer-led methods and processes. Dilts and Hate (Chapter 8) recall that the limited adoption of IPM technologies by farmers was one important factor which prompted those involved to seek alternative means of encouraging farmers to consider the IPM concept and develop alternative technologies. The community agricultural worker approach described by Thapa (Chapter 11) was also developed in response to a similar set of problems.

An absence of prior extension or research systems can prompt the development of more farmer-led approaches. As explained by Pham Xuan Du (see Chapter 4), the extension approaches adopted by VACVINA in Vietnam grew out of the fact that government extension services for small-scale farmers were very limited, having been established only in 1993. Because of a lack of any basis on which to build such an extension service, much reliance was placed on local knowledge and local human resources in the search for new approaches.

Lack of an extension system in Vietnam (Pham Xuan Du)

The first obstacle encountered in choosing appropriate techniques stemmed from the fact that gardening systems had been neglected for decades. Therefore there were no research findings available for the establishment and management of such small-scale bio-intensive farming systems. Most of the technologies available at the time were elaborated for farming on a bigger scale in state farms and farm co-operatives. This was the reason we had to sum up the relevant local knowledge available.

Factors internal to the extension system

Relationships with the community

Good relationships between outsiders and insiders are seen to be vital to the success of farmer-led agricultural development and may require considerable investment of time by both sides.

However, Shinde and Rangnekar warn of the dangers of developing relationships built on dependence. When communities continue to depend on outside agencies and people, a lack of initiative among farmers and their organizations can result.

185

Dependency feelings in Rajasthan (Shinde and Rangnekar)
In many areas lack of initiative amongst farmers is observed and a dependency syndrome has developed amongst the rural population who have got used to initiatives from the government for problem solving and expect heavy subsidies for any activity. However, we find that not much effort is made to understand the reasons behind such attitudes and the lack of confidence. Often this attitude is related to utter poverty prevailing in the society, sometimes to the bad experiences and exploitation faced by the families and the neglect of the area. Where people's major concern is subsistence, one can hardly expect them to suggest future development approaches and participate in planning.

Good relationships with the community may depend in large part on the outsiders' knowledge of local socio-cultural and physical aspects of small-scale farming systems. An understanding of the local cultures, indigenous knowledge and technologies is important. Part of the success of the farmer field school approach in Indonesia, described by Dilts and Hate in Chapter 8, stems from the extended hands-on field training given to extension workers in rice growing and IPM.

Adoption of a learning process approach
Adoption of a learning process approach, including embracing error, self-critical monitoring and evaluation, with good feedback and readjustment mechanisms, is favourable to farmer-led extension approaches. This was clearly demonstrated by Kamp in his description of the evolution of CARE's fish-farming project in Bangladesh (Chapter 11).

Decentralization of authority and flexibility in decision making
Decentralization of authority and flexibility in decision making can be critical in farmer-led initiatives, because they allow local flexibility to respond to farmers' demands. De Freitas describes how public sector extension agents in Santa Catarina, Brazil, now have the freedom to create and innovate in order to adjust to local conditions. The working methodology is the only factor which remains well defined. Garg believes that rigid staffing structures and budgetary processes are two of the weaknesses that current efforts to reform public sector extension services in Rajasthan need to address.

Problems with public extension services in Rajasthan (Garg)
The system has a lot of weaknesses... It is too rigidly structured. The rigidity in structure has come basically from two sources. First, the extension personnel are organized in cadres. Consequently, promotion, pay, and responsibility depends on the rank and place in the cadre, not on the qualifications, experience, and motivation of the worker. Second, the system works in accordance with the budgetary system of the state. Consequently, the response time taken in effecting change is too long.

The tightening financial health of the government has affected the vitality and flexibility of the extension agencies. The control over expenditures connected with travelling cuts at the root of the system which was meant only for reaching out to farmers. The disinclination of the state to create further posts also leads to critical gaps and frustration over the lack of promotions. The proportion of salaries has reached about 94 per cent of total establishment costs, clearly indicating an immobilized extension machinery.

186

Sunset clauses on external support

Sunset clauses on external support are argued by some as a means of focusing on the sustainability and empowerment of groups and communities. For example, in the Nepal Agroforestry Foundation project (Pandit, Chapter 5) and CARE's FarmLink programme in Egypt (Farouk and Worsley, Chapter 11), timelines are established for the withdrawal of external support to groups and communities. Likewise, Cansancio stresses that the public sector's co-ordinating role in the Upland Development project in the Philippines has to be taken over by the farmers' associations so that the organization does not continue to support one area indefinitely.

Factors internal to the community

Local organizations and traditions

The existence of community groups, even if not previously concerned with agricultural problems, can facilitate farmer-led extension efforts. Holt-Gimenez (Chapter 4) suggests that farmer solidarity is one of the main pillars of the *campesino-a-campesino* movement. The Nicaraguan Farmers' Association was the first institution in Nicaragua to engage in farmer-to-farmer extension.

Traditions of communal activities or labour are, in many cases, a prime influence on the adoption and effectiveness of farmer-led extension and research efforts. According to Cansancio and Kilalo respectively, *alayon/bayanihan* working groups in the Philippines Upland Development project, and *harambee* communal labour traditions in Kenya, have had positive effects on farmers' activities in their respective projects.

Local organization in the Philippines (Cansancio)

The farmers were able to establish a viable organization, the Upper Bala Upland Farmers Development Association, Inc., and register it with the Security Exchange Commission. The officers concerned are responsible for making solutions to the problems. They have also formed seven committees each headed by the chairman. These committees cover: infrastructure, co-operatives, livelihood, agroforestry/soil and water conservation, livestock dispersal, and health and sanitation.

The chairman is responsible for undertaking activities in co-ordination with the officers and members within the organization. In order to speed up the development of the 650 ha total project area and other activities, the association was divided into five sectors, each headed by a sector leader. Each sector formed an *alayon/bayanihan* work group that will undertake different activities therein. They procured their food from the *alayon* canteen established by their association at *sitio* Kabuhu-an, which was later converted into a co-operative.

Mutual-help groups in Kenya (Kilalo)

There is an indigenous self-help process referred to as *ngua* in the people's vernacular. *Ngua* refers to infrequent support given by neighbours and friends for a one-time activity. The person to be supported provides the day's meals for all who have come to help. Often, there can be as many as 60 people who participate.

Kuwadana is another indigenous self-help system. *Kuwadana* consists of three or four people who have agreed to work together, mainly for farming. This process continues throughout the year, but unfortunately, it is strong at the start of the partnership; then it is slowly eroded by the élitist, selfish attitude of individualism. The 'we' concept strongly stressed by indigenous systems has now been replaced by the 'me' point of view. The motto, 'If I have, I help you to have too so that we can live in harmony', is no longer popular. The partnership has challenged villagers to review what they were losing and what is replacing it.

In Nepal, Bimoli and Manandhar (Chapter 9) describe how existing training-and-visit farmer groups were restructured to enable the problem census technique to be used to identify and prioritize farmers' problems and needs, and develop potential solutions.

Below, Peacock shows how easily a traditional approach can be adapted for project purposes, often on the initiative of local people themselves.

Savings associations in Ethiopia (Peacock)
During the course of project activities, staff and collaborators learned of a traditional method used by women in Welayta to save money and help each other. Known locally as *eddir*, this involves small amounts of money saved regularly by a small, informal, group of women. The money can be allocated to women in the group in turn, or given or lent to those in need. Members of goat groups in Areka, Welayta, spontaneously organized themselves into a 'Women's Self-Help Goat Society', with each member contributing a small sum during each of their weekly meetings. Some groups decided to set aside a portion of their savings to purchase goats for other needy women. Project staff were impressed with the efforts of these women and were eager to suggest it to groups in other areas. The idea was shared with other extension staff during the regular project training courses and quickly spread to all project sites where it was enthusiastically adopted. Groups leaders are now being helped with leadership, as well as trained in basic bookkeeping skills.

Similarly, Kilalo describes below a dispute-resolution community organization that was restructured to incorporate agricultural concerns and interest groups in a community project supported by World Neighbors in Kenya.

Using existing local institutions in Kenya (Kilalo)
The programme leaders studied the indigenous institution *weni mwana*, which was very active in the area and could mobilize most of the community. Its role was mainly to settle disputes, keep the peace, and resolve other matters of concern in the community. *Weni mwana* is a Taita institution. Translated into English, it means 'the institution that addresses our issues and our problems'. The fascinating thing about this institution is the way it handles community problems and issues by bringing together men, women, and the young to settle disputes or discuss issues. Those people attending are encouraged to air their views freely without intimidation. Attendance is open to everyone. Usually a binding decision is reached. The facilitators of this process are *njama ya weni mwana* or the 'council of elders', whose major role in a *weni mwana* gathering is to listen and ask questions. Before the meeting, the council studies the issues and problems to be discussed. This institution, though indigenous, is officially recognized by the government, and the decisions made have frequently been adopted. The *weni mwana* handles land, family, and petty theft disputes. Issues that arise in the diagnosis require organization and mobilization of the people.

188

The existence of capable community organizations may influence planners in locating a project in a particular community. Maningding states this was a determining factor in siting the IPM farmer field school project in Benguet, Philippines.

Community organizations in the Philippines (Maningding)
The government formed a committee to save the vegetable industry in Benguet. It was then very timely because IPM through the farmer field school had been very successful in rice. Using the same concept, national authorities believed that it could also work in Benguet. The municipality of Atok, Benguet, was then selected as the pilot area because of the support given by the mayor and the presence of a well organized co-operative of farmers.

In the absence of existing community organizations, new organizations can be created. This requires careful design and the participation of local people from the outset if they are to feel that they belong to the organization. This is illustrated by Restrepo's tale of Corpotunía, a local non-profit development corporation supported by the Carvajal Foundation in Colombia.

Building local institutions in Colombia (Restrepo)
A big gap was created between the people in the town and the rural area. Farmers were not members of Corpotunía's board of directors and did not participate in the decision-making process when important matters were discussed. The only community representatives on the board were people from the town, and their contact with the rural area was nil. Even though the relationship with the farmers was broad, it was limited to extension activities... Corpotunía amended its statutes to make it possible for people from the community to become members... However, almost no one joined, due to a lack of ownership and fear of acquiring more obligations, and people preferred to pay higher prices as non-members.

Levels of education
The levels of education among farmers can also be an important influence on the adoption and success of farmer-led extension. However, some argue that more formal education is an advantage, whilst others argue the reverse. This debate is illustrated here by two authors. Cansancio suggests that low levels of education can be a problem faced by farmers in maintaining farm plans and keeping records. In response, Murwira describes an example from the ITDG-supported project in Zimbabwe where low levels of education among farmers were not a disadvantage.

Education levels in the Philippines (Cansancio)
The farmers find it hard to make farm plans and keep records due to low educational attainment. Only a few have attended high school, and they are loaded with positions of different organizations in the community, so they become ineffective in performing their duties and responsibilities.

Literacy in Zimbabwe (Murwira)
When both farmers and gardeners were asked by project staff to select representatives of their choice to go on exposure visits, they sought clarification from the staff as to whether they should select only literate people. The idea of selecting literate people to attend courses and participate in look-and-learn visits was something which has been imposed on them by

staff of the Department of Community and Co-operative Development. The project staff advised that it was better for them to select those people whom they felt would be able to grasp issues quickly and provide the necessary feedback to the rest of the community.

Reflecting the community's choice, representatives who went on exposure visits to similar geographical areas included both the literate and the illiterate. On their return a feedback meeting was arranged. The literate spoke first, but the audience had problems understanding their reports, which involved mainly reading notes taken during their visits but which lacked the necessary flow. It seems that in the process of taking notes they missed part of the explanations given by their hosts. So failing to pay attention to what was being said and concentrating on writing notes led to some representatives not being able to understand what was happening in these projects.

When a greater part of the audience failed to get the story, the illiterate participants stood up one by one to explain what they had seen. The information was coming from their memories alone and they did not rely on notes to describe what happened. In order to illustrate what they had seen, they drew diagrams and pictures on the ground and gave examples using things in their environment and known to most of the members of the community. It was easier for the community to understand the information shared by the illiterate participants. For this reason, they were better informed and were in a better position to make their own choices.

Given this experience, the project staff feel that low levels of education should not always be viewed as a constraint to active participation by farmers in development.

Farmer mobility

Many farmer-extensionists or researchers have limited mobility beyond their own community and therefore cannot reach a large number of other farmers. For example, Pandit (see Chapters 5 and 12) estimates that less than 30 per cent of the Nepalese community agricultural workers provide agro-veterinary extension services outside of their own village. Sinaga and Wodicka (see Chapter 12) note that it has taken 15 years for the Tananua programme to reach 3000 farmers, and that this represents less than 5 per cent of the entire island population.

Factors common to the extension system and the community

Genuine participation in and control of the system by farmers
This is self-evidently important in farmer-led agricultural development. Indeed, Holt-Gimenez (see Chapter 4) argues that outsiders should participate in farmers' development agendas, but that farmers need to control the decisions on the planning and implementation of development activities. However, he questions outsiders' ability to participate in, rather than patronize, farmers' agenda and programmes.

Participatory analysis, planning, and implementation techniques
Participatory analysis, planning, and implementation techniques are, almost by definition, necessary if outsiders are to engage in farmer-led extension. Numerous examples of the use of such techniques are described in the preceding chapters.

Role changes for farmers, extensionists and researchers

Successful farmer-led extension and research systems often require significant role changes: farmers become extensionists and researchers, extensionists become facilitators instead of teachers, and researchers become backstoppers and supporters of the farmers' research. Thapa provides an example of such a switch in roles.

Changing roles in Nepal (Thapa)

New levels of farmer participation were introduced at this time. These included the use of village workshops to help farmers analyse and set priorities based on their needs. The project abandoned the definition of options, and left the selection of innovations entirely open to farmers. The reduced analytical role of CARE staff has enabled farmers to better state their needs and act on their own initiative.

Farmer-extensionists provide for:

o local agro-ecological, socio-economic and cultural knowledge and understanding
o a common language (in both linguistic and cultural senses) with farmers
o demonstration of what can be done with similar resources and background
o the ability to expand project activities
o cost-efficiency
o the potential for long-term project sustainability.

Using farmer extensionists, however, is not necessary for farmer-led extension efforts, as shown by projects that do not rely upon them — for example some of the IPM farmer field schools. Likewise, the farmer-to-farmer extension approaches described in Chapters 3 – 7 may not be sufficient to ensure that research, technologies and extension systems meet farmers' needs. For example, Okumu (1995) describes a case in Kenya where farmer-to-farmer extension relied upon externally provided technologies that proved too labour-intensive for widespread adoption by farmers.

Many feel that there is a positive link between farmers being involved in experimentation and those who become involved in extension. The farmer field schools (Chapter 8) are based on the idea that farmers are more likely to adopt and spread a practice if they discover it themselves. Bunch (below) and Kamp (see Chapter 11) argue that if farmers do the research, it is more likely that the technology will be adopted more widely.

Farmers as researchers (Bunch)

The people-centred agricultural development (PCAD) process teaches villagers how to experiment and teach each other through the most efficient teaching process we know: learning by doing. Repeatedly, year after year, farmers manage experiments. Some of them also come to work as extensionists, teaching farmers in other villages what they themselves have learned. And the success of the innovations they learn through the PCAD process motivates them to continue experimenting and continue sharing what they know... New pests attack crops, seeds degenerate, input prices rise, old markets dry up and new ones appear. The only way farmers can maintain both productivity and profitability in a modern, rapidly changing environment is to be constantly trying out new technologies.

191

Incentives for farmers

There is a lively debate on whether material incentives should be given to farmers to engage in extension or research (see Chapter 7). Incentives to those contributing to communal works may be useful, especially in the early stages of the project, because they help the poorest community members to participate. Unfortunately, they can also lead to participation for the wrong reasons, and the work may end if they are withdrawn. However, upon completion of an extension programme, the presence and input of the professional extension workers will also be withdrawn. If a programme has used farmer-extensionists, at least some human resource remains in the community — even if extension work is much less intense without compensation. Selener, Chenier and Zelaya (Chapter 7) and Baile (see Chapters 5 and 6) argue that incentives for farmer extensionists may be important for the sustainability and scaling-up of a programme.

Training and other opportunities for learning and sharing

Training for farmers, extensionists and research staff is vital where an existing system of agricultural service provision is attempting reform. Such training should be undertaken locally, at times convenient to trainees, using participatory dialogue, discussions, demonstrations and facilitation of farmers' own research and extension efforts, rather than lectures, talks or slide-shows. Such characteristics are illustrated by Peacock's (Chapter 10) description of how the training of female farmers in Ethiopia was adapted to the participants' needs in various ways. Pandit (see Chapter 5) and others also stress the importance of follow-up training and argue against on–off training sessions.

Training can have other benefits apart from the immediate one of learning. Ishii-Eitemann and Kaophong below describe how a training programme on integrated pest management in Thailand stimulated linkages among various organizations and individuals.

Effects of training in Thailand (Ishii-Eitemann and Kaophong)

Participants in the IPM training learned an enormous amount about ecological approaches to pest management through the 'learning-by-doing' non-formal education methods. When evaluating the condition of their fields and their management options, farmers based their decisions on a more comprehensive assessment of interrelated ecological factors than they did prior to the training. Thus, for example, farmers were more likely to observe the life cycle of the insect or weed pest, recognize the presence or absence of life stages which could threaten crop yield, and compare the effect of chemical versus non-chemical interventions on both pests and their natural enemies.

Six months after the completion of the IPM training, Save the Children observed subtle progress in co-operation between the former participants of the training. At least two of the international NGOs have entered into an extended partnership with the same government extensionist who had participated in RISA's 1994 training, bringing the enquiry-based farmer field school methodology to primary school agro-environmental education in 1995.

Word of the success of the IPM training has spread through the local NGOs' network, encouraging another group of NGOs in the northeast of Thailand to request that the

192

Department of Agricultural Extension send the same now-popular extensionist to lead the IPM sessions of their alternative agriculture training.

One local training NGO, which had the previous year eschewed co-operation with the government and heaped scorn upon the department's IPM training capacities, now actively seeks the department's support and participation in its NGO training. A district-wide farmers' association which had sent representatives to the 1994 IPM training requested RISA to assist them in 1995 in obtaining further technical support from local government to implement additional ecological field training in their villages. RISA staff knew that the Department of Agricultural Extension was organizing a new series of farmer participatory research activities, with an emphasis on ecological weed management in rice. After discussion with RISA, the department chose to locate one of its pilot sites in the district of this farmers' organization, and designated the lead extensionist to work directly with 30 farmers from several villages in the district.

Many other opportunities for learning and sharing information are described in previous chapters, including farmers' meetings, events and cross-visits (Chapter 5), visits to research sites (Farouk and Worsley, Chapter 11) and farmer field schools (Chapter 8).

14 Lessons and conclusions

IN THIS FINAL chapter, we attempt to do two things. First we go back from the particular to the general. We try to stand back from the detail presented in the preceding chapters, and to classify the experiences into broad categories. Second, we examine the potential for expansion of the approaches within each category, the types of constraints they face, and how these might be overcome.

Categorizing the experiences

The experiences presented in this volume fall into three broad categories:

o those in a 'pure' farmer-to-farmer vein, often found in areas where appropriate government services are almost non-existent, and in some areas reaching the status of a 'movement' among farmers
o those (very few cases) aiming to set up input supply services on a sustainable, priced basis, or examining how the provision of technical information might be improved to suit dynamic market conditions
o those (the majority) which fall into more of a 'farmer-led' than pure 'farmer-to-farmer' mode, and are concerned in various ways with generating more and better responses from government services.

We take each of these in turn.

Farmer-to-farmer extension in its 'pure' form
Usually promoted by NGOs or individuals, this approach originated in areas where government services were chronically weak or recommended technologies were inappropriate. The longest-standing examples are found in the *campesino-a-campesino* movement in Central and South America (Holt-Gimenez; Lopez; Selener, Chenier and Zelaya), and its derivatives elsewhere, including the World Neighbors programme in Sumba, Indonesia (Sinaga and Wodicka). Also included are the Nepal Agroforestry Program (Pandit), programmes on soil and water conservation and upland farm management in the Philippines (Bhuktan, Killough and Basilio), and the VACVINA programme in Vietnam. Many of these latter drew on lessons from earlier World Neighbors projects. They are described in Chapters 4–7.

Many of the features now commonly associated with farmer-to-farmer extension, including group-based learning, cross-visits, farmer-trainers and so on, originated in these experiences.

195

In some settings, especially in Latin America, the approach is driven by farmers' sense of solidarity with each other and has come to be regarded as a 'movement'. Although it contains strong elements of self-learning, and working at a group rather than individual level (especially where the management of soil and water resources is concerned), in some cases it relies heavily on the ability of the external facilitator (whether NGO or individual) to offer appropriate technology options, much as described by Bunch (1982).

Those of a sceptical mind-set might regard farmer-to-farmer extension in this mode as having low future potential for growth, limited perhaps to areas (such as the outer islands of Indonesia) still unreached by government extension services, or to topics (such as agroforestry) which compartmentalized approaches in government find difficult to address.

Elements of 'pure' farmer-to-farmer extension are found also in a very different context: the various cases describing farmer field schools and their derivatives (Dilts and Hate; Kingsley and Musante; Maningding, Chapter 8; Kamp, Chapter 11) rely in many of the same ways on experiential, field-based learning, cross-visits, and so on. However, they differ in three important respects:

o They are generally located in contexts of good infrastructure where government extension services are strong, but have been promoting inappropriate chemical-based technologies.
o They require a structured learning approach, and a reliable source of technical information which (as in the case of IPM) can be highly specialized and complex.
o In some settings, part of their 'mission' is to engage the interest of government services in what farmer field schools have to offer.

For these reasons, farmer field school-type approaches may be thought to have more potential for general uptake than farmer-to-farmer extension in its original mode. However, the fact should not be overlooked that their success has depended on highly skilled and committed support teams and on the introduction of strong support policies in response to concern over pollution and human health issues due to high pesticide use (for example, the case of IPM in Indonesia).

Relating farmer-led extension to the market
Experiences falling within the 'pure' farmer-to-farmer category generally derive strongly from the cultivation of a spirit of voluntarism from within highly motivated groups. Two experiences expand the options available to farmers in ways which do not rely on group formation or voluntarism, but instead, help to introduce market-like solutions, or to put in place the preconditions for markets to function efficiently. First, ActionAid modified its community agricultural worker scheme in Nepal (Thapa, Chapter 11), away from a philosophy purely of voluntarism and towards one based on payment for some of the services which community agricultural workers provide. This, it is hoped, will enhance the prospects of these workers' having enough income to continue after ActionAid's withdrawal.

In Egypt, CARE's FarmLink project (Farouk and Worsley, Chapter 11) has been concerned with helping small-scale farmers to respond to the liberalization of the economy, and to the subsequent reduction in public sector extension services. In particular, it has been putting community-selected 'innovative farmers' in touch with research services and farmers in other areas who may have interesting technologies. In this way, the innovative farmers can (a) bring back these technologies for use on their own farm and on those of other community members, and, equally importantly, (b) develop links with farming systems and practices elsewhere which may be of value for the future.

Farmer-led approaches and the public sector
These can be categorized into two broad types: some attempt to transform the public sector from within, whereas the remainder seek to do so by generating pressure from outside. In each of these broad types, there are important differences in the scope of individual efforts.

Transforming the public sector from within. The problem census/problem solving methodology in Nepal described by Bimoli and Manandhar (Chapter 9) presents opportunities for transforming the current training and visit extension system, yet remains limited to questions of designing and accessing appropriate technologies. A similar scheme in Bangladesh described by Bhuiyan and Walker (Chapter 9) has greater scope for influencing policy design, given that it is at the heart of new decentralization measures.

Generating external pressure on public sector organizations. The ITDG Chivi Food Security project (Murwira *et al.*, Chapter 11) has strengthened local communities' capacity not only to identify and meet their own needs, but also to draw more fully on the government resources available in order to obtain appropriate technologies. The FarmAfrica goat project (Peacock, Chapter 10) went further: it sought from government not only relevant technical support, but also more positive policies towards small ruminants and towards women in development.

Some of the efforts towards NGO-government collaboration described in Chapter 10 are similarly limited to attempted collaboration on technology issues, and have been characterized by considerable tension: Ishii-Eitemann and Kaophong, for instance, describe how the differences in perceptions, technical background and expectations made it difficult for an NGO and government officials to work together on integrated pest management. Garg describes how government efforts in India to contract NGOs to implement extension services in selected areas provoked negative responses from all sides: NGOs saw the provisions as too restrictive, and as an attempt by government to acquire their services 'on the cheap'; lower-level government staff saw it as a threat to the security of their positions. A small number of cases of collaboration have now been implemented under this scheme. However, other collaboration is successfully taking place outside the scheme (Shinde and Rangnekar). Considerable time and effort has been devoted to creating a forum for NGO-government collaboration in Rajasthan (Sharda and Ballabh) and to stimulating 'process' learning of how and why activities progress in certain directions. This has increased awareness of NGO and government activities and in a limited number of cases has led to new collaborative efforts. But questions remain over, for instance, the future of the forum once the initial introductory phase is over; the extent to which (especially) the larger NGOs are willing to engage with government, and the extent to which government services can free themselves from 'targets' in order to become more responsive to local needs.

The CIDSE project in Vietnam (Nguyen Kim Hai, Chapter 10) is perhaps the most ambitious in the scope of its relations with government. At the government's invitation, it has responded to a void in policies and structures following the demise of the command economy. It has worked patiently with government and local organizations not only to generate technologies oriented towards farmers' needs, but also to ensure that policies, resource-allocation strategies and human resource development harmonize towards the same objective.

Multi-agency approaches towards technology generation and dissemination are much more difficult to introduce where there are strong institutional positions and vested interests. Perhaps government agriculture departments belong more firmly in this category than most. Multi-agency collaboration in preventive health care and functional literacy, for instance, has been more widespread than in agriculture; in response to environmental pressures, even some forest departments have become open to new approaches. Nowhere are such vested interests and entrenched positions stronger than in India. Even here, however, there is considerable debate in the public sector on the appropriate role of different types of organization in research and extension, and how they might work together.

Prospects for expansion

All types of farmer-led extension face a number of generic constraints:

o All involve considerable investment in the development of human resources and of local institutions. The financial resources to achieve this are a relatively minor part of the overall requirement in the early stages of expansion. More important are the specific skills required among trainers and extension staff to ensure that extensionists' and farmers' skills in leadership, negotiation and conflict resolution develop in a participatory and sustainable fashion.

o Once the human resource and institutional conditions are in place, financial constraints may become binding. But the lack of rigorous assessments of the economic costs and benefits of farmer-led extension will deter large-scale investment by development finance organizations. Nevertheless, economic evaluations alone will not tell the full story. Many farmer-led extension experiences increase the confidence, self-esteem, status and credibility of those involved. Although real, they may be hard to see — let alone quantify. And before such an assessment can be made, a clear account of the sequence of events is needed, giving the previous conditions, cause and effect, and so on. The assessment can then be seen in context rather than in a vacuum.

o Farmer-led extension gives more power to farmers to determine the public-sector agenda for extension (and in some cases possibly also research). This implies a reduction in the power of others (usually those in the public sector itself). This has other implications, though these rarely work through in practice, especially in public-sector extension: reward criteria and assessment procedures should depend more closely on how technologies perform in farmers' fields, and farmers should contribute to assessing performance. Any one of these — let alone all taken together — implies a significant shift in the balance of power. The public sector will have to give clear and repeated signals of its willingness to accept such shifts if those seeking to make it more responsive to farmers' requirements are not to be discouraged.

o There are overriding technology constraints in some areas. Farmer-to-farmer extension establishes itself most rapidly in areas where two or three technical changes which are well proven elsewhere can be introduced quickly. Yet such technologies are rarely available for the more difficult agro-ecological zones, such as the semi-arid areas of sub-Saharan Africa.

Farmer-to-farmer extension
The scope for the expansion of this mode, in the 'pure' form typified by the *campesino-a-campesino* movement, is likely to be limited to those areas for which new technologies are available, but are unlikely to be offered to farmers through public-sector extension services. Providing that there is an adequate spirit of voluntarism among farmers, and that a support organization such as an NGO can offer at least initial support, then farmer-to-farmer extension can not only substitute for what the public sector fails to provide, but can also create a capacity among farmers themselves to experiment and share technical information.

Despite the fact that they have operated under somewhat different agro-ecological and infrastructural conditions, farmer field schools face many of the same requirements in respect of scaling up as does farmer-to-farmer extension: it requires specialist human resource and institutional development, and a strong spirit of voluntarism among farmers. The fact that economic and other evidence of the success of the method is available, together with the fact that hitherto it has largely addressed issues of primary environmental concern to international funding agencies, together suggest that there are less likely to be funding constraints in the path of farmer field schools than in other types of farmer-led extension.

Relating farmer-led extension to the market
This is a relatively minor category of experience. In our view, there is substantial scope for NGOs and other organizations to support farmers as they come to terms with rapidly changing market conditions. However, a major constraint here lies in the lack of interest and aptitude on the part of many NGOs in assisting farmers to

integrate with the market, as well as potential dangers of farmers' suffering losses due to their incorporation into, for example, highly volatile export markets.

Farmer-led approaches and the public sector

Apart from the generic considerations (outlined above) of shifts in the balance of power, and changes in reward systems, a number of other constraints need to be removed if farmer-led extension is to gain ground in making the public sector more demand-responsive:

o Public sector actors will, in many circumstances, be faced with new roles and corresponding new skill requirements. The emphasis will be less on technical expertise and more on the capacity to find answers that respond to farmers' requirements; less on teaching and more on joint learning; less on prescription and more on joint diagnosis. Diagnostic skills and more participatory training methods are among the many that will have to be introduced into the curricula for government staff if they are to succeed in these new approaches.

o Changes in resource allocation patterns will also be desirable, with less emphasis on the provision of subsidies or inputs, and more on bringing groups of farmers together for joint learning, cross-visits and so on.

o Change will also be needed in the level of local control over resource allocations. Farmer-led extension is unlikely to succeed if decisions cannot be taken without prior clearance from headquarters. However, governments are increasingly coming under pressure to reduce the amount of central funding being channelled to the rural sector. In response, they are decentralizing decision making, and the resources to implement those decisions, to local government units. Although not without problems, this does potentially enable farmers and their organizations to have a larger voice in setting agricultural development priorities. Several of the methodologies presented here (among others Kingsley and Musante, Maningding, Chapter 8; Bhuiyan and Walker, Bimoli and Manandhar, Chapter 9; Peacock, Chapter 10) are being used in situations where power is being decentralized.

Providing that these preconditions are met within the public sector, farmer-led extension has good prospects of influencing the design and implementation of public sector programmes.

Clearly, as evidenced by the diversity of approaches presented in this book, there will be no set prescriptions or 'models'. Institutional roles and combinations which work well in some conditions will not necessarily do so in others. Further, much flexibility will be required to allow different kinds of organizations to find their most productive roles. For instance, some of the larger NGOs may find it more appropriate to provide technical and other support to smaller NGOs than to undertake work directly themselves with farmer groups. Others may find it easier to influence government through advocacy (on environmental matters, for instance) than through jointly implemented projects.

200

Appendix 1: Workshop participants

THIS BOOK IS an outcome of a July 1995 workshop on farmer-led extension at the International Institute of Rural Reconstruction in the Philippines. Addresses of workshop organizers and participants are given below.

Workshop organizers

Dr John Farrington, Director, Rural Resources and Poverty Research Programme, Overseas Development Institute, Portland House, Stag Place, London SW1E 5DP, UK; tel +44-171-393 1600, fax +44-171-393 1699, e-mail odi@gn.apc.org, internet http://www.oneworld.org/odi/

Mr John Jackson, World Neighbors-Philippines, 5 Road 13, Pag-Asa, Quezon City, Philippines; tel +63-2-962 414

Ms Debra A.Johnson, World Neighbors, 4127 NW 122 Street, Oklahoma City, OK 73120-8869, USA; tel +1-405-752 9700, fax +1-405-752 9393

Mr Scott Killough, International Institute of Rural Reconstruction, Silang, Cavite 4118, Philippines; tel +63-46-414 2417, fax +63-46-414 2420, +63-2-522 2494, e-mail iirr@phil.gn.apc.org

Ms Mila Resma, Training Division, International Institute of Rural Reconstruction, Silang, Cavite 4118, Philippines; tel +63-46-414 2417, fax +63-46-414 2420, +63-2-522 2494, e-mail iirr@phil.gn.apc.org

Ms Vanessa Scarborough, 108 Great Portland Street, London SW1E 5DP, UK; tel +44-171 637 8603

Dr Daniel Selener, Director, Regional Office for Latin America, International Institute of Rural Reconstruction, Av. America 4451 y Pasaje Muirriagui Donoso, Apartado Postal 17-08-8494, Quito, Ecuador; fax +593-2-443 763, e-mail daniel@iirr.exc.ec

Mr Stefan Wodicka, World Neighbors, PO Box 71, Ubud, Bali, Indonesia; tel/fax +62-361-975 707, fax +62-361-975 120

Participants

Dr Ruth Alsop, Environment and Production Division, IFPRI, 1200 17th Street, Washington DC 20036-3006, USA; tel +1-202-862 5687, fax +1-202-467 4439

Mr Pedro Aspiras, c/o AGTALON, Nalsian, Manaog, Pangasinan, Philippines

Prof. George Axinn, College of Agriculture and Natural Resources, Michigan State University, 323 Natural Resources, East Lansing, Michigan, USA; fax +1-517-353 8994, e-mail 22331gha@msu.edu

Mr Pedro Baile, SADOPECO, Sta. Misericordia, Sto. Domingo, Albay, Philippines

Mr Pankaj Ballabh, Vidya Bhawan Krishi Vigyan Kendra, P.O. Badgaon, Udaipur 313 011, India; tel +91-294-60313, fax +91-294-524 800

Mr Carlos Basilio, 10 Concio Apts, Mayondon, Los Baños, Laguna 4030, Philippines; tel +63-49-536 4754, 912-322 2673, 912-335 4937, fax +63-2-813 5697, 49-536 2914, e-mail csb@compass.com.ph

Dr Nasiruddin Bhuiyan, Additional Director, Dept of Agricultural Extension, Ministry of Agriculture, Khamarbari, Dhaka 1215, Bangladesh; tel +880-2-326 114

Dr Jit Bhuktan, Monitoring & Evalation Expert, HDIF UNDP P.O.Box 650, #6 Natmauk Road, Yangon, Myanmar; tel +95-1-542 911 to 19, fax +95-1-292 739, e-mail jit.p.bhuktan@undp.org

Mr Badri Prasad Bimoli, Project Co-ordinator, Dept of Agricultural Development, Agricultural Extension Project II, Harihar Bhawan, Lalitpur, Nepal; tel +977-1-523 318, 522 082, fax +977-1-522 439

Mr Roland Bunch, COSECHA, Apartado 3586, Tegucigalpa, Honduras; tel +504-76-6150, fax +504-76-6240

Mr Jose Cansancio, Forest Community Organizer, Region 11 CENRO-Digos, Department of Environment and Natural Resources, Davao del Sur, Philippines; fax +63-714-877590

Prof. J.Lin Compton, Professor of Extension Education, University of Wisconsin, 226 North Mill St., Madison, Wisconsin 53706, USA; tel +1-608-263 2082, fax +1-608-262 7751, e-mail lcompton@macc.wisc.edu

Dr P.Das, Deputy Director-General (Agric. Extension), Indian Council of Agricultural Research, Krishi Anusandhan Bhawan, Pusa Gate, New Delhi 110 012, India; tel +91-11-573 1277, fax +91-11-387 293

Ms Pratima Dayal, c/o Resident Commissioner of Uttar Pradesh, 401 Ambadeep Building, 14 Kasturba Gandhi Marg, New Delhi 110 001, India; tel +91-11-331 3338, fax +91-11-371 5604

Mr Valdemar Hercilio de Freitas, Projecto de Recuperacao do Recursos, Naturais em Microbacias Hidrogratificos, Caixa Postal 502, Itacorubi, Florianopolis, Sta. Catarina, ECP 88030, Brazil; tel +55-48-234 0066, fax +55-48-234 1024

Mr Brij Mohan Dixit, Deputy Director of Agricultural Extension, Government of Rajasthan Agriculture Dept, Sikh Colony, Udaipur, Rajasthan 313 001, India

Mr Khaled Ehsan, ICLARM Dhaka, House 20, Road 9/a, Dhanmondi, Dhaka, Bangladesh; fax +880-28-83416

Dr Peter Nzie Ewang, Programme Co-ordinator/Senior Lecturer, School of Rural Community Development, University of Natal, Private Bag, X01 Scottsville, Pietermaritzburg 3209, South Africa; tel +27-331-260 5792, fax +27-331-260 5495, email robinson@srcd.unp.ac

Mr Ahmad Farouk, CARE International–Egypt, 18 Hoda Sharawi St., Bab El Louk, P.O. Box 2019, Cairo 11511, Egypt; tel +20-2-393 5262, 393 2756, fax +20-2-393 5650

Dr Chris Garforth, Agricultural Extension and Rural Development Dept, University of Reading, 3 Earley Gate, Whiteknights Road, Reading RG6 2AL, UK; tel +44-1734-318 884, fax +44-1734-261 244, e-mail c.j.garforth@reading.ac.uk

Mr Subash Garg, c/o Director of Agriculture, Government of Rajasthan, Krishi Bhavan, Jaipur 302 005, India; fax +91-141-380 088

Mr Glenn Genovate, c/o Atallah Kuttab, Save the Children–Philippines, PO Box 4448, Manila Central Post Office Building, Liwasang Bonifacio, Metro Manila, Philippines; tel/fax +63-2-527 3750

Dr Abdul Ghani, World Bank, 3/a Paribagh, Dhaka, Bangladesh; tel +880-2-861056 fax +880-2-863 220

Mr Simon Hate, FAO–IPM Office, Jl Taman Marga Satwa Raya 61, Ragunan, Jakarta, Indonesia; tel +62-21-789 0288, fax +62-21-780 0265

Mr Eric Holt-Gimenez, SIMAS, Apartado A-136, Managua, Nicaragua; tel/fax +505-2-225 652, e-mail simas@nicarao.apc.org

Mr Hu Huabin, Kunming Institute of Ecology, Chinese Academy of Sciences, 25 Jiaochang Road, Kunming 650 223, PR China; tel +86-871-515 4135, fax +86-871-332 4834

Prof. Chris Igodan, Dept of Agricultural Extension and Rural Development, University of Fort Hare, Private Bag X1314, Alice, South Africa; fax +27-404-31730

Dr Friedrich Kahrs, GTZ, PO Box 5180, 65726 Eschborn, Germany; fax +49-6196-797 280

Mr Kevin Kamp, CARE International–Bangladesh, GPO Box 226, Dhaka, Bangladesh; tel +880-2-814 195, fax +880-2-814 183

Mr Mohan Kanda, Joint Secretary (Extension), Dept. of Agriculture and Cooperation, Ministry of Agriculture, Krishi Bhawan, New Delhi 110 001, India; tel +91-11-138 4902, fax +91-11-138 1176, 382 137

Ms Mien Kaomini, Forest and Nature Conservation Research and development Center, Jl. Gunung Batu 5, PO Box 165, Bogor 16001, Indonesia; tel +62-251-322 829, fax +62-251-315 222

Mr Rajesh Kapoor, Aga Khan Rural Support Programme (India), Choice Premises, Swastik Cross Road, Navrangpura, Ahmedabad, Gujarat 380 009, India; tel +91-79-464 730, 642 7729, fax +91-79-464 862

Mr Rajiv Khandelwal, ODI Research Associate, c/o V.S.Surana, 32 Ahinsapuri, Fathepura, Udaipur 313 001, India; tel +91-294-522 846, fax +91-294-525 399

Mr Wilfredo Listones, Mag-Uugmad Foundation, Inc., 784-H San Roque Ext., Mambaling, Cebu City, Philippines; tel +63-2-97617, fax +63-2-220 197

Mr Teo Llena, Mag-Uugmad Foundation, Inc., 784-H San Roque Ext., Mambaling, Cebu City, Philippines; tel +63-2-97617, fax +63-2-220 197

Mr Gabino Lopez, COSECHA, Apartado 3586, Tegucigalpa, Honduras; tel +504-762 256, fax +504-762 354

Mr Peter Malvicini, Dept. of Education, Kennedy Hall, Cornell University, Ithaca, NY 14853, USA; tel +1-607-255 7905, fax +1-607-255 2207, email pgm1@cornell.edu

Dr Prahlad Narain Mathur, Division of Agricultural Extension, Indian Agricultural Research Institute, 312 Krishi Anusandhan Bhawan, Pusa Gate, New Delhi 110 012, India; tel +91-11-578 9102, 578 1905, fax +91-11-576 6420, 575 1719

Mr Simon Mchunu, Cornfields Land Trust, PO Box 1601, Eastcourt 3310, South Africa; tel +27-3622-2530

Mr Kudakwasne Murwira, Intermediate Technology Development Group, 7 Jason Moyo Avenue, PO Box 1744, Harare, Zimbabwe; tel +263-4-795 232, 796 420, fax +263-4-796 409

Mr Nguyen Kim Hai, CIDSE–Vietnam, 38 Au Trieve Street, Hoam Kiem District, GPO Box 110, Hanoi, Vietnam; tel +84-4-254 834, 250 265, fax +84-4-250 266, email cidsehan@netnam.org.vn

Mr Nguyen Ngoc Lung, Director, Silvicultural Department and Forestry Extension Unit, Ministry of Forestry, Hanoi, Vietnam; fax +84-4-213 781, 241 779

Prof. Ulrich Nitsch, Dept. of Extension Education, SLU, Box 7013, S-750 07 Uppsala, Sweden; tel +46-18-672 612, fax +46-18-673 502

Mr Sivelile Nompozolo, Agricultural and Rural Development Research Institute, University of Fort Hare, Private Bag X1314, Alice, Eastern Cape, South Africa; tel +27-404-31154, fax +27-404-31730, e-mail nompo@ufhcc.ufh.ac.za

Mr Robert Nugent, IPM Officer, FAO-Philippines, PO Box 3700 MCPO, 1277 Makati, Philippines; tel +62-2-818 6478, 813 4229, fax +63-2-812 7725, 810 9409, email ipm-manila@cgnet.com

Mr Noel Oettle, Farmer Support Program, University of Natal, Private Bag X01, Scottsville 3209, South Africa; tel +27-331-68385 to 87, fax +27-331-68485

Mr Bishnu Hari Pandit, Executive Director, Nepal Agroforestry Foundation, P.O. Box 9594, Kathmandu, Nepal; tel +977-1-524 257, fax +977-1-222 026

Mr Pang Yong, Yunnan Upland Management, 50 Milesi, Kunming 650 032, PR China; tel/fax +86-871-514 6912, 414 4819

Dr Christie Peacock, FarmAfrica, 9–10 Southampton Place, London WC1A 2EA, UK; tel +44-171-430 0440, fax +44-171-430 0460

Mr Pham Xuan Du, VACVINA (National Association of Vietnamese Gardeners), C2B Thanh Cong, Hanoi, Vietnam; tel. +84-4-345 216, 344 779, fax +84-4-353 144

Dr Harry Potter, First Secretary (Natural Resources), Aid Management Office, British High Commission, United Nations Road, Baridhaka, Bangladesh; fax +880-2-883 474, 883 719, email amod.hlp@oda.gnet.gov.uk

Quach Ngoc An, Department of Agricultural Extension, Ministry of Agriculture and Food Industry, 2 Ngoc Ha-Bac Thao, Hanoi, Vietnam; tel +84-4-237 033, fax +84-4-236 403

Mr Jorge Ivan Restrepo, Fundacion Carvajal, Calle 2a Oeste No. 24F–73, Apartado 6178, Cali, Colombia; tel +57-2-3554 2949, fax +57-2-3554 2892, e-mail fucarvaj@mafalda.univalle.edu.co

Mr Angel Roldan, Programa de Acción Forestal Tropical, Progreso 5, Col. del Carmen, Coyoacan 04110 DF, Mexico; tel 52-5-658 3112, 658 6324, fax +52-5-658 3556, 554 3599

Mr Ahsan Ali Sarkar, Additional Secretary, Ministry of Agriculture, Bangladesh; tel +880-286 7040, fax +880-283 1649, 224 3208

Dr H.C.Sharda, Chief Training Organizer, Krishi Vigyan Kendra (KVK), Vidya Bhawan Society, Badgaon, Udaipur 313 011, India; tel +91-294-560 313, tel/fax +91-294-524 800

Dr D.N.Shinde, BAIF Development Research Foundation, 49 Kumbhanagar, Sector No. 4, behind T.N. Hostel, Udaipur 313 001, India; fax +91-294-584 467

Mr Nelson Sinaga, Yayasan Tananua, Jl. H Horo Matawai, PO Box 13, Waingapu, Nusa Tenggara Timur, Indonesia; tel +62-386-22055, fax +62-361-975 120

Mr Manohar Singh, Seva Mandir, Fatehpura, Rajasthan 313 001, India

Mr Nar Bikram Thapa, Action Aid–Nepal, Lazimpat, GPO Box 6257, Kathmandu, Nepal; tel +977-1-410 929, 419 115, fax +977-1-419 718, email vishal@aanepal.mos.com.np

Mr Tran Van Son, Department of Agricultural Extension, Ministry of Agriculture and Food Industry, 2 Ngoc Ha-Bac Thao, Hanoi, Vietnam; tel +84-4-433 485, fax +84-4-745 4319

Mr Laurens van Veldhuizen, ILEIA, c/o ETC Foundation, Kastanjelaan 5, P.O. Box 64, 3830 AB Leusden, The Netherlands; tel +31-33-943 086, fax +31-33-940 791, e-mail ileia@antenna.nl

Mr Mark Walker, Agricultural Support Services, Project Dept. of Agricultural Extension, British High Commission, United Nations Road, Baridhara, Dhaka, Bangladesh; tel +880-2-8832 5347, fax +880-2-883 416, 883 519

Mr Zhong Bingfang, Centre for Integrated Agricultural Development, Beijing Agricultural University, Beijing 100 094, PR China; tel +86-10-258 2337, fax +86-10-258 5866

Appendix 2: Papers cited and summarized

BELOW IS A list of the papers submitted to the organizers of the 1995 workshop in the Philippines, on which this book is based.

The full text of papers marked with an asterisk (*) is published in ODI's *Agricultural Research and Extension Network Paper* 59 (Scarborough 1996), available from ODI. The other papers are available on request from IIRR (see address at the beginning of the book).

	Excerpted in chapter
Alsop, Ruth, Rajiv Khandelwal, Elon Gilbert and John Farrington, *The Human Capital Dimension of Collaboration among Government, NGOs and Farm Families: Comparative Advantage, Complications and Observations from an Indian Case.*	
Arora, S.K., *Distance Learning for Farmers: The MANAGE Way.*	11
Aspiras, Pedro, *AGTALON – Agro-technical Assistance and Livelihood Opportunities in the North.*	
Baile, Pedro, *Farmer-to-Farmer Extension: Pedro Baile's Experience.*	5, 6 *
Baraz, Erol and Ufuk Kirmizi, *Notes on Union of Turkish Chambers of Agriculture Progress Farmer Project.*	
Bhuiyan, N. and Mark Walker, *The Problem Census: Participatory Public Sector Agricultural Extension in Bangladesh.*	9
Bhuktan, Jit Pradhan, Scott Killough and Carlos Basilio, *Farmer-to-Farmer Extension: An Analytical Review of Some Selected Experiences.*	4, 5, 6, 7
Bimoli, B.P. and D.N.Manandhar, *A Farmer-Centred Extension Approach in Nepal.*	9 *
Bunch, Roland, *People-Centred Agricultural Development: Principles of Extension for Achieving Long-Term Impact.*	12, 13 *
Cansancio, Jose D., *Upland Development Pilot Project of the Department of Environment and Natural Resources, Philippines.*	13
Compton, J.Lin, *Responding to Farmer Initiative: A Case Study of Decentralised, User-Oriented Extension in Nepal.*	
Dayal, Pratima, *Agriculture Extension Services in India: A Perspective for the National Agriculture Technology Project.*	
de Freitas, Valdemar Hercilio, *A Watershed as Planning Unit in Soil Conservation and Extension Management.*	12
Dilts, Douglas R. and Simon Hate, *IPM Farmer Field Schools: Changing Paradigms and Scaling-up.*	8, 13 *

References

Acharya, Meena, and Lynn Bennett, 'The rural women of Nepal: An aggregate analysis and summary of eight village studies', *The Status of Women in Nepal*, Vol.2, Field Studies, Part 9, Centre for Economic Development and Administration, Tribhuvan University, Kathmandu, 1981.

ActionAid–Nepal, *Annual Progress Report*, ActionAid–Nepal, Kathmandu, 1992.

Adhikari, B., and B.Baniya, *A Research Study on Food Self-Sufficiency and Farm Productivity*, ActionAid–Nepal, Kathmandu, 1991.

Ameur, C., *Agricultural Extension: A Step Beyond the Next Step*. World Bank Technical Paper 247, World Bank, Washington DC, 1994.

Antholt, Charles H., 'Agricultural extension in the 21st century: Lessons from South Asia', in Rivera, W. and Dan Gustafsen (eds), *Agricultural Extension: Worldwide Institutional Evolution and Forces for Change*, Elsevier, New York, 1991.

———— *Getting Ready for the Twenty-First Century: Technical Change and Institutional Modernisation in Agriculture*, World Bank Technical Paper 217, World Bank, Washington DC, 1994.

Arnaiz, Maria E.O., *Farmers' organizations in the technology change process: An annotated bibliography*, Network Paper 53, Overseas Development Institute, Agricultural Research and Extension Network, London, 1995.

Arnold, J.E.M., and W.C.Stewart, *Common Property Resource Management in India*, Tropical Forestry Papers, Oxford Forestry Institute, Oxford, 1991.

ASSP, 'Jessore Pilot Programme: Process Evaluation Report', Project Report 52, Dhaka, 1995.

Axinn, George H., *New Strategies for Rural Development*, Rural Life Associates, Kathmandu and East Lansing, 1978.

———— *Guide on Alternative Extension Approaches*, Food and Agriculture Organization of the United Nations, Rome, 1988.

Axinn, George H., and Nancy W. Axinn, 'An African village in transition: Research into behavior patterns', *Journal of Modern African Studies* 7(3), 1969.

Axinn, George H., and Sudhakar Thorat, *Modernizing World Agriculture: A comparative study of agricultrural extension systems*, Praeger, New York, and Oxford and IBH, New Delhi, 1972.

Axinn, Nancy W., 'Involving women farmers in FSR/E — Separate projects vs integrating gender: The South Asian experience', Paper presented at the 10th Annual Symposium, Association for Farming Systems Research/Extension, Michigan State University, 1990.

Basnyat, B.B., 'Nepal's agriculture, sustainability and intervention: Looking for new directions'. Ph.D. thesis, Wageningen Agricultural University, Wageningen, Netherlands, 1995.

Bawden, Richard J., 'Systems Thinking and Practice in Agriculture', *Journal of Dairy Science*, 74:2362–73, 1991.

Belshaw, D., P.Blaikie and M.Stocking, 'Identifying Key Land Degradation Issues and Applied Research Priorities', Winpenny, J.T. (ed.), *Development Research: The Environmental Challenge*, Overseas Development Institute, London, 1991, pp.66–91.

Brokensha, D.W., and P.D.Little (eds), *Anthropology of Development and Change in East Africa*, Westview Press, Boulder, 1988.

Bunch, Roland, *Two Ears of Corn: A Guide to People-Centred Agricultural Improvement*, World Neighbors, Oklahoma City, 1982.

Bunch, R. and G.López, 'Soil recuperation in Central America: Measuring the impact three to forty years after intervention.' Paper presented at the International Institute for Environment and Development's International Policy Workshop in Bangalore, India, November–December 1994.

Byrnes, K.J., 'Review of AID experience with farming systems research and extension projects', United States Agency for International Development, Washington DC, 1990.

Campilan, D.M., 'Learning to change, changing to learn: Managing natural resources for sustainable agriculture in the Philippines uplands', Ph.D. thesis, Wageningen Agricultural University, Wageningen, Netherlands, 1995.

Chambers, Robert, *Rural Development: Putting the Last First*, Longman, London, 1983.

—— *Challenging the Professions: Frontiers for Rural Development*, Intermediate Technology Publications, London, 1993.

Christoplos, I., and U.Nitsch, 'Extension and learning', *Forest Trees and People* 24, 1994, pp.8–13.

Clark, John, *Democratizing Development: The Role of Voluntary Organizations*, Kumarian Press, West Hartford, 1991.

Cloud, Kathleen, 'Women, development, equity, and efficiency: In pursuit of constrained bliss', in Clubb, Deborah and Polly C.Lignon (eds), *Food, Hunger, and Agricultural Issues*, Winrock International Institute for Agricultural Development, Morrilton, Arkansas, 1989.

Cornwall, A., I.Guijt and A.Welbourn, *Acknowledging Process: Challenges for Agricultural Research and Extension Methodology*, IDS Discussion Paper 333, Institute of Development Studies, Brighton, UK, 1993.

Crouch, B., 'The Problem Census: Farmer Centred Problem Identification', Haverkort, B., (ed.) *Joining Farmer Experiments: Experiences in Participatory Technology Development*, Intermediate Technology Publications, London, 1991.

Davidson, J., 'Gender and environment: Ideas for action and research', Winpenny, J.T. (ed.), *Development Research: The Environmental Challenge*. Overseas Development Institute, London, 1991, pp.137–144.

Esman, Milton J., and Norman Uphoff, *Local Organizations: Intermediaries in Rural Development*, Cornell University Press, Ithaca, 1984.

Farrington, John, 'Review of "Beyond Farmer First", edited by I Scoones and J Thompson' ODI *Agricultural Research and Extension Network Newsletter* 31, 1995, pp.15–21.

Farrington, John, A.Bebbington, K.Wellard with D.J.Lewis. *Reluctant Partners? Non-governmental Organizations, the State and Sustainable Agricultural Development*, Routledge, London, 1993.

211

Farrington, John, and A.Martin, *Farmer Participatory Research: A Review of Concepts and Practices*, Agricultural Research and Extension Discussion Paper 19, Overseas Development Institute, London, 1987.

Farrington, John, and John Nelson. 1997. *Using Logframes to Monitor and Review Farmer Participatory Research*. Network Paper 73, Overseas Development Institute, Agricultural Research and Extension Network, London, 1997.

Freire, Paulo, *Education for Critical Consciousness*, 2nd. ed., Ramos, M.B., L. Bigwood and M. Marshall (trans.), Sheen and Ward, London, 1989.

Garforth, C., 'Rural People's Organisations and Agricultural Extension in Northern Thailand: Who Benefits?' *Journal of International Development* 6(6), 1994, pp.707–20.

———— *Building on Diversity: Prospects for Public Sector Agricultural Extension in Bangladesh* AERDD Working Paper 95/1, Agricultural Extension and Rural Development Department, Reading, 1995.

George, Susan, *A Fate Worse than Debt*, Penguin Books, London, 1988.

———— *The Debt Boomerang*, Westview Press, Boulder, 1992.

Goldsmith, A.A., 'Institutions and Planned Socioeconomic Change: Four Approaches', *Public Administration Review* 52(6), 1992, pp.582–7.

Gustafson, D.J., 'Developing Sustainable Institutions: Lessons from Cross-Case Analysis of 24 Agricultural Extension Programmes', *Public Administration and Development* 14(2), 1994, pp.121–34.

Hancock, Graham, *Lords of Poverty: The Power, Prestige, and Corruption on the International Aid Business*, Atlantic Monthly Press, New York, 1989.

Holt-Gimenez, E., and Mora Cruz, 'Farmer-to-Farmer: The Ometepe Project', Alders, C., B.Haverkort and L.van Veldhuizen, *Linking with Farmers*, Intermediate Technology Publications, London, 1993.

Jazairy, I., M.Alamgir and T.Panuccio, *The State of World Rural Poverty*, Intermediate Technology Publications, London, 1992.

Jiggins, Janice, *Changing the Boundaries: Women-Centered Perspectives on Population and the Environment*, Island Press, Washington DC and Covelo, California, 1994.

Kardam, Nuket, *Bringing Women In: Women's Issues in International Development Programs*, Lynne Rienner, Boulder, 1991.

Kenmore P.E., *How Rice Farmers Clean Up the Environment, Conserve Biodiversity, Raise More Food, Make Higher Profits: Indonesia's IPM Programme, A Model for Asia*. FAO Rice IPC Programme, Manila, 1991.

Korten, D.C., *Community management: Asian experience and perspectives*, Kumarian Press, West Hartford, 1987.

Korten, D.C., and R.Klauss (eds), *People-Centered Development*, Kumarian Press, West Hartford, 1984.

McCalla, Alex F., *Agriculture and food needs to 2025: Why we should be concerned*, Washington, DC: Consultative Group on International Agricultural Research, 1994.

Meadows, Donella H., Dennis L.Meadows, Jorgen Randers, and William W.Behrens III. *Limits to Growth: A Report for the Club of Rome's Project on the Predicament of Mankind*, Universe Books, New York, 1972.

Mody, B., *Designing Messages for Development Communication: An Audience Participation-Based Approach*. Sage Publications, New Delhi, 1991.

212

Mosse, D., *Authority, Gender and Knowledge: Theoretical Reflections on the Practice of Participatory Rural Appraisal*, Agricultural Research and Extension Network Paper 44, Overseas Development Institute, London, 1993.

Nasiruddin, 'Report on the Problem Census Process: Evaluation with Farmers'. Planning and Evaluation Wing, Department of Agricultural Extension, Dhaka, 1995.

Okumu, Samual, 'Farmer-to-farmer extension process in four different areas of the Kitui and Ukambani development programmes in Kenya', Paper presented at the Workshop on Farmer-Led Extension, International Institute of Rural Reconstruction, Silang, Cavite, Philippines, July 1995.

Pandit, B.H., Nepal Agroforestry Foundation Support Programme: Evaluation of an NGO Support Programme in Kunwari and Gaikhura Villages of Ramechhap District of Nepal, M.Sc. thesis, AIT, 1994.

Pincus J., *Farmer Field School Survey: Impact of IPM Training on Farmers' Pest Control Behaviour*. Integrated Pest Management National Programme, Jakarta, 1991.

Pretty, J.N., *Regenerating Agriculture: Policies and Practice for Sustainability and Self-Reliance*, Earthscan, London, 1995.

Ramkumar, S.N., 'The analysis of farmer information systems for feeding dairy cattle in two villages of Kerala state, India', Ph.D. thesis, University of Reading, Reading, UK, 1994.

Rivera, W.A., and D.J.Gustafson (eds), *Agricultural Extension: Worldwide Institutional Evolution and Forces for Change*, Elsevier, Amsterdam and London. 1991.

Rogers, A. 'Third Generation Extension: Towards an Alternative Model' *Rural Extension Bulletin* 3, 1993, pp.14–16.

Rogers, E.E., *Diffusion of Innovations*, Free Press, New York, 1983.

Rola, A.C., and P.L.Pingali, *Pesticides, Rice Productivity and Farmers' Health: An Economic Assessment*, International Rice Research Institute, Manila, 1993.

Röling, N., 'Extension and the sustainable management of natural resources' Paper presented at the 11th European Seminar on Extension Education, Arhus, Denmark, 30 August–4 September 1993.

Röling, N., and E.van der Fliert, 'Transforming Extension for Sustainable Agriculture: The Case of Integrated Pest Management in Rice in Indonesia', *Agriculture and Human Values* 11(2), 1995, pp.96–108.

Sabirin, 'Laporan Kegiatan Tahun 1993', Unpublished report by Pesticide Action Network North Sumatra, Medan, 1994.

Scarborough, Vanessa (ed.), *Farmer-Led Approaches to Extension*, Network Paper 59, Overseas Development Institute, Agricultural Research and Extension Network, London, 1996.

Sen, Amartya Kumar, *Poverty and Famines: An Essay on Entitlement and Deprivation*, Clarendon Press, Oxford, and Oxford University Press, New York, 1981.

Sen, Gita and Caren Grown, *Development, Crises, and Alternative Visions: Third World Women's Perspectives*, Monthly Review Press, New York, 1987.

Shiva, Vandana, *Staying Alive: Women, Ecology, and Survival in India*, Kali for Women, New Delhi, and Zed Books, London, 1988.

———— *Most Farmers in India are Women*, FAO, New Delhi, 1991.

SIMAS, *Canasta Metodológica*, SIMAS, Managua, Nicaragua, 1995.

Swaminathan, M.S., Statement at the 1994 International Conference on Population and Development in Cairo, cited in *Ceres* 151, Vol. 27(1), 1995, p.11.

Umali, D.L., and L.Schwartz, *Public and Private Agricultural Extension: Beyond Traditional Frontiers*, World Bank Discussion Paper 236, World Bank, Washington DC, 1994.

UNDP, *United Nations Human Development Report*, United Nations Development Programme, New York, 1993.

Uphoff, Norman T., *Local Institutional Development: An Analytic Sourcebook with Cases*, Kumarian Press, West Hartford, 1986.

——— *Learning from Gal Oya: Possibilities for Participatory Development and Post-Newtonian Social Science*, Cornell University Press, Ithaca and London, 1992.

USAID, 'Project evaluation of Lesotho agricultural production and institutional support (LAPIS)' United States Agency for International Development, Washington, 1989.

van de Fliert, E. and L.R.I.Velasco, 'Project review report for action learning to promote improved environmental management and advocacy (IEMA) through popular participation with Indonesian NGOs'. Unpublished report prepared for USAID and World Education Inc., Jakarta, 1994.

van Veldhuizen, Laurens, and Ann Waters-Bayer, 'Participatory technology development: Extension for learning', Paper presented at the Workshop on Farmer-Led Extension, International Institute of Rural Reconstruction, Silang, Cavite, Philippines, July 1995.

Yinghui, Y., 'China: Rural Reform and Agricultural Extension', *Rural Extension Bulletin* 3, 1993, pp.24–8.

Zijp, W., 'From Agricultural Extension to Rural Information Management', *Interpaks Digest*, 1(1), 1992, pp.1–3.